Parents in modern America

A sociological analysis

THE DORSEY SERIES IN ANTHROPOLOGY
AND SOCIOLOGY

EDITOR   ROBIN M. WILLIAMS, JR.   *Cornell University*

Parents in modern America

A sociological analysis

by

E. E. LeMASTERS

University of Wisconsin

1970

THE
DORSEY
PRESS   HOMEWOOD, ILLINOIS

IRWIN-DORSEY LIMITED   GEORGETOWN, ONTARIO

First Printing, January, 1970
Second Printing, May, 1970
Third Printing, January, 1971
Fourth Printing, July, 1971
Fifth Printing, September, 1971

Library of Congress Catalog Card No. 73–98255

Printed in the United States of America

*For my wife, Billie, and our
two sons, Bill and Gary*

The relationship between parents and children is no less difficult, no less fraught with drama, than that between lovers. The growing child, developing into an independent individual, surprises and annoys its parents. What once was a charming plaything becomes an adversary.

ANDRÉ MAUROIS
Lelia: The Life of George Sand

Preface

T HIS book is about parents—not children. In essence, it attempts to focus on what happens to parents in the child-rearing process, whereas most of the studies in this field concern themselves primarily with what happens to the children.

The approach in this study is sociological rather than psychological or psychiatric—that is, we are interested in the parenthood role as a social system and in the attempts of so-called "normal" fathers and mothers to perform in the system. Any pathology in the study is assumed to be in the parental role itself and not in individual parents. We are aware, of course, that some fathers and mothers are "sick" or incompetent, but they are not our primary interest in this study.

We assume, along with Williams, Lerner, and other observers,[1] that American parents appear to be under considerable stress. It would be difficult to prove empirically that American fathers and mothers are having more problems today than they had in 1860 or even 1760—or that they find their parental role any more difficult than Russian or Swedish or Japanese parents. In other words, American parents *seem* to be having serious problems, but we really don't know how different this is from what it was like in an earlier period of our national history. In any event, this analysis proceeds on the assumption that being a father or mother in modern America is a difficult and complex social role.

We first became seriously interested in parents while doing a doctoral thesis at Ohio State University—the research problem was to evaluate a large, federally financed, parent-education project in a midwestern metropolitan community. Among other things, we discovered in that

---

[1] The references for this statement will be found in the various chapters of the book.

research that parent educators really cared very little for parents themselves: the ultimate concern was with the child. We also discovered that the parent educators in this project (some of the best in the country) were hopelessly class-bound in their approach to parents. As Brim documented some years later,[2] they assumed that all fathers and mothers were middle-class—or aspired to be middle-class. The result was, as the research demonstrated, that they were only able to reach middle-class parents.

After World War II our interest in parents was renewed when we served as a Dean of Students in a state university system in the East. In interviewing fathers and mothers whose sons or daughters had gotten into serious difficulty on campus, we were impressed with the efforts these parents had put forth to discharge their parental responsibility—and very often they seemed to have done quite well in their other major social roles (marital and occupational). In other words, many of them—perhaps the majority—did not appear to be incompetent human beings: they had simply not been able to manage a given son or daughter. It was also clear that they had often succeeded with other children—it was this particular child that had baffled them.

We have been pondering this matter ever since the Dean of Students experience and this book is the result.

In writing this book it has been very difficult to remain objective—we have had some of the same problems Kenneth Clark encountered as an "involved observer" in writing about Harlem.[3] As a parent we have often been offended and angered by stories in the mass media accusing American fathers and mothers of warping and smothering what should have been a perfect child. Reading the attacks on parents that emerged in the 1940's and the 1950's, one would think that America *lost* World War II. As a matter of fact, it was precisely during the last several decades (since World War I) that America became a world power at the very time that our fathers and mothers were accused of rearing two generations of weaklings. Would any one accuse Russian parents of gross malfunctioning as that country became a world power after 1920?

In many ways, then, this book is a defense of American parents. It is not entirely objective, but neither have the attacks on parents been entirely objective.

It is hoped that the book will prove useful in marriage and family courses, perhaps also in some child development classes. Parents' discussion groups should find it interesting. Public libraries may find it a useful addition to their shelves of books on "how to understand your child." If

---

[2] See Orville G. Brim, Jr., *Education for Child Rearing* (New York: Russell Sage Foundation, 1959). We regard this study as a classic in its field and have used its findings extensively in various chapters.

[3] See the Preface to *Dark Ghetto* (New York: Harper & Row, Publishers, 1965).

young people could be encouraged to read it they might learn how to understand their parents.

No one should conclude from this book that the writer has suffered any particular trauma as a parent. We regard our two sons as pretty good representatives of their generation and hope they feel that way about us.

We regret that this book does not convey the thrill and the excitement of being a parent. Like the modern novelists and the playwrights, we have focused on the problems of modern parents, not their joys. For those parents who do not have any problems, our hat is off—they are indeed unusual in our society.

Madison, Wisconsin   E. E. LeMasters
December, 1969

Acknowledgments

W E wish to record an appreciation of two great undergraduate teachers of sociology: Read Bain and W. Fred Cottrell of Miami University (Ohio). They first introduced us to the idea that one could study social systems as well as individual human beings.

Among our many stimulating colleagues in the School of Social Work at the University of Wisconsin we wish to pay special tribute to Professors Martin Loeb and Alfred Kadushin for their many insightful comments on the parent role in our society.

We would like to thank the following publishers, periodicals, and authors for granting permission for us to quote from their material: The American Sociological Association, The Free Press, Grosset & Dunlap, Inc., Harper & Row, W. W. Norton & Company, Inc., Russell Sage Foundation, Simon & Schuster, Inc., Yale University Press; *Daedalus, Saturday Review;* Robert Bell, Orville Brim, Jr., James Coleman, Kingsley Davis, Geoffrey Gorer, Max Lerner, Ferdinand Lundberg and Marynia Farnham, David Riesman, Leo Rosten, and Paul Woodring.

Finally, we want to thank Mrs. Mary Hood for her careful typing of the final draft.

E. E. L.

Table of contents

fessionals—not your peers. No margin for error. Parents can't quit. Modern parents are expected to rear children that are not only different from the parents but *better*. Role theory and parenthood. Summary and conclusion.

chapter
one

Parents in
modern America

I̲ɴ his autobiography, Norbert Wiener, one of the true geniuses of our time, confesses his humility in his attempts to cope with the baffling complexities of parenthood. He writes: "Thus, like all families, we had our problems to consider and our decisions to make. I am neither certain of the correctness of the policies I have adopted nor ashamed of any mistakes I might have made. One has only one life to live, *and there is not time enough in which to master the art of being a parent.*"[1]

In writing this book the author was inspired (or motivated) by hundreds of interviews with parents who echoed the feelings of Norbert Wiener—a man who could design a computer modeled on the human brain but who found parenthood a mystery and a confusion.

Many of the parents we talked with—perhaps a majority—were quite competent in their jobs and in the other areas of their lives, yet they felt insecure and inadequate as parents.

Talking with these fathers and mothers the writer found himself haunted by the question: *why* do these people find parenthood so difficult? How can a man run a corporation and fail miserably as a father?[2] How can a woman be regarded as a superior teacher in a suburban school system and be told by her daughter that she is a poor mother?

Max Lerner, in an interesting book, has written: "It is evident that in no other culture has there been so pervasive a cultural anxiety about the rearing of children."[3] The writer shares this feeling and this book may be

---

[1] Norbert Wiener, *I Am a Mathematician* (New York: Doubleday & Co., 1956), p. 224. Wiener, a child prodigy, is often given credit for being the brain behind the development of the modern computer. [Italics not in original.]

[2] All of the case illustrations used in this book refer to actual parents, but certain details may have been altered to protect their identity.

[3] Max Lerner, *America as a Civilization* (New York: Simon and Schuster, 1957), p. 562. We cite this book often in this study because we regard it as one of the

regarded as one sociologist's attempt to account for this cultural complex.

In this first chapter we wish to explore some of the features of our society that seem to pose problems for parents. In subsequent chapters most of these variables will be analyzed in depth—here we only wish to sketch them in.

The reader should remember that this book does not attempt to deal with the *personal* or *individual* problems that any given father or mother might have—on the contrary, we are concerned with the problems that *most* American parents seem to have. In other words, it is a sociological, not a psychiatric, study.

In reviewing the literature on parents it seemed to us that the vast majority of the material was concerned with children—not with parents. We were impressed by an observation of Brim that most family writers seemed to think that parents operated in a social and cultural vacuum because so little was said about the social situations confronting fathers and mothers.[4]

It also seemed to us that the American father was virtually ignored by most of the writers.

In this book, then, we wish to look long and hard at the social system —or systems—in which American parents operate; we want to analyze the problems that plague *most* of these fathers and mothers—not just the inadequate ones; we want to talk with fathers as well as mothers, to lower and upper class parents as well as middle class ones.

Not much will be said about children—the libraries are full of books about them.

We will begin, in this first chapter, by noting some of the features of our society that constitute the social framework in which American fathers and mothers must function.

Sociological factors that affect parents

In his classic 1940 paper, "The Sociology of Parent-Youth Conflict,"[5] Kingsley Davis discussed 11 variables that he believed to be related to the problems that American parents have. These are as follows:

---

better attempts to delineate American civilization. For another analysis, see Robin M. Williams, Jr., *American Society* (2d ed.; New York: Alfred A. Knopf, 1960).

[4] For a discussion of the failure of parent specialists to consider the social conditions under which parents function, see Orville G. Brim, Jr., *Education for Child Rearing* (New York: Russell Sage Foundation, 1959), chap. 3, "Causes of Parent Behavior." This is the definitive analysis of parent education in the United States and is cited often in this book. One sociologist who made a consistent effort to understand the social forces affecting parents was the late James H. S. Bossard of the University of Pennsylvania. See his *The Sociology of Childhood* (New York: Harper & Brothers, 1948), also other volumes he wrote over a period of years.

[5] Kingsley Davis, "The Sociology of Parent-Youth Conflict," *American Sociological Review*, 5 (August, 1940), pp. 523–535. Although published in 1940 this paper was

1. *The rate of social change.* It seems to be obvious that parents in a relatively static society would have less difficulty than those in which social change is rapid and deep—as in the United States. In a slowly changing society parents would be closer to their children—the generation gap would be minimized. In such a society parents need only to produce children like themselves. The models do not change so often or so drastically as they do in modern America.

2. *The decelerating rate of socialization of the parent in contrast to that of the child.* Davis is referring to the fact that the learning curve of the parent is almost the exact opposite of that of the child: during adolescence, for example, when the boy or girl is in the process of discovering sex, the parent may be well past the peak of his or her interest in sex. In terms of learning theory the child reaches a peak of psychological and social change at a time when the average parent is learning and changing less and less.

    If the child is learning about the same things that the parent learned earlier no great problems may arise—but in societies such as the United States social change is so rapid, and so deep, that the new generation doesn't learn the same things the parents learned. One exasperated mother put it this way: "How in the hell am I supposed to help my kids with their homework when even *adding* and *subtraction* have changed?"

    It will be seen in later chapters that rapid and deep social change poses serious problems for American parents.

3. *A combination of physiological and psychological differences between parent and child.* This is a sort of *gestalt* effect—the parent is not only different physiologically from the child, but also psychologically and culturally.

4. *Adult realism versus youthful idealism.* Davis argues that as parents mature they tend to compromise their ideals—they still teach them to their children but only partially believe in them—or they have become cynical about their ideals being practical.

    Youth, in contrast, take the ideals seriously and are upset when they find their parents giving only lip service to such ideals as racial equality.

    It does not help to tell the child—"Wait until you are as old as I am and then you will understand." This only widens the gap between parents and child.

5. *The nature of parental authority.* Davis cites Simmel to the effect "that authority is bearable for the subordinate because it touches only

---

being reprinted as late as 1965; see Hyman Rodman, *Marriage, Family, and Society* (New York: Random House, 1965). It is also available in Herman D. Stein and Richard A. Cloward (eds.), *Social Perspectives on Behavior* (Glencoe, Ill.: The Free Press, 1958). In many ways this paper was the original impetus behind the present book.

one aspect of his life."[6] But in a primary group such as the family, parental authority extends over all phases of the child's life. The wise parent, of course, limits his exercise of authority as much as he can— but in the last analysis the father and/or mother is responsible for all phases of the child's life as long as the youngster is not of legal age.

6. *Conflicting norms.* In a rapidly changing, pluralistic society children can often challenge parents as to what constitutes moral or good behavior. Not only do the two generations hold different norms, but *within* each generation the standards also vary. This greatly complicates the enforcement of discipline.

7. *Competing authorities.* Parents are not the only source of wisdom and propriety in modern society—the schools, mass media, the youth peer groups—all of these tell the child what he should think and how he should behave. Fathers and mothers are always in competition with these forces when they seek to influence their children.

8. *Poor age grading.* We lack a series of clear steps by which boys and girls move from the status of a child to that of an adult. A male college student put it this way to the writer: "The local movie theater decided I was an adult when I was 12 and has been charging me adult prices ever since. The Bureau of Motor Vehicles gave me the nod to drive a car at 16—but if I had been living in Texas I could have driven at 14. The draft board says I mature at 18, but the bars, the marriage license bureau and the voting authorities say I'm not a man until 21. It is very confusing."

9. *Concentration within the small family.* Davis argues that in larger family systems authority and its related feelings are more diffused among several adults than in our intense nuclear system.

   Not only are the parent-child feelings very intense in our society, but the smallness and detachment of our family units make them vulnerable to dissolution, thus adding to parent-child tensions.

   Riesman[7] argues that the margin for parental error shrinks as the family system becomes smaller—each child becomes more crucial. An only child put this to the writer in these words: "I am all the children my parents have. If I get into trouble *all* of their children are in trouble. It is not a very comforting thought."

10. *Open competition for socio-economic position.* The adult status of children in our social class system is not finally settled at birth. Children have a chance to improve their social position and in the process parent-child conflicts may be generated.

11. *Sex tension.* Davis contended that sex "tensions not only make the

---

[6] Davis (p. 40 in Stein and Cloward book).

[7] David Riesman et al., *The Lonely Crowd* (New Haven: Yale University Press, 1961 ed.), p. 49.

adolescent capricious, but create a genuine conflict of interest between the two generations."[8]

These, then, are the features of Western society that Davis believed to be sociological factors in creating parent-youth conflict. Since 1940, when Davis was writing, American society has undergone deep and pervasive changes—some of which may have simplified the role of parent while others made it more difficult. Let us look first at the negative impact of recent social change on American parents and then we will close the chapter with a review of the positive aspects of recent social change as it affects parents.[9]

Negative aspects of recent social change on parents

Higher standards for parents

It is the belief of the writer that parents are being judged by higher standards—by their children, by professionals such as schoolteachers and social workers—and by parents themselves.

There seems to be no way to prove or disprove this empirically. It seems logical, however, to assume that in a society in which other standards are being raised that those applied to parents would be elevated also. We refer to school standards enforced on elementary and secondary students, higher living standards, and others.

In the writer's own life it seems quite obvious that parents in the 1920's were not expected to have their children's teeth straightened—only the very wealthy ever did that. But today even blue-collar parents are expected to make sure that the teeth of their offspring are not crooked.

Illustrations of this sort could be added endlessly—what was good enough for children in 1900 or 1920 is not good enough today—and this means that fathers and mothers are judging themselves more harshly. This may be a crucial factor in explaining why American fathers and mothers feel so inadequate.[10]

The concept of progress

In most human societies, according to social scientists, it is enough if parents produce and rear children as good as the parents are—biologically

---

[8] Davis, *op. cit.* (p. 43 in Stein and Cloward book).

[9] See chap. 11 of this book for an extensive analysis of parents and social change.

[10] We are in the same position as Davis, Lerner, and Williams in that while we believe American parents to be more uneasy than parents in most other modern societies we are unable to prove the assertion. For the Williams discussion, see Williams, *American Society, op. cit.* chap. 4, "Kinship and the Family in the United States."

and socially.[11] But in modern America this is not good enough: the children have to be *superior* to the parents. This may be functional for the society, but it may also help to produce a negative self-image in parents.

The cult of the child

Lerner writes about the "cult of the child" in American society[12]—parents are expendable but children are "precious"—the salt of the earth. To the extent that this is true of our society it has to have a negative impact on parents as well as all other older persons; it means that any person not a child is a second-class citizen in America. This may be one of the reasons why people in the United States don't want to become old—they know what that means.

Judgment by professionals

It is one thing for parents to be judged by their peers (other parents) but it is quite a different experience to have your efforts evaluated by professionals. It seems that increasingly fathers and mothers in our society have to submit to the judgment of school counselors, social workers, clinical psychologists, speech therapists, psychiatrists, and a host of other experts if anything happens to the child.

This was certainly not the case when our parents and our grandparents were rearing their children. In those days a parent could hold up his head if he did what other parents in the community regarded as right and decent, even if his child did get into difficulty. A grandmother of ours—the mother of 15 children—had a rebellious son who ran away from home at the age of 14 and was not seen again for 10 years. As we recall family history nobody called this woman a bad mother; after all, her other 14 children had not found it necessary to run away from home. It was simply felt in the community that some boys are more restless than others and that these things had to be expected. This was judgment by our grandmother's peers.

A few years ago a friend of ours also had a boy run away—he simply took off at age 16 and was not heard from for 18 months. Meanwhile the parents had consulted a child guidance clinic and came away burdened with guilt. They were led to believe that boys don't run away from good parents.

---

[11] Bell points out that in most human societies parents are not expected to rear children who are "different" from the parents; they are only expected to produce images of themselves. See Robert R. Bell, *Marriage and Family Interaction* (rev. ed.; Homewood, Ill.: The Dorsey Press, 1967), p. 405.

[12] For a discussion of "the cult of the child" see Lerner, *op. cit.*, pp. 560–570.

It would be interesting to know how many boys have left home in America since 1800. This was apparently quite common during frontier days when restless sons would decide to "go West."[13]

It is a fact that the boy who ran away from our grandparents eventually came home and always claimed that he left home not because of anything his parents had ever done but because he wanted to see the world. It is also true that he was very close to his parents once he had returned to his native community.[14]

We live in a world of specialists, some of whom are very helpful to parents. But fathers and mothers are *amateurs* in their parental roles, not professionals.

Our criminal courts provide that an accused person be judged by a jury of his peers. It seems to us that parents are entitled to the same consideration.

Marital instability

It is often assumed that fathers and mothers operate as a team in their parental role in our society. This may still be true for a majority of American parents but it is not true of a sizable minority. This is discussed at length in chapter nine but it needs to be noted here that 20 to 40 percent of American parents see their team broken at some time or other.

Rearing children is difficult in our society with the best of marriages, but one can only imagine what it is like for couples whose marriages are failing or have already broken.[15]

New roles for American mothers

Since grandmother's day American mothers have taken on new community roles and new economic roles—they raise money for Red Cross and about one third of them are employed outside of the home.[16] In many ways they have more responsibility than their mothers and grandmothers ever had. Maybe some of them try to do too much but that is the world they find themselves living in.

---

[13] An interesting description of the process of families "splitting up" as the sons left for the West may be found in Lura Beam, *Maine Hamlet* (New York: Wilfred Funk, 1957).

[14] This man was our favorite relative. He had spent years touring with a "wild west" show and used to perform for us children on his infrequent visits.

[15] For discussion of parents in unusual circumstances, see chap. 9. "Parents without Partners," in this volume.

[16] The most complete analysis of the employed mother in our society is that by F. Ivan Nye and Lois Wladis Hoffman, *The Employed Mother in America* (Chicago: Rand McNally & Co., 1963).

America is no longer a rural society

The rural and small-town America of 1900 or even 1920 must certainly have posed fewer problems for parents than our urban society of today. In fact, we not only live in cities: over half of us now reside in metropolitan centers.[17]

On the farm, children could be kept busy with chores, while in the city they have nothing to do. The long school vacations pose very real problems for urban parents, but on the farm these recesses simply provided more hands to do all the things that have to be done on a farm. It is significant that less than 10 percent of all American parents were engaged in farming as of the 1960's.[18]

In chapter 11 the impact of urbanization on parents will be discussed at greater length. Here we simply note that the critics of American parents need to remember that the child rearing "laboratory" is vastly more complex today than it was 50 years ago.

Rise of the mass media

Parents today are only one of several powerful influences on their children—at least this is so once the youngsters are old enough to read the comics, go to movies, listen to the radio, or watch television. Madison Avenue would like to have us believe that television doesn't influence children but parents are skeptical. It is a bit difficult to grasp why advertisers would spend hundreds of millions of dollars on television programs for children if they didn't influence anybody.[19]

Parents and children today both are so immersed in messages from the mass media that they are scarcely aware of it.

It seems clear that Hollywood and the local rock 'n' roll radio station do not worry as to whether or not they support the values that parents are struggling to promote. The mass media are commercial enterprises and they promote what sells. If this happens to be sex, as in the movies, or violence, as on television, that is not their concern—parents are supposed to see that their children avoid such movies and such programs. And some

---

[17] The U.S. Census for 1960 reported 53 percent of the population living in metropolitan areas with a central city of at least 50,000. Another 16 percent lived in smaller cities that were not part of a metropolitan area. Thus 69 percent of American families as of 1960 were urban.

[18] As of the 1960 U.S. Census, 9 percent of the population lived on farms. This has declined slightly since then according to news reports.

[19] For an analysis of the impact of television on children, see Wilbur Schramm et al., *Television in the Lives of Our Children* (Stanford: Stanford University Press, 1961).

parents, of course, are able to do just that. But lots of other parents are not so skillful or so fortunate.

We were reminded of this recently when we took time to read a state information sticker on a cigarette machine. It read: "Minors are prohibited by state law from purchasing cigarettes from this machine. *Parents will please cooperate.*" Parents should cooperate! In an earlier America, cigarette vending machines were illegal; you had to prove your age to buy cigarettes over the counter.

It is perfectly obvious that the legislators who authorized these machines were primarily interested in only one thing—the easier sale of cigarettes. They were certainly not concerned about helping parents prevent or control smoking among teenagers.

Why not have a beer machine, or a martini dispenser, with the same hypocritical sticker stating "Parents will please cooperate"?

Emergence of the youth peer group

One of the most dramatic developments of modern urban America has been the phenomenal rise to power and influence (also affluence) of the youth peer group.[20] In rural America young people might spend one evening a week together, but most of their time was absorbed by the work on the farm. Today, however, high school students and other young people may spend several hours *daily* within a subsociety often labeled "teen age society." These young people have their own mass idols, their own music, their own clothes, their own language—in a very real sense they have created their own world.

Parents find that to buck this youth peer group is not an easy matter. More will be said about this later, but it needs to be remembered that this youth peer group is a new force in American society that parents (as well as university administrators) have to reckon with.[21] It is the writer's belief that only the more skillful parents can challenge the youth peer group with any consistent success.

Parents today have to deal with the experts on child rearing

After World War I, psychiatry, sociology, anthropology, and psychology (the behavioral sciences) became very prominent in the United

---

[20] For useful discussions of teenage culture in our society see: Jessie Bernard (ed.), *Teen-Age Culture*, special issue of *The Annals*, 338 (November, 1961); James S. Coleman, *The Adolescent Society* (New York: The Free Press, 1961); also Grace and Fred M. Hechinger, *Teen-Age Tyranny* (New York: William Morrow & Co., 1963).

[21] A faculty committee at the University of Wisconsin reported in 1967 that American universities were moving in the direction of giving up their *in loco parentis* (parental) function for their students. But fathers and mothers cannot yield responsibility just because the going gets rough.

States.[22] The psychiatric casualties of the war and concern about the causes of war led the more intelligent members of our society to turn to the sciences of man in an effort to understand human behavior.

This development soon raised serious questions about the methods parents were using to rear their children.

Two specific threads in this new behavioral science tended to bother parents: (1) Freudian theory, which revolutionized the concept of what children were like and took the position that what parents did (or did not do) in the first five years of the child's life would shape the person forever; and (2) the conclusion of sociology and anthropology that children were born with few (if any) instincts, that their eventual behavior would essentially reflect the socialization they received (or did not receive) from their family and other social institutions. This extremely plastic view of the child frightened the more intelligent parents and left them apprehensive. Later on, if their child did not turn out well, they were saddled with guilt.

It is the writer's thesis, discussed in chapter 3, that these new behavioral sciences have not, as yet, been of much help to parents. Much of the research has not been good enough to stand up over the years with the result that the recommendations to parents on child rearing methods have changed from one decade to the next.[23] This has resulted in the term *child rearing expert* becoming almost a national joke in our society.

There were undoubtedly many different factors involved in the developments discussed above, just as there were many different results—both positive and negative. But one result was that traditional parental methods, based on hundreds of years of experience, were discarded (or at least downgraded) before a mature and reliable science of child rearing became available. Thus a great many of the more progressive parents were caught between the old and the new. To a considerable extent this situation still prevails.

Poor preparation for parental roles

In a study of young parents,[24] the writer was impressed by the frequency of the comment, "We didn't know what we were getting into." Even though this sample included only couples who had wanted a baby,

---

[22] The development of child rearing experts is treated in different places by Lerner, *op. cit.*, Brim, *op. cit.*, and also by Daniel R. Miller and Guy E. Swanson, *The Changing American Parent* (New York: John Wiley & Sons, 1958).

[23] See, for example, the research of William H. Sewell, "Infant Training and the Personality of the Child," *American Journal of Sociology*, 58 (1952), pp. 150–159; also Martha Wolfenstein, "Trends in Infant Care," *American Journal of Orthopsychiatry*, 23 (1953), pp. 120–130.

[24] E. E. LeMasters, "Parenthood as Crisis," *Marriage and Family Living*, 19 (1957), pp. 352–355. The writer was first made aware of the widespread interest in parental

the actual process of becoming parents had posed problems and stresses they had not anticipated.

It seemed to us that these couples had received very inadequate preparation for the parental role. Most of the husbands felt that they had had no preparation whatsoever for the father role, and even a majority of the wives felt that their preparation for the role of mother had been quite inadequate.

One obvious factor in this feeling of not being prepared for the parental role was the almost complete failure of our high schools and colleges to include this subject in their courses of study.

Another factor, less obvious, was that these parents had grown up in relatively small families and had had very little experience caring for younger brothers and sisters.[25]

A third factor was the existence in our culture of a very real "romantic complex" about children (especially babies) and parenthood. If you interview parents whose children are 15 to 20 years of age, they will usually admit that the parent role is perhaps the most challenging thing they have ever done in their lives—exciting, thrilling, exhausting, and (at times) heartbreaking. These are not bitter or cynical parents; they are just realistic. They remind the writer of war veterans: they find the experience unforgettable but are not enthused about going back and going through it again.

Young parents lack any of this feeling of what parenthood involves. And when they begin to find out they often experience a temporary state of shock or disbelief. As one young mother, an honors graduate from a famous women's college, put it to us: "I just couldn't believe that the baby could upset me the way she did. But when she cried so much during the first few weeks and the doctor couldn't find out what was wrong, I thought I would lose my mind."

This concludes the discussion of features of our society that the writer believes pose problems for parents.

In order to balance the picture somewhat let us look briefly at some of the developments in modern America that have been supportive to fathers and mothers in this crucial role.

---

problems by the reception given this paper. Feature stories appeared in such newspapers as *The New York Times* and *The Chicago Tribune;* the paper was summarized for a group of newspapers in Australia; several hundred reprints were requested from all over the world; as late as 1968 (11 years after publication) feature stories were still appearing in mass magazines and metropolitan newspapers based on the findings of this paper.

[25] For a discussion of the parental role played by older siblings in the large family, see Salvador Minuchin et al., *Families of the Slums* (New York: Basic Books, 1967), p. 219.

Positive features of American society
in relationship to parents

Modern medicine

There can be no doubt that the substantial progress made in understanding and controlling childhood diseases has lifted some of the fear and agony from the hearts and shoulders of parents. One has only to remember back a few years when polio stalked the land to appreciate this type of progress.

The dramatic decline in infant mortality since 1920 has alone saved millions of parents from tragedy and despair.

As a branch of modern medicine child psychiatry has undoubtedly helped some parents, but the writer feels that other parents have actually been damaged by the inadequate scientific base upon which psychiatric diagnoses are made.

Greater affluence in the society

In an urban society parenthood is an expensive business. Since more parents have more money in the 1960's than ever before in our society they should be in a better position to finance their child rearing efforts.

This is undoubtedly true, yet only a few interviews with affluent parents are needed to uncover some of the hazards of this affluence. One father said to the writer: "It worries me that kids today get almost everything they want just by asking for it. My wife and I have tried not to spoil our children, yet I'm afraid they haven't learned the value of a dollar. Things come too easy for them these days." This father had grown up in a family of modest means and was concerned that some of the lessons he had learned as a child were being denied his children.

Better means of contraception

For a long time most American parents have used some means of limiting the size of their families.[26] This was one of the strategies employed by the various immigrant groups to climb out of the lower income levels.

But until recently a significant margin of error in family planning was almost inevitable because of the contraceptive methods used. The pill has improved family planning, but even more simple and effective means of birth control are promised in the future.

---

[26] About 85 percent of American married couples plan their families at least in part. See Ronald Freedman, Pascal K. Whelpton, and Arthur A. Campbell, *Family Planning, Sterility and Population Growth* (New York: McGraw-Hill Book Co., 1959), p. 79.

This should mean that the great majority of parents in our society will have their children because they *want* them—certainly one of the prerequisites for successful performance of the role of father or mother.

Miscellaneous positive factors

Most American parents are no longer immigrants reared in a society quite different from the one in which they are trying to rear their children.[27] Most of the fathers and mothers today have another advantage in that they grew up in an urban community; they are not migrants from the farm trying to rear their sons and daughters in the strange world of the city.[28]

There are, however, striking exceptions to the above statement—southern black parents recently moved to the urban jungles of the north and the west; southern rural whites from Appalachia and elsewhere trying to make a new start in Chicago or Detroit or some other city where the jobs are supposed to be; American Indians resettled in Chicago or Denver or some other city; and Puerto Rican parents trying to make the long jump from the island to the mainland. These parents and their problems are very real and very dramatic, but they comprise a relatively small proportion of all American parents.[29]

Most fathers and mothers today have more education than their parents had—and in a society that places so much stress on formal education one would like to think that this should be an advantage.

Some general observations

Earlier in the chapter the point was made that modern America lacks consensus-based, clearly articulated age grading steps which would define for both young people and their parents the specific point in the maturation cycle occupied by the child at any given time. When such age grading exists, for example, that children enter the first grade at six years of age, the parent and the child both know what the next step in growth consists of and when it will occur. An even better example, mentioned earlier, is the legal age of driving an automobile, a step clearly enunciated in most of the 50 states.

---

[27] See Oscar Handlin, *The Uprooted* (Boston: Little, Brown & Co., 1952).

[28] The writer's father, for example, grew up on a small farm and attended school for only three years; the mother lived in a small rural village until her marriage; later on the parents moved to a small city of 12,000 population where they reared their four children. In contrast, the writer grew up in an urban world and is rearing his children in an urban world.

[29] For a systematic analysis of the problems of minority group parents in our society see chap. 6.

In the writer's personal experience as a parent, and based on interviews with other parents, situations of this nature which have been clearly defined seem to produce relatively little conflict between parents and their children. But in many other areas, such as dating and the hours to be observed in dating, there seems to exist considerable leeway and variation in many local communities. This produces a situation in which parents and young people must bargain and haggle. This in itself may not be undesirable but it places parents who do not possess great skill in handling their children at a considerable disadvantage. In an ideal social system even the average person can manage his role assignments—this is the plan for most armed forces units, for example—but the absence of age grading sets up situations which only the superior parent can manage.

Another observation that might be pertinent at this point is the fragmentation of family functions in our society: other social institutions such as the school have been expanding their responsibilities since World War I, which means that it is not always clear whether parents or teachers (or somebody else) are supposed to do certain things for children.[30] A good example of this may be found in the area of sex education: in some school systems young people are given excellent courses in human reproduction, the part that sex plays in marriage, and other aspects of human sexuality. In such communities the function of parents in sex education might be limited to the inculcation and/or discussion of values. But in other communities the parent would have to assume the entire responsibility for sex education—or else concede it to the adolescent peer group and the mass media.

Here, again, superior parents would probably not experience too much difficulty, but less adequate parents would find the situation difficult to cope with.

The transfer of functions from the family does not necessarily represent social decline, nor does it foretell the demise of the American family. Childbirth, for example, has been almost entirely shifted from the home to the maternity ward since 1900 with benefits to both family and society. Such transfer of function, however, does produce a more specialized type of family, as Pitts has pointed out.[31] A specialized family system may be desirable and more efficient, but it has to perform its specialty, not just exist.

---

30 The standard reference on the changing functions of the American family is W. F. Ogburn and M. F. Nimkoff, *Technology and the Changing Family* (Boston: Houghton Mifflin Co., 1955). For a more recent analysis, see Robert F. Winch, *The Modern Family* (rev. ed.; New York: Holt, Rinehart, and Winston, 1963), Pt. 2. "The Family in America and Its Functional Matrix."

31 See Jesse R. Pitts, "The Structural-Functional Approach," in Harold T. Christensen (ed.), *Handbook of Marriage and the Family* (Chicago: Rand McNally & Co., 1964), pp. 51–124.

One of the reasons why many parents feel inadequate in modern America is the pervasive nature of negative news media stories about fathers and mothers: one seldom reads or hears or sees any items about successful parents—we only know about those that have failed. It is as if the only business news available would be that about firms that have gone bankrupt, whereas in truth most of the news about private corporations in our society today tells how successful they have been in the current year.

It is true that a few outstanding newspapers, such as the *Christian Science Monitor*, make a determined effort to report positive news about the American family, but for the most part the stories about parents and their children in the mass media are tragic and sad. This may make some parents feel superior but it hardly encourages most of us to think that we are on a winning team.

Constants and variables in parenthood

In the paper by Davis cited earlier a distinction is made between the constants (or universals) in parenthood and the variables (factors found only in certain societies at specific periods in history). An example of a constant would be the physiological differences found between the parent and child—the fact that each is at a different stage of physical growth or decline but yet must accommodate themselves to each other. This would be true of parenthood in any society, and yet social factors might still be operative to some extent: persons age faster in most so-called primitive societies than in most modern societies, and attitudes toward aging also vary from one culture to another.

An example of a variable would be social change: not only its rate but also its depth would vary from one society to another and from one historical period to another within the same society.

In this book we are primarily concerned with the variables in parenthood: the particular characteristics of our society that seem to affect the role of father and mother.

To some extent parenthood in any society is probably traumatic for both parent and child—at least this seems to be the point of Feuer who comments: "The conflict of generations is a universal theme in history . . . ."[32]

Conclusions and summary

In this first chapter some of the structural features of American society that affect parents were analyzed in a preliminary fashion. Since most of

[32] Lewis S. Feuer, *The Conflict of Generations* (New York: Basic Books, 1969), p. 68.

these cultural patterns will be discussed in greater depth in subsequent chapters no effort was made at this point to examine them systematically.

In the early part of the chapter we drew heavily on the classic 1940 paper by Davis; in the later sections cultural characteristics were noted which were not dealt with by Davis.

In the balance of the book systematic analysis will be attempted on those features of our society that constitute the social setting in which fathers and mothers must function.

chapter

two

Folklore
about parenthood

S OME years ago Thurman Arnold wrote a very interesting and provocative book called *The Folklore of Capitalism.*[1] In this study Arnold
was analyzing folk beliefs or myths about the American economy. His
thesis was that capitalism in the United States had changed so drastically
in the last century that hardly any of the traditional theories about it were
relevant any more—and yet they were constantly being quoted by persons
who opposed any change in the government's economic policies.

In later years John Galbraith has taken up where Arnold left off and
uses the term *the conventional wisdom* to describe beliefs about American
society that he regards as erroneous.[2]

The clinical psychologist Albert Ellis has also used this approach in
analyzing American attitudes and beliefs about sex.[3]

In a previous book about the American courtship and marriage systems the present writer made extensive use of the concept of folklore.[4]

The reception of the Arnold and Galbraith books leads one to believe
that this type of analysis is interesting and worthwhile.[5]

In this chapter an attempt will be made to analyze folk beliefs about
parenthood. In any civilization there is always a large body of folk belief

---

[1] Thurman Arnold, *The Folklore of Capitalism* (New Haven: Yale University Press,
1937).

[2] John Kenneth Galbraith, *The Affluent Society* (Boston: Houghton Mifflin Co.,
1958). For another treatment of folklore, see William J. Lederer and Don D. Jackson,
The Mirages of Marriage (New York: W. W. Norton, 1968).

[3] Albert Ellis, *The Folklore of Sex* (New York: Charles Boni, 1951).

[4] E. E. LeMasters, *Modern Courtship and Marriage* (New York: The Macmillan
Co., 1957).

[5] For a brief and popular discussion of myths in our society see Leo Rosten, *The
Many Worlds of Leo Rosten* (New York: Harper & Row, 1964), especially pp. 206–208.

about anything very important. As the term *folklore* or *folk belief* is used here, it means simply widely held beliefs which are not supported by the facts. Usually, these beliefs tend to romanticize the truth, although in some cases the reverse might be true: reality might not be as bad as the folk belief would imply.

It is the writer's contention that persons living in modern civilizations are apt to think they do not believe in folklore, whereas in actual fact they do. Thus they are apt to think their behavior is based on sound rational principles when in reality it is not.

The approach will be to state the folk belief and then to subject it and its implications to systematic analysis.

1. That rearing children is fun. No one can teach high school or college courses in the family without being impressed by this belief that rearing children is fun. It derives from the notion that "children are cute" (to be analyzed later). Young people are often heard to say: "Oh I just can't wait to have children." The odd thing is that *parents* don't talk that way. This leads one to the conclusion that this belief reflects folklore and has no substantial basis in reality.

The truth is—as every parent knows—that rearing children is probably the hardest, and most thankless, job in the world. No intelligent father or mother would deny that it is *exciting*, as well as *interesting*, but to call it "fun" is a serious error. The idea of something being fun implies that you can take it or leave it, whereas parents do not have this choice. Fathers and mothers must stay with the child and keep trying, whether it is fun, or whether they are enjoying it or not. Any comparison to bowling or listening to jazz records is strictly coincidental.

We do not mean to deny that a great many parents enjoy their work and that they derive a certain amount of satisfaction from it. But to describe what parents do as fun is to miss the point. It would be like describing the sweat and tears involved in the artist's creation as fun. The life of Thomas Wolfe or that of almost any serious artist will convey the point.[6]

Now that his military service is well in the past, the author of this book can truthfully say that he enjoyed his years in the U.S. Naval Air Corps and that he would not have wanted to miss the experience. But it is also true that on almost any day of those three years he would have accepted his immediate discharge had it been offered. This feeling is very common to the millions of men who served in the armed forces during World War

---

[6] Persons who think it is fun to be a great writer should read the following: Andrew Turnbull, *Thomas Wolfe* (New York: Charles Scribner's Sons, 1967), and the book about Eugene O'Neill by Arthur and Barbara Gelb: *O'Neill* (New York: Harper & Brothers, 1962).

II (or any other war, for that matter). We think the sentiment also describes very accurately the feelings of millions of fathers and mothers.

The truth is somewhat as follows: rearing children is hard work; it is often nerve-racking work; it involves tremendous responsibility; it takes all the ability one has (and more); and once you have begun you can't quit when you feel like it. It would be helpful to young parents if they could be made to realize all of this before they enlist—or before they are drafted, as the case may be.

In pursuing the analogy between military service and parenthood, the writer has often heard parents refer to married couples who have no children as draft-dodgers. The sentiment is similar to that which veterans of the armed forces have toward able-bodied men who somehow escaped military service in the last war (any last war will do). The veteran feels that military service is a rough experience but that it has to be endured for the sake of the country; his feeling toward men who did not have this experience is ambivalent: in a sense he resents their escaping what he had to go through, but in another sense he recognizes that there may have been valid reasons why they were not in the armed forces.

Parents are also ambivalent toward nonparents: since children represent the future of the society it is reasonable to expect that all of us would make some contribution to that future, and this, of course, nonparents have not done;[7] but there is also a sense in which parents envy the nonparents— their freedom, their less strenuous way of life, their lack of responsibility for another human being's welfare.

This does not mean, however, that most parents regret having had children any more than it means that veterans regret having served their country. Of course, we don't hear much from the men who were killed or maimed in the wars, and we also don't hear too much from parents who have suffered much the same fate rearing their children.

2. *That children are sweet and cute.* When young people see small children they are apt to remark: "Your children are so cute!" It is true, of course, that small children *are* cute (at times), but this hardly exhausts the subject—or the adjectives parents use to describe their children when they are *not* being cute.

Several years ago the author published the results of a study of young parents entitled "Parenthood as Crisis."[8] In this report it was stated that parents in our society have a romantic complex about child rearing and

---

[7] Nonparents, however, may well have made other valuable contributions to the future of the society. A classic example would be the spinster schoolteacher of an earlier era who devoted her life to helping children get an education.

[8] E. E. LeMasters, "Parenthood as Crisis," *Marriage and Family Living*, 19, (1957). See also Arnold W. Green, "The Middle Class Male Child and Neurosis," *American Sociological Review*, 11 (1946), pp. 31–41.

that they tend to suffer from a process of disenchantment after they become parents. When this study was summarized in *The New York Times* a flood of mail descended on the writer from parents, with the vast bulk of it agreeing with the findings of the study. The response to this dry scientific paper (first published in a professional journal) led the writer to feel that he had struck a responsive chord in the collective bosom of American fathers and mothers.[9]

3. *That children will turn out well if they have "good" parents.* Logically, this should be so, and one would certainly like to believe that it is so. For that matter, it probably is *usually* a correct statement—but not always. Almost everyone knows of at least one nice family with a black sheep in the fold. It seems to be a rare family, indeed, that has not had some tragic experience with at least one child (assuming the family consists of several children).

It would be comforting to think that parents can guarantee happiness and success (the twin gods of our civilization), but the sad truth is that they cannot. Children are so complex, and so different, and our society is so complicated, that fathers and mothers simply do not have the "quality control" one finds in industrial production. Parents with skill and ability, of course, probably have a better batting average than those of us with more modest talents—but even the good parents do not bat a thousand.

Someone has observed that marriage is perhaps the only game of chance at which both players can lose.[10] It might be that rearing children should be added to this list.

It would be fascinating and interesting (and perhaps frightening) to know what the actual success and failure rate is in rearing children in modern America. The writer has seen no respectable research (including his own) which would answer this question, and in a certain sense it cannot be answered because the terms are so hard to define.[11] When has a parent been successful with any given child? At what age do we judge the product—adolescence, early adulthood, middle age, or the life span? Do we include material success, physical health, mental health, spiritual health, or what?

In an extremely unscientific manner the writer has surveyed a few

---

[9] A more recent study of new parents came to different conclusions. See Daniel F. Hobbs, Jr., "Transition to Parenthood: A Replication and an Extension," *Marriage and the Family*, 30 (August, 1968), pp. 413–417. Although Hobbs refers to his study as a replication of the earlier study by LeMasters, an important difference is that the LeMasters sample was limited to middle-class parents. This does not appear to be true of the Hobbs sample.

[10] Someone else commented to the writer that marriage may also be the only game of chance in which both players *can win.*

[11] In their study of married couples in Detroit, Blood and Wolfe report that only 3 percent of the sample said they would not want any children if they had their life to live over again. See Robert O. Blood, Jr. and Donald M. Wolfe, *Husbands and Wives* (New York: The Free Press, 1960), p. 137. It is interesting to note that of the 909 spouses interviewed for this study not one was a male.

families with very sobering results. Winston Churchill and his wife, for' example, seem to have been successful with only two of their children, yet both of these parents have been remarkably successful in the other areas of life.[12] Franklin D. Roosevelt and Eleanor Roosevelt, certainly two of the most loved and revered Americans of the modern era, seem to have been only moderately successful in rearing their children—and this appraisal comes from Democrats, not Republicans.[13]

It is true that families of the above type have most unusual family stresses because of the heavy burden carried by the father and mother in discharging their many public responsibilities, but the writer has also studied some families at very modest social levels with somewhat similar results: three families selected at random agreed that only about half of their children had turned out very well—not in material matters but as human beings. One wonders whether the parental batting average in modern America would exceed 50 percent. But of course in baseball .300 is considered to be an exceptional batting average. The problem in parenthood is that fathers and mothers are not supposed to fail with any child, no matter what the difficulties.

4. That girls are harder to rear than boys. It seems to be true, at least, that parents worry more about daughters than about sons. A study by Mirra Komarovsky of Barnard College reveals that girls in middle-class families were supervised more closely than their brothers.[14] There seems little doubt that this is generally true in our society.

The reason, no doubt, is that daughters can get pregnant and sons cannot. If you think about it, however, this is rather superficial reasoning on the part of parents, for premature pregnancy (serious as it still is) is only one of the hazards faced by American young people.[15] If we consider such a thing as alcoholism, for example, with its predominantly male addicts, parents could well afford to shift some of their concern from their daughters to their sons. Personally, if we had to make a choice, we would rather

---

[12] On the difficulties of child rearing in the Churchill family see Jack Fishman, *My Darling Clementine* (New York: David McKay Co., 1963). This is the story of Mrs. Winston Churchill and their married life; also Randolph Churchill, *Twenty-One Years* (Boston: Houghton Mifflin Co., 1965), the story of his childhood; also Randolph Churchill's book, *Winston S. Churchill* (New York: Houghton Mifflin Co., 1966). This latter volume details how seldom Winston Churchill ever saw his upper upper class parents when he was a child.

[13] All of the Roosevelt children have now been divorced at least once, which does not necessarily indicate failure in life but is quite a different record from that of their parents. Some of the parental problems of the Franklin D. Roosevelts are discussed in *This Is My Story* by Eleanor Roosevelt (New York: Harper & Brothers, 1937) and in Elliott Roosevelt, *As He Saw It* (New York: Duell, Sloan & Pearce, 1946).

[14] Mirra Komarovsky, "Functional Analysis of Sex Roles," *American Sociological Review*, 15 (1950), pp. 508–516.

[15] For sons the hazards from automobile accidents are far greater than for daughters—three times greater according to this writer's insurance agent. The documentation behind these statements about sons and daughters in our society will be found in chap. 7, "The American Mother," and chap. 8, "The American Father."

have a daughter get pregnant without benefit of marriage license than we would to have a son become an alcoholic.

There is also evidence from the monumental study by Burgess and Wallin, of the University of Chicago, that boys (or young men) approach marriage in our society less realistically than do girls—and with a greater chance of failing as marriage partners.[16] Here, again, if we had a choice, we would rather have a daughter become pregnant before marriage than to have a son ruin his marriage.

One last bit of evidence on this point: the Kinsey research group found that men (sons) were less able to practice sexual monogamy than were their wives (daughters).[17] This too would lead one to suspect that modern parents would do well to transfer some of their concern and supervision from their girls to their boys. The interested reader will find a great deal more on this subject in Ashley Montagu's book, *The Natural Superiority of Women*.[18] As a sociologist the writer tends to distrust the word *natural* in the title of this study, but Montagu seems to prove his point: that daughters are doing much better than sons in our society in the 20th century.

5. *That today's parents are not as good as those of yesterday.* It is impossible to prove or disprove this sort of belief, of course, but it does seem to be prevalent. The truth is, as shown elsewhere in this study,[19] that standards applied to parents today have been raised, and it is also true that the laboratory in which parents have to operate (the modern world) has become infinitely more complex. All of this tends to create the impression that parents as a group have deteriorated since the good old days of the 18th or 19th century. This sort of argument is usually clinched (at least to the satisfaction of the critic) by reference to the family of John Adams or Jefferson. Actually, nobody knows what most parents were like in the old days, but if we can compare them to what doctors and other practitioners of the era were like, it seems possible that they were not supermen or superwomen but just plain fathers and mothers sweating out every child.

There is always a tendency to romanticize the past, and this seems to have done a very real disservice to modern parents.[20]

6. *That child rearing today is easier because of modern medicine, modern appliances, child psychology, and so on.* According to this belief,

---

16 See Ernest W. Burgess and Paul Wallin, *Engagement and Marriage* (Philadelphia: J. B. Lippincott Co., 1953), p. 565.

17 On the Kinsey data on adultery among husbands and wives in their sample see: Alfred C. Kinsey, *Sexual Behavior in the Human Female* (Philadelphia: W. B. Saunders Co., 1953), chap. 10.

18 See Ashley Montagu, *The Natural Superiority of Women* (rev. ed.; New York: The Macmillan Co., 1968).

19 See chap. 4, "Role Analysis of Parenthood."

20 One of the leading family sociologists, William J. Goode of Columbia University, takes the position that we have no reliable history of the American family. See his

modern mothers have an easy time of it because of the weekly diaper service and the automatic dishwasher. Actually, the truth is probably just the opposite: that mothers today are in much more of a rat race than their grandmothers ever dreamed of. Middle-class mothers, in particular, have become poorly paid cab drivers, racing from one place to another trying to get all of the children to their various appointments, helping to run the PTA, being a buddy to their husbands—plus holding a full or part-time job in many instances.[21]

The odd thing is that modern medicine and modern child psychology have really made matters worse in some ways, for we now are more aware of all of the terrible things that can happen to children and are expected to recognize them early enough to take the proper preventive action. Example: the writer has crooked teeth. He has never, however, held his father and mother responsible for this. With his own two sons, however, it is expected that he and their mother will take the necessary action to prevent their children from having such teeth. This, of course, will cost a small fortunte if an orthodontist has to improve on nature—but in addition to the financial outlay will be the concern as to whether "we have done the right thing about Bill's teeth," and so on. The writer's parents never had to shoulder such burdens.[22] And *their* parents had it even easier.

It is true, of course, that there are times when the pediatrician or the surgeon or the child psychiatrist can make you glad you are living in the 20th century instead of the 18th. But for every such moment modern parents pay dearly—and not just in terms of money. They pay in terms of awareness and fear and responsibility and in ways their ancestors never thought of.

7. *That children today really appreciate all the advantages their parents are able to give them.* Oddly enough, the reverse seems to be true: that children today are less appreciative and not more so. Numerous observers of the American family have come to this conclusion.[23]

College students are very frank about this: they regard what they have received as their *right* and not as something to be thankful for.[24]

In a sense, this same sort of psychology is characteristic of all of us

paper, "The Sociology of the Family," in *Sociology Today*, edited by Robert K. Merton et al. (New York: Basic Books, 1959), p. 195.

[21] For a popular account of the hectic schedule of many American mothers see Betty Friedan, *The Feminine Mystique* (New York: W. W. Norton, 1963). This subject is pursued in greater depth in chap. 7, "The American Mother."

[22] Actually, in all fairness to our parents, they at least preserved the writer's teeth, even though they are crooked, whereas they themselves never saw a dentist in their childhood.

[23] See David Riesman et al., *The Lonely Crowd* (rev. ed.; New Haven: Yale University Press, 1961), chap. 2, "From Morality to Morale: Changes in the Agents of Character Formation." See also Max Lerner, "Children and Parents," *America as a Civilization* (New York: Simon and Schuster, 1957), pp. 560–570.

[24] This statement is based on an unpublished study of college seniors done by the writer at Beloit College, Beloit, Wisc., in 1958.

living in the modern world; we take for granted inside toilets and painless dentistry and religious freedom and simply complain when the system fails to deliver what we have come to consider as our birthright. Thus parents derive very little satisfaction from giving children all the modern advantages: they only feel guilty when they *can't* deliver the goods.

8. *That the hard work of rearing children is justified by the fact that we are going to make a better world.* This is a comforting thought, and one that most parents need desperately to believe, but there is very little evidence to sustain it. It has more to do with hope than reality.

Actually, a great many schoolteachers and other persons who work with children believe they are getting worse, not better. And except for material progress it is hard to see how the modern world is better than the one preceding it.

One can always hope, of course, that this new generation will be braver, wiser, and happier than their parents have been. It is doubtful, however, that this will prove to be true.

9. *The sex education myth: that children won't get into trouble if they have been told the facts of life.* One mother said to the writer: "I don't see how such a thing (premarital pregnancy) could have happened to our daughter. She has known where babies come from since she was six years old."

This indicates how naive some parents in our society are about the mystic power of sex education, which at best usually covers only the physiology of reproduction. Nothing is said about passion or seduction or the role of unconscious factors in heterosexual interaction. It seems to be assumed by such parents that sex is always a cold calculating act—as if Freud had never written a word to the contrary.[25]

The truth is that much (if not most) human sexual behavior is non-rational and only partly subject to continuous intellectual control. If this were not the case illegitimate pregnancies in our society would be much fewer than they are and Kinsey's data on adultery would be less massive.[26]

A great many human societies, such as the Latin cultures, have always assumed that sex was too powerful for most humans to control and they therefore arranged that persons for whom sexual relations were taboo were never left alone together.[27] Our society is relatively unique in that we

---

25 See Sigmund Freud, *Sexuality and the Psychology of Love* (New York: Collier Books Edition, 1963). Almost any page will do.

26 Kinsey reported a significant amount of adultery by both wives and husbands ·in his sample—but considerably higher rates for husbands than for wives. See Alfred C. Kinsey et al., *op. cit.*, pp. 409–445. In this second volume Kinsey summarizes the data on men from the first volume and compares it with the data on women compiled for the second volume.

27 For the Italian view of sex as too overpowering for individuals to control see Luigi Barzini, *The Italians* (New York: Atheneum Press, 1964); also Irving R. Levine, *Main Street, Italy* (New York: Doubleday & Co., 1963).

have adopted just the opposite policy—at least for single persons: they are permitted (and even expected) to spend hundreds of hours alone without ever having sex relations until they marry. Research tells us, of course, that considerable proportions of them do have sexual relations before marriage, but only a relatively few ever get pregnant. Or if they get pregnant they marry before the birth of the child.[28]

The writer believes in sex education and thinks it belongs in every school and college curriculum, also in every family. But one should not expect too much of sexual knowledge: attitudes and values and passion and a host of factors determine the sexual behavior of any person at any given time with a particular partner. It could well be that the art of seduction has as much to do with premarital sexual relations as sex education does. Certainly the subconscious and unconscious factors analyzed by Freudians have to be taken into account in understanding why people behave the way they do sexually.

10. There are no bad children—only bad parents. This, in the opinion of the writer, is one of the most destructive bits of folklore relating to parenthood. As Max Lerner points out, parents have become the bad guys in modern America while children and teachers and other custodians and child-shapers (such as the television station owners) have become the good guys.[29] And just as on television, the bad guys always lose.

Actually, Brim has analyzed a rather lengthy list of factors other than parents which affect the destinies of children.[30] These include: genetic factors, siblings, members of the extended family such as grandparents, schoolteachers, playmates, the youth peer group, and so on. He concludes that parents have been held unduly responsible for shaping the destiny of their offspring.

Lerner takes the position that parental critics tend to be "child worshippers"—the child can do no wrong, all children are potentially perfect (or near perfect), and that parents should be able to rear *any* child successfully if they only knew enough and only tried hard enough.[31]

The writer is inclined to the view that some children are doomed almost from the point of birth: try as they will, their parents seem destined to fail in their efforts to solve the various problems that arise during the child rearing process. In an earlier America this was conceptualized as fate, but in contemporary America there is no such thing as fate; fate is just another word for poor parental role performance. It seems to us that this is folk-

---

[28] Christensen's research indicated that perhaps 20 percent of all first births in our society were conceived before marriage. See Harold T. Christensen, *Marriage Analysis* (New York: Ronald Press, 1950), p. 153.

[29] Lerner, *op. cit.*, pp. 560–570.

[30] See Orville G. Brim, Jr., "The Influence of Parent on Child," *Education for Child Rearing* (New York: Russell Sage Foundation, 1959), chap. 2.

[31] This discussion is in the section cited previously.

lore or mythology. It also seems to us to be very unfair to parents who have made valiant efforts to help their children attain a decent and productive life.

These matters will be discussed at some length in the next chapter on "Parents and the Behavioral Sciences."

11. *That two parents are always better than one.* Adoption agencies and psychiatrists have usually (if not always) taken the position that a child must have both a father and a mother to grow up properly, yet it would be interesting to know how many Americans have survived reasonably well with only one parent—President Nathan Pusey of Harvard University is an example that comes to mind. Another is John W. Gardner, recently Secretary of Health, Education, and Welfare in the Johnson Administration.[32] It is not intended here to argue that it isn't nicer to have two parents rather than one; the issue is whether it is absolutely necessary that a child have both a father and a mother in the home to grow up properly. Our hunch is that it is not.

In a recent paper Alfred Kadushin, a recognized authority on child welfare, has reviewed the evidence on the one-parent family in our society and has concluded that the data do not justify the assumption, widely held, that such families are predisposed to pathology. As the result of papers such as this some adoption agencies are reviewing their traditional policy of not permitting single adults to adopt children.[33]

With only a casual effort the writer has located and identified over 50 adults who appear to live perfectly normal adult lives (that is, they perform at least adequately their major adult roles) who were reared by only one parent or one-parent substitute: fathers, mothers, older brothers or sisters, aunts, uncles, grandmother, grandfather. And with even less effort we have identified hundreds of adults who have failed in one or more major adult roles but who had both parents present during the child rearing process.

It would seem that there is much we don't yet know as to what it takes for children to grow up normally.

12. *That modern behavioral science has been helpful to parents.* The

---

[32] *Time Magazine* for January 20, 1967, reported that Gardner's father died when Gardner was just a year old and that his mother had been married to three different men after that. Gardner's response to this environment was to become an athlete, a Marine in World War II, and one of the ablest administrators in modern America (according to *Time*).

[33] See Alfred Kadushin, "Single-Parent Adoptions: An Overview and Some Relevant Research." Paper presented to the Northwest Regional Conference, Child Welfare League of America, May, 1968. To be published but available in mimeographed form from the School of Social Work, University of Wisconsin, Madison, Wisc. See also a review of the research on this point in Robert R. Bell, *Marriage and Family Interaction* (rev. ed.; Homewood, Ill.: The Dorsey Press, 1967), p. 420.

writer considers this to be folklore or mythology. For the details see the next chapter. Our basic contention is that psychiatry, sociology, and the related fields have functioned largely to make parents feel more guilty and inadequate. We also argue, with Brim, that the research on which most professionals in the parent education field have based their programs has been relatively poor research.[34]

13. *That love is enough to sustain good parental performance.* Bruno Bettelheim has argued that love is not enough.[35] His main point is that love has to be guided by knowledge and insight and also tempered with self-control on the part of the parent.

It is quite probable, however, that the reverse proposition is true: that no amount of scientific or professional knowledge about child development will do parents (or their children) any good unless it is mixed with love for the child and acceptance of the parental role.

14. *That all married couples should have children.* This seems to be a dubious proposition and one that few (if any) social workers or psychiatrists would support. There are undoubtedly married couples who enjoy each other and can sustain a satisfying marriage but who are not cut out for parenthood. Marriages of this sort are sometimes broken by the arrival of the first child.

One of the tragedies of the baby boom in America since World War II has been the compulsive nature of parenthood: everybody has to join the club, and the sooner the better. One young married woman who didn't feel ready to plunge into rearing a family as yet said to the writer: "I feel so conspicuous not being pregnant after two years of marriage that I am embarrassed to go to my bridge club. *All* of the girls my age have already had at least one baby and some of them have two."

Having children has become fashionable in modern America and it takes a very strong man or woman to ask themselves whether they are qualified to be a father or mother. Yet the fact remains that there is nothing magic about marriage which guarantees love for children or the capacity to be an adequate parent.[36]

15. *That childless married couples are frustrated and unhappy.* This might seem only natural and logical, yet one has to take it with a grain of salt. Judging from the experience of adoption agencies, who see a great many married couples who desire children but don't have any, it seems perfectly evident that these couples are frustrated and unhappy

---

[34] Brim, *op. cit.* This is a careful review of the research related to parent education and almost every chapter includes criticism of the research methods employed in parental studies.

[35] See Bruno Bettelheim, *Love Is Not Enough* (Glencoe, Ill.: The Free Press, 1950).

[36] Bell points out that biological parenthood does not guarantee the presence of other qualities required of parents. See Robert R. Bell, *op. cit.*, p. 386.

at not being able to be parents.[37] And one of the functions of such organizations is to help meet this need of childless couples. But at the same time adoption agencies have learned from long and bitter experience not to accept at face value the notion that childless couples only need children to make their lives happy and complete. Some couples may be seeking a child in a desperate effort to save their marriages; others seek children to fill the void of their unhappy and empty lives; and still others only imagine that they want a child—parenthood might be the last experience in the world which would be good for them, their marriage, or the adoptive child.

Actually, some childless couples seem to be quite happy in their marriages and their personal lives. They have accepted life as they find it, have perhaps wanted children at some point in their marriage or perhaps never planned on having children, but in any event they have evolved a satisfying way of life without adding the role of parent to their other roles. Some of the married women in this group have demanding careers, some have suffered some disability that makes them doubt their ability to care for children, and others simply do not see themselves as being good parents. One such wife said to the writer: "I can understand that for most persons being a father or mother would be one of the most interesting and rewarding experiences of life. But in our family there was so much misery and so much bickering about children that I never had any desire to rear children myself. I simply don't think I would be any good at it. And my husband feels the same way."

It is an interesting fact that in the Chicago studies of married couples that came out of the pioneering work of Ernest Burgess, some of the highest marital compatibility scores were made by childless couples.[38] It is also an interesting fact that a great many married couples *with* children are unhappy and frustrated. Thus those of us who are parents have to be somewhat careful about feeling sorry for those couples who don't have any children. They may feel the same way about us.

16. That children improve a marriage. There is abundant statistical evidence that children stabilize marriages,[39] but this isn't quite the same as improving them. It is obvious, of course, that children deepen and

---

[37] See Alfred Kadushin, *Child Welfare Services* (New York: The Macmillan Co., 1967), chap. 10 on adoption.

[38] In the pioneer study of marital adjustment and its prediction the conclusion was reached that couples with no children or one child rate their marriages significantly higher than couples with two or more children. See Ernest W. Burgess and Leonard S. Cottrell, Jr., *Predicting Success or Failure in Marriage* (New York: Prentice-Hall, Inc., 1939), pp. 258–259. See also a later study, Ernest W. Burgess and Paul Wallin, *Engagement and Marriage* (Philadelphia: J. B. Lippincott Co., 1953), pp. 712–713.

[39] Cavan observes: "The rate of divorce among childless couples is almost double that for couples with children." See Ruth Shonle Cavan, *The American Family* (3rd ed.; New York: Thomas Y. Crowell, 1963), p. 426. With the increasing acceptance

enrich millions of marriages in the United States, but it is less obvious that some married couples have their worst conflicts over their parental role. There are also some marriages which are destroyed by children. It is certainly true that most married couples try harder to preserve their marriage because they have children, but this doesn't prove that the husband-wife relationship itself is made more congenial by the presence of children. It only means that they are willing to endure more frustration to provide a stable family environment for their offspring.

17. *That American parents can be studied without interviewing fathers.* This is scientific folklore if you will. In reviewing material for this book the writer was amazed to discover that most of the empirical studies of American parents failed to interview the fathers in the sample.[40] Most of the studies simply state blandly that it was not possible or convenient to interview fathers and then go on to generalize about parents as if fathers were simply carbon copies of mothers. Otto Pollak is almost the only student of parents who rejects this notion.[41] Indeed books on the American father are almost nonexistent.[42] As a father, and as a family sociologist, the writer does not accept the proposition that only mothers need to be interviewed in studying modern American parents. And in one major study, *Crestwood Heights*, in which fathers *were* included in the study, major differences in values and child rearing methods were discovered to exist between mothers and fathers.[43] More will be said about this later in chapter 8, "The American Father."

The social function of folklore about parenthood

It is a truism in sociology that one of the functional imperatives of any society (or any social group) is that of replacement: the production and

---

of divorce in our society it is expected that children will not prevent divorce as they have in the past.

[40] A good example is the widely quoted study *The Changing American Parent* by Daniel R. Miller and Guy E. Swanson (New York: John Wiley & Sons, 1958). All of the 582 "depth" interviews were with mothers. In the study *Husbands and Wives* by Robert O. Blood, Jr. and Donald M. Wolfe, all of the 909 interviews were with wife-mothers. In another well-known study, *Patterns of Child Rearing*, by Robert R. Sears et al. (Evanston, Ill.: Row, Peterson & Co., 1957), 379 mothers were interviewed but not one father. The writer is very skeptical of marital and parent samples that auto-matically exclude one half of those who might be in the sample (husbands and fathers). It is our belief that the two sexes are not that similar in our society.

[41] Otto Pollak seems to concur with this writer on the exclusion of husbands and fathers from studies and social work treatment programs. See Otto Pollak, *Integrating Sociological and Psychoanalytic Concepts* (New York: Russell Sage Foundation, 1956), *passim*. It should be added that Brim, *op. cit.*, also includes fathers in his analysis.

[42] Most of this volume was written before the appearance of *Fatherhood: A Socio-logical Perspective* by Leonard Benson (New York: Random House, 1968). We have incorporated some of Benson's conclusions in chap. 8, "The American Father."

[43] John R. Seeley et al., "Parent Education: Resocialization," *Crestwood Heights* (New York: Basic Books, 1956), chap. 9.

training of the people who will make tomorrow possible.[44] Along with defense of the group from attack, the replacement function is indispensable.

It follows from the above that every society makes sure that reproduction (parenthood) will take place. Most societies, in addition, try to make sure that persons will only reproduce in some approved fashion—usually through some system of marriage. Random reproduction is approved or permitted in very few human societies, according to Murdock.[45]

When a social function is relatively rigorous, as parenthood seems to be in our society, a rich ethos or romantic folklore evolves to make sure that the role is not avoided by most adults. This can be seen in relationship to military service—almost nobody in their right mind would volunteer for service in the armed forces, yet in a majority of American wars, the Civil War, World War I, and World War II, large numbers of young men have offered their lives for their country. Flags, bands, and the concept of patriotism have been part of the process by which men have been willing to assume the role of soldier. Of course, in the event that these means of persuasion don't work, compulsion (in the form of a draft system) is resorted to.

In the case of parenthood, all sorts of sanctions are provided to encourage men and women to have children and rear them: parents receive preferential tax treatment, they have priority in applications for public housing, they receive higher pay in the armed forces, but above all they receive great public acclamation. "Isn't it too bad that they never had any children?" is a statement often heard. It is regarded as a tragedy if a man or woman should prove to be sterile, yet it is usually not considered a tragedy if a couple has more children than they can take care of.[46]

We do not wish to be misunderstood in these observations: we have two children, we volunteered to have them, and we would do so again. The only point is that parenthood is so surrounded by myth and folklore and public approval that most parents don't actually know what they are getting into until they are already fathers and mothers. This is also true of most men in the armed forces. And that is precisely the function of folklore—to make sure that most of us do not avoid or evade roles that have to be assumed and performed if our society is to survive.

---

[44] Strictly speaking, we are referring to two separate functions here: that of reproduction or replacement, and that of socialization or training for adult roles. See Kingsley Davis, *Human Society* (New York: The Macmillan Co., 1949).

[45] George Peter Murdock, *Social Structure* (New York: The Macmillan Co., 1949).

[46] In an award-winning program produced by the University of Wisconsin Television Station, WHA channel 21, a black man with 12 children is without a decent house in which to live. His wife has also died. The film leaves the viewer with the feeling that the man does not regret having 12 children—his only regret is that he does not have a good house to live in. This film is called "Pretty Soon Runs Out" and was televised in March, 1969.

Summary and conclusion

In this chapter we have been considering some of the folk beliefs (or myths) which cluster about parenthood in our society. It is not difficult to understand why these beliefs should exist: they tend to sustain parents in what is at best a very difficult and discouraging job; furthermore, they explain (or seek to explain) many of the mysteries which the experts have not been able to explain to the satisfaction of most parents. These beliefs in some instances represent tradition, while in other instances they represent so-called scientific fact.

Given the inadequate state of knowledge about parenthood and child rearing in our society it is not surprising that otherwise intelligent fathers and mothers are found harboring folk beliefs and scientific fallacies about parenthood and child rearing. The fact remains, however, that some of these beliefs can be harmful at times and damage the morale of conscientious parents. Some of the case studies in later chapters should illuminate this point.

chapter
three

Parents and the
behavioral sciences

I n this chapter we wish to examine the rise of the behavioral sciences during the 1920's and the decades after that in an effort to assess their impact on parents and the parental role. Under the term *behavioral science* we are including sociology, psychology, psychiatry, and social anthropology. We recognize that some persons might include more or less disciplines under the heading of behavioral science but these suit the purposes of this chapter and are included for that reason.

The writer's own doctoral degree is in sociology and he recognizes that some of the negative statements made about this discipline in the pages to follow will not meet with favor from all of his professional colleagues. He also had considerable work at the doctoral level in social and cultural anthropology and dislikes criticizing this group as much as he dislikes negating any of the work of his fellow sociologists. All he can say is that the comments are made with admiration for both groups and that perhaps it is better for a member of the family to make them than some outsider.

Not being a psychiatrist the writer has less pain in taking them to task, and judging from the sociological literature of recent years this has become almost a form of recreation or psychic therapy in professional sociology. Most psychiatrists seem to have pretty good defense mechanisms against such attacks, however, and the writer is convinced that the analysts and other members of the psychiatric profession will manage to survive this critique too.

The procedure in this chapter will be to examine first the impact of sociology, psychology, and anthropology on modern American parents, with a separate section on psychiatry after that.

The impact of sociology, psychology, and
anthropology on modern American parents

In the last several decades of our society, beginning roughly in the 1920's, the social and behavioral sciences have become a major force in America. Literally thousands of sociologists, psychologists, psychiatrists, social workers, educators, child development specialists, and anthropologists have been studying children and drawing conclusions about their parents. Their findings have appeared in a vast stream of books, magazine articles, professional journals, and newspaper stories.[1] One can hardly read a magazine or newspaper today without seeing at least one article on child rearing and/or parents. This is a relatively new development in human society and one can hardly doubt that it has had considerable impact on fathers and mothers.

As a behavioral scientist himself the writer must of necessity believe, as most Americans believe, that this mass of research and observation will eventually be in the best interests of all of us—but at the same time it is hard to escape the conclusion that so far its main impact on parents has been to make them feel more confused and inadequate than ever.

In a recent talk the writer had with a pediatrician, the physician was deploring the mass of articles on children's diseases in the news media. "Every time *The Reader's Digest* comes out with a story on some new disease or wonder drug," he said, "my telephone rings for days. Every mother has diagnosed her child as having the disease, or as needing the new drug, and she merely wants me to confirm the diagnosis. I wish they would stop publishing that stuff."

There is some logic to what he says. It is hazardous to release to the public partial bits of research that only a well-trained professional can evaluate properly. In the behavioral sciences, for example, the nature of the sample studied is crucial to professionals reading the material, but very few readers of the public press are able to evaluate sampling design. In questionnaire studies the nature of the questions asked is crucial, but newspaper men are not noted for their sophistication in these matters and their readers even less so. The same sort of problem could be cited about any research method used in obtaining data about people.

In attempting to assess the impact of behavioral science on modern American parents the writer has identified several concepts or developments since the 1920's which he feels have been essentially negative in their influence on fathers and mothers. These are discussed below.

1. Overemphasis on environmental factors in behavior. John Watson's

---

[1] According to Foote and Cottrell there were 1,031 papers published on the American family during the period 1945–1954. See Nelson N. Foote and Leonard S. Cottrell, *Identity and Interpersonal Competence* (Chicago: University of Chicago Press, 1955), pp. 231–290.

extreme version of environmentalism in psychology during the 1920's easily led to the conclusion that parents could do anything with any child if the parents were only skillful enough.[2] It is true that professional psychologists soon outgrew such simple theories of personality but Watson and his followers had considerable influence on the new profession of advertising—and mass advertising has influenced *all* Americans in some ways.

Sociologists embraced environmentalism in their theories of social interaction and personality. They discarded any belief in human instincts and evolved essentially a plastic personality model that was largely the product of its social environment.

2. *Underemphasis on man's organic nature.* Sociologists in particular tended to ignore the fact that man is an animal and that all of his behavior has some relationship to his organic nature. It is true that the anthropologists were much more careful in this matter but this aspect of anthropology did not seem to influence sociologists to any great extent.[3]

It is also true that psychologists stayed much closer to organic factors in their research, an example being their interest in intellectual capacity in children and means of measuring it. But outside of IQ tests and other measurements of motor skills it is hard to see how the knowledge of man's physical nature has entered into modern clinical psychology as it filters down to parents in clinics or guidance centers.[4]

Sociologists have tended to assume a random distribution of organic factors in human populations and hence they have felt that these variables could be ignored in studying human behavior. This can be seen in their

---

[2] This early version of environmentalism is found in J. B. Watson, *Behaviorism* (New York: W. W. Norton, 1925). For a review and critique of this personality theory see Calvin S. Hall and Gardner Lindzey, *Theories of Personality* (New York: John Wiley & Sons, 1957), chap. 11.

[3] In a well-known text the anthropologist Gillin devotes the first 171 pages to man's organic nature and his biological relationships to other mammals and other primates. See John Gillin, *The Ways of Men* (New York: Appleton-Century-Crofts, 1948). In a cursory survey of sociology textbooks the writer found little coverage of man's organic nature and his relationship to other animals. For example: Out of 556 pages of text Sutherland and Woodward devote 15 pages to man's organic nature. On p. 101 they refer to "the elimination of heredity folklore." See Robert L. Sutherland, Julian L. Woodward, and Milton A. Maxwell, *Introductory Sociology* (5th ed.; Philadelphia: J. B. Lippincott Co., 1956). Another well-known text gives two pages out of 642 to man's organic nature—see Leonard Broom and Philip Selznick, *Sociology* (2d. ed.; Evanston, Ill.: Row, Peterson & Co., 1958). A widely used text by Arnold Green, *Sociology* (2d ed.; New York: McGraw-Hill Book Co., 1956), devotes 14 pages to man's organic nature out of 557 pages.

[4] It is interesting to note that in the survey of personality theories by Hall and Lindzey, cited above, that the Index lists only two pages devoted to man's organic nature (p. 569). The terms *organism* and *organismic* are used frequently in the various chapters but refer to gestalt theory: that numerous factors are involved in human behavior, but these references do not spell out man's biological inheritance as the above analysis by Gillin does. For an excellent review of man's organic nature see

discussion of racial groups, yet it has by no means been proven scientifically that all of the major biological groups at the human level are identical. It is very likely true that the rabid racists are wrong and that no one biological group has all of the superior traits or abilities, but this is not the same as assuming that the groups are essentially identical in their organic nature. Alex Inkeles has stated bluntly that he thinks this matter needs to be reexamined by sociologists.[5]

3. *Overemphasis on cultural factors.* Sociologists and anthropologists in particular have tended to believe that almost any behavior at the human level can be explained by reference to culture patterns,[6] and yet in complex societies such as the United States there is almost endless variation in behavior within families, within social classes, within the sexes, within subcultures, and so on. It is not enough to explain the uniformities in behavior: the variations have to be accounted for also.

4. *Oversimplified reasoning from the group to the individual.* Parents are not confronted with a statistical aggregate, they are faced with a particular child or a small group of particular children. Any statistician will admit that when the size of any given cell is very small in quantitative research that the chances of error being present are very great. Thus we can generalize about boys when we are analyzing thousands of cases, but any given boy may not be masculine at all—he may actually be more representative of the feminine sample than of the male sample. Yet in discussing sexual deviation the usual line of reasoning is that somehow the parents through their mishandling have changed a natural male into a sex deviate.[7] If a daughter is sexually promiscuous the same type of

---

Weston LaBarre, *The Human Animal* (Chicago: University of Chicago Press, 1954). A mass of material on the similarity of human behavior to that of other animals has appeared in recent years: see Konrad Lorenz, *On Aggression* (New York: Harcourt, Brace & World, 1963), Robert Ardrey, *The Territorial Imperative* (New York: Atheneum Press, 1966), and others.

[5] For a good (and rare) discussion of this see Alex Inkeles, "Personality and Social Structure," in *Sociology Today* edited by Robert K. Merton et al. (New York: Basic Books, 1959), pp. 249–276.

See also Dennis H. Wrong, "The Over Socialized Conception of Man in Sociology," *American Sociological Review*, 26 (1961), pp. 183–193.

[6] An example of this is Mead's argument that male and female behavior is essentially the result of cultural conditioning. See Margaret Mead, *Male and Female* (New York: William Morrow & Co., 1949).

For a critique of the "cultural explanation" of human behavior see Elliott Liebow, *Tally's Corner* (Boston: Little, Brown & Co., 1967), pp. 208–209.

In commenting on the shift from genetic or biological explanations of behavior to a cultural theory, Brim writes: "One characteristic after another of the person was transferred, so to speak, from the domain of inheritance to the territory of environment." See Orville G. Brim, Jr., *Education for Child Rearing* (New York: Russell Sage Foundation, 1959), p. 33.

[7] In a United Press story dated August 1, 1957 (one of many in the author's files), it was reported that "two psychiatrists said today that parents can be blamed in most cases if their children grow up to be sex deviates." The reporter, who had been

logic is in order: the girl is assumed to have been normal or typical of women in her sexual drives and interests and that somehow the parents have managed to distort this.

It is very tricky reasoning from group behavior to individual behavior but some writers don't worry about it very much.

5. *Poor sampling.* Kinsey was constantly belabored for his sampling deficiencies in his studies of American sexual behavior, yet there are relatively few studies of parents and their children that will stand close scrutiny of their sampling method or the conclusions that can be drawn from such a sample.[8] Social class bias is usually present, age factors are not held constant, religious affiliation is usually a problem, urban-rural composition is at variance with the general population, and so on. The universe studied may be very limited but the conclusions drawn are often quite sweeping—especially so when the study is reported in the general press.

6. *The research design itself is poor.* Behavioral science at best is not apt to be too good. Brim, Orlansky, Sewell and others have found it possible to criticize almost every study of parents and children published during the past several decades in the United States from the point of view of research design.[9] Control groups are not usually employed, samples are inadequate, questions are vague, interviews are brief, hypotheses are not explicitly stated or else they are evolved after the data are collected and tabulated.

These limitations may not do much harm within the profession and the studies may indeed be worthwhile, but by the time the findings reach the general public they have often become the "scientific finding of an eminent research specialist."

---

attending a professional conference, went on to say that the study was based on 16 cases. No control group was used. Story published in the *Beloit Daily News*, Beloit, Wisc.

   8 Vincent notes that Kinsey's data are often questioned on sampling grounds but other studies with even more bias in their sample are quoted without criticism. See Clark Vincent, *Unmarried Mothers* (Glencoe, Ill.: The Free Press, 1961), footnote pp. 27–28.

   9 See Brim, *op. cit.*, various chapters. This is the most complete critique of "scientific research" on child rearing that this writer has found. An earlier work by Orlansky also contains a voluminous review and evaluation of the research material given out to parents in our society in recent decades; see Harold Orlansky, "Infant Care and Personality," *Psychological Bulletin*, 46 (January, 1949), pp. 1–48. The sociologist Sewell has done well-designed field research on children which failed to support many Freudian theories about breast feeding and other child rearing practices; see William H. Sewell, "Infant Training and the Personality of the Child," *American Journal of Sociology*, 58 (September, 1952), pp. 150–159. Wolfenstein, through an analysis of federal government bulletins on child rearing, has been able to demonstrate that the advice given parents has fluctuated from one decade to the next; see Martha Wolfenstein, "Trends in Infant Care," *American Journal of Orthopsychiatry*, 33 (1953), pp. 120–130.

7. *American fathers and husbands are usually not studied.* The writer has been appalled in reviewing the studies of American parents to see that only people like Brim and Pollak seem to worry about husbands and/or fathers.[10] Goode, for example, in probably the best empirical study of divorce we have had, did not find it possible (or necessary?) to include any of the divorced men in his sample.[11] Miller and Swanson, Sears, and others, in quite elaborate studies of American "parents" (sic) did not find it necessary to interview any fathers.[12]

The failure to include husbands and fathers in such research is disturbing enough, but one seldom finds that the research team has been very upset by the absence of any males in the sample. The two sexes are surely not that homogeneous in America, not even in the 1960's.

8. *Social environment has been equated with parental influence.* It is one thing to assume (or conclude) that personality is the net result of social interaction and exposure to cultural patterns, but it is quite another thing to assume that the social world of the child is the net result of the interaction *with parents*. It is true that in the early years the outside world is mediated by and through the family, but as Clinard has pointed out, there are forces such as the youth peer group, siblings, and mass media.[13] Parental influence is not even synonymous with *family* influence, let alone *social environment*.

The net result of this sort of approach is to saddle fathers and mothers with complete responsibility for the molding or shaping of their children.[14]

9. *The failure to account for accidental combinations of events that affect children and parents.* In interviewing parents the writer has been impressed with the fact that in some cases an odd combination of events seems to have determined what happened to a child or a parent. These might be conceptualized as "statistical freaks" that normally would not occur but occasionally do. Thus a child will meet a peer group member at exactly the point in life when a father or mother is unable to give the child close supervision and then it happens that this particular peer

---

[10] For Brim's discussion of the father's role see Brim, *op. cit.*, pp. 36–38 and 69–70. For Pollak's analysis of the neglect of fathers in child guidance clinics see Otto Pollak, *Social Science and Psychotherapy for Children* (New York: Russell Sage Foundation, 1952).

[11] See William J. Goode, *After Divorce* (New York: The Free Press, 1956), p. 21.

[12] For a review of several studies of parents that did not include interviews with any fathers see chap. 8 of this volume—"The American Father."

[13] See Marshall B. Clinard, *Sociology of Deviant Behavior* (rev. ed.; New York: Rinehart & Co., 1968), p. 133.

[14] The anthropologist Gorer has commented: "In American psychoanalytic thinking the child is born faultless, a *tabula rasa*, and any defects which subsequently develop are the fault of uncontrollable circumstances or of the ignorance or malice of its parents who mar what should otherwise be a perfect, or at least a perfectly adjusted, human being." See Geoffrey Gorer, *The American People* (rev. ed.; New York: W. W. Norton, 1964), p. 70.

group member is the one that could influence the child at this time in a negative way. A girl on the rebound from her parents, for example, could meet a nice boy in college to express her revolt but becomes friendly with a young man who is able to influence her in almost any direction. It is easy, of course, to argue with the psychiatrists that there must have been some reason why she took up with this particular boy, but the fact is that all of us at some point in life have been so desperate for a relationship that we have accepted anybody who offered himself or herself—and sometimes we have met some very nice people that way. But other persons do not seem to have been so fortunate.

The writer believes that there are such things as statistical accidents that affect children and parents but apparently most behavioral scientists don't. At least they don't refer to it in their research findings.

Summary

It would easily be possible to expand this discussion almost endlessly— as indeed it has been done by some severe critics of behavioral science in the United States.[15] The writer's purpose has not been to condemn the effort to study human behavior systematically and scientifically but rather to point out that the general public (in this case parents) can be hurt if the research is not well designed and well conducted and accurately reported in the public press. It is hard to argue that this has been the case with studies of parents and children published in the United States since the 1920's.[16]

Psychiatric theory and parenthood

It probably is true that most American parents know very little about Sigmund Freud and his personality theory, but the fact remains that

---

[15] A scathing attack on social science was contained in a best seller by William H. Whyte, Jr. See *The Organization Man* (New York: Simon and Schuster, Inc., 1956). He writes: "scientism is the promise that with the same techniques that have worked in the physical sciences we can eventually create an exact science of man. In one form or another, it has had a long and dismal record of achievement." See p. 26 of the Anchor Books edition (New York: Doubleday & Co., 1957).

Another attack on social science was published in another best seller, *The Feminine Mystique* by Betty Friedan (New York: W. W. Norton, 1963).

For a third attack see *The Experts* by Seymour Freidin and George Bailey (New York: The Macmillan Co., 1968). The dust jacket of this book has the following statement: "A scathing indictment of the opinion makers who flood the press, the networks and the policy-makers of our government with their special brand of instantaneous wisdom."

It is an interesting fact that these attacks have all sold very well.

[16] This statement is based on works by Brim, Wolfenstein, and Orlansky, *op. cit.*

their performance of parental roles has often been measured against the major principles developed and taught by Freud. This results from the fact that American psychiatry and American social work have been largely Freudian since World War I.[17]

It is the writer's impression that American teachers and school administrators have been less Freudian than social workers but this point is open to dispute. In his attack on the followers of Freud, LaPiere claims that American school programs have also been widely subject to the theories of Freud.[18]

Regardless of the position one takes on this point, it is certainly true that child guidance centers, psychiatric clinics, and professional child welfare agencies have used Freudian theory in their case diagnoses and in their consultations with parents. If this is true it means that American parents who got into difficulty performing their parental roles have been judged largely within the framework of Freudian personality theory.

It also seems to be true that many of the books which have criticized American parents—such as the best seller by Strecker after World War II[19]—have been written by psychiatrists whose training was essentially Freudian.

For the above reasons it is essential that we take a good look at Freudian theory *from the parents' point of view*. This is not an evaluation of Freudian theory as it applies to marriage or psychotherapy: we are looking at it from the point of view of fathers and mothers. How adequately does it explain behavior, both that of the child and that of the parent? How helpful has it been to parents? How destructive? Has it been practical for most American parents?

These are difficult questions and the writer has no illusions about his ability to answer them adequately. But they are important questions that need to be asked and perhaps a beginning can be made here.

---

[17] The writer recognizes that not all psychiatrists are followers of Freud. We cite Freudian theory here because we feel it has had the most impact on American parents. Miller and Swanson, for example, report that of 146 articles on psychoanalysis indexed in *The Reader's Guide to Periodical Literature* for the years 1910–1935 that only 27 were basically negative. They concluded that millions of American parents must have been subjected to psychoanalytic influence during this period. See Daniel R. Miller and Guy E. Swanson, *The Changing American Parent* (New York: John Wiley & Sons, 1958), pp. 185–186.

[18] See Richard LaPiere, *The Freudian Ethic* (Duell, Sloan & Pearce, 1959). For a scholarly evaluation of Freudian theory see R. R. Sears, *Survey of Objective Studies of Psychoanalytic Concepts* (New York: Social Science Research Council, 1943), Bulletin No. 51.

[19] Edward A. Strecker, M.D., *Their Mothers' Sons* (Philadelphia: J. B. Lippincott Co., 1946). Strecker blames the psychiatric casualties of our military forces in World War II on the American mother.

Contributions of Freudian theory to American parents

First, let us attempt to analyze the positive contributions made by Freudian theory to American parents, after which some of the negative results will be discussed.[20]

1. A more realistic view of the child.   No one has done more than Freud and his followers to end the romantic view of children held by some of the previous generations of parents. Freud saw the child as self-centered, aggressive, impulsive, and ruthless. It was up to the parents to make a human being of the infant. This put a great responsibility on parents, but it also gave them a more realistic understanding of the job to be done.

Freudian theory also made it easier to understand why parents were not always successful in child rearing by showing how complicated personality development is. Some people feel that Freud took all the romance out of parenthood, that his view of the human infant is too gloomy. While there is some truth in this, it is the writer's view that a romantic view of the child in the long run is more destructive to parents than a down-to-earth realistic view. There is no way to settle this point scientifically. The reader will have to take his choice.

2. A more realistic view of parents.   It is so easy to become lyrical about parents—mothers in particular. All new parents are portrayed as happy and delighted, ecstatic, and so forth. Very often this is true at the point of birth. But if you follow the lyrical mother home from the maternity ward you will soon see her confused, perplexed, and frustrated. She and her husband (if she has one) will still have their moments of delight, to be sure, but they will also wonder what on earth they have gotten themselves into.[21]

The truth is that parenthood requires such maturity, insight, stamina, and self-control that it soon exposes any personality weaknesses the parent may have. Unfortunately, there is nothing about biological paternity which removes any of the personal problems of the father and/or mother. It may be, however, that becoming a parent motivates some people to work harder at handling their personal problems, thus performing a sort of therapy of a limited nature.

It is also true, however, that parenthood disturbs some fathers and mothers and makes them less adequate. Freud, it seems to us, gave an honest report on the parent-child relationship, thus preparing some parents for what was ahead. Often the parent himself or herself had not read any Freudian books, but the basic ideas became so widely diffused in the society that almost everybody had some knowledge of them.

---

[20] A convenient summary of the basic Freudian theory may be found in Hall and Lindzey, *op. cit.*, chap. 2.

[21] See E. E. LeMasters, "Parenthood as Crisis," *Marriage and Family Living,* **19** (1957), pp. 352–355.

Here, again, a price has to be paid for realism, but the writer believes it to be less than the price paid for romanticism.

3. *Insight into sibling relationships.* Parents are often shocked by the amount of conflict and hostility which exists between siblings. They had hoped that their family would be just one big loving group, as one mother said to us, and so often this is not the whole picture. Freud had considerable insight into this sort of thing and his concepts have helped parents, social workers, physicians, and others to understand the presence of negative feeling inside the family group.

4. *Insight into childhood sexuality.* The sexual play and curiosity of children can be disturbing to parents and other adults (such as school-teachers). After Freud's work it was much easier to understand this aspect of the child's interests. The writer feels that Freud could have used a better terminology in describing the sexual interests of children, but at least he did not ignore this sort of behavior or label it "abnormal"—to Freud the child who did not express curiosity about his sexual equipment and its use was the abnormal one.

5. *Insight into the key function of emotion in rearing the child.* Freud got us out of the arid intellectual or rational view of human behavior, so popular in the 18th and 19th centuries, and put emotion into its proper perspective. It is almost impossible since Freud to be a parent and ignore the child's feelings—or those of the parent either.

6. *Insight into the nonrational aspects of human behavior.* While this may overlap a bit with the previous point it is not exactly identical. In this part of his work Freud stressed the nonrational things that people do: their little idiosyncrasies, their defense mechanisms, their rationalizations, their neuroses. This view is often disturbing, but it is hard to understand much of what children and parents do if you view them otherwise.

These are some of the positive contributions of Freudian theory to parents as the writer sees it. Now let us look at some of the negative impact of this body of knowledge on the parental role.

Negative impact of Freudian theory on modern American parents

1. *It placed too much responsibility on parents.* Freudian theory was part of the broad theory of environmentalism considered in this chapter. Along with Watsonian psychology, and the personality theories of American sociologists, it held that the child was essentially the product of parental influence.[22] Freud probably placed greater emphasis on the role

---

[22] Clarence Darrow, the great criminal lawyer, is credited with developing the theory of environmentalism as a defense for certain types of crime—such as the famous Loeb-Leopold murder trial of the 1920's. But Darrow did not equate the influence of parents with environment—he indicted the entire society in which the child was reared. See *Attorney for the Damned,* edited by Arthur Weinberg (New York: Simon and Schuster, Inc., 1957); also Irving Stone, *Clarence Darrow for the Defense* (New York: Doubleday & Co., 1941).

of siblings in personality development than the sociologists and psychologists did, but even there parents were the ultimate culprits because they were supposed to create a family climate in which sibling relationships would be healthy or constructive.

It is the writer's contention that parents are only one set of factors which determine the outcome of the child's life[23] and that Freudian theory was one of the instruments used to enslave the modern parent. It may well be true that Freud himself did not intend that his concepts should be used in this way but this does not mean that they were *not* used to that end. In the same vein one can find that the teachings of Christ have been used at various times in the United States to justify the enslavement of the Negro by the white race, yet we can hardly imagine that Christ had this in mind when he was teaching his ethical system.[24]

It is true, of course, that Freud described the child as having "instinctual" drives and needs, and in this sense Freud viewed the human infant as being less passive than the sociologists, the psychologists, and the cultural anthropologists. But Freud's instincts did not automatically produce any specific behavior—even the sexual instinct in Freudian theory is subject to endless conditioning and modification. Thus the concept of instinct as used by Freud did not relieve parents of any responsibility because the end-product was still undetermined at the point of birth. This was a somewhat different use of the concept of instinct than had been customary in biology and earlier psychology.[25]

2. In Freudian theory parents are responsible for what happens to the child even after it becomes an adult. In psychoanalysis childhood never really ends: adults only live out in a sort of dreamlike trance what happened to them in the first four or five years of life. They never really outgrow their childhood—they only relive it in different forms. Thus parents are forever saddled with guilt and responsibility because mistakes made in the first few years are never really outgrown or outlived. They may be modified by expensive and long-term psychotherapy but their influence is permanent.

As the writer reads the history of parenthood in America this was not always the case. Parents were expected to do the best they could with children but at some point children became adults and were responsible for their own destiny. And if they believed in God even miracles could be wrought—without benefit of psychotherapy. There was also the notion of fate as having something to do with what happened to people in this world as well as the next.

---

[23] Brim, *op. cit.*, develops this thesis in chap. 2.

[24] See Lerone Bennett, Jr., *Black Power USA: The Human Side of Reconstruction 1867–1877* (Chicago: Johnson Publishing Co., 1967).

[25] Hall and Lindzey, *op. cit.*, review Freud's use of the concept of instinct. See pp. 36–41.

3. Freudian theory overemphasized the preschool years as determinants of adult personality. Some critics of Freud have labeled this "diaper determinism":[26] that nothing happens after the first few years which was not predetermined in the early years of life. Brim, however, cites several studies to the effect that people in modern society *do* change in behavior as they move into adult status—experiences in the nonfamily world (such as military service) have an impact which is not within the realm of parents to control. The peer group in urban society is powerful, as are occupational roles and marital relationships.[27]

It is true that the parent has the child first, but behavior is not always the result of first experiences. Sometimes the *last* event is crucial. On the same logic one could lean toward the genetic theory of personality because the genes precede what the parents do. Yet most of the behavioral scientists and psychiatrists have been willing to forget genetic factors and as a rule have emphasized them little in their studies of personality.

4. Freudian theory made psychosexual development too tentative and too hazardous. It is hard to believe that the human race would have survived this long if reproduction were as tentative as some analysts have made it out to be—that is, that any boy or girl might become homosexual if the right stimuli were supplied (or not supplied) at the right moment. Mead has argued that male and female behavior are largely the product of cultural patterns; but the cultural patterns themselves have to be explained also.[28] Polyandry, for example, has never had wide distribution in human society but polygyny has. This sort of data can hardly be explained by simple reference to "cultural determinism." Brim has commented on this to the effect that it may be possible to make a girl out of a male infant but it seems a lot easier to make a boy out of him in most societies.[29]

Our point here is simply that psychiatric theory in general and Freudian theory in particular have overemphasized the tentative nature of psychosexual development and that human behavior is not that plastic. To the extent that psychiatric theory is correct it places an additional responsibility on fathers and mothers. And to the extent that it is not true parents are held responsible for behavior which they did not cause.

---

[26] The writer first heard this expression used by the late Howard Becker, sociologist at the University of Wisconsin. We do not know the origin of the expression.

[27] These data are summarized by Brim, *op. cit.*, chap. 2.

[28] Mead's thinking on this is summarized in *Male and Female*. She fails to explain what Murdock discovered: that plural wives have been common in human society whereas plural husbands have been quite rare. See George P. Murdock, *Social Structure* (New York: The Macmillan Co., 1949). Mead also fails to explain why female prostitution has been widespread in human society whereas male prostitution has been relatively rare. It is not enough to simply say that this is the result of culture. Why did the cultural patterns develop that way instead of some other way?

[29] Brim, *op. cit.*, p. 34.

In the Freudian system there seems to be nothing *guaranteed* about the child's psychosexual development—it all depends on what the parents do, how they do it, when they do it, how often they do it—or what they don't do. There is no automatic unfolding of the male or female traits as earlier generations apparently thought.

Actually, this is probably far too tenuous a picture of human growth and development. It could probably be demonstrated, if the research were adequate, that *most* people would be seriously neurotic or psychotic if their personalities were as malleable as the Freudians and other psychiatrists have described them. In a very real sense, all child rearing is traumatic, not only for the child but also for the parents.[30] But most adults do manage to stay out of mental hospitals and to perform their basic roles in society.

In recent years writers such as Orlansky and Spock have rejected this fragile view of human nature and have pointed out that the human infant is pretty tough and capable of surviving almost incredible experiences.[31] One rarely finds this point of view in psychiatric agencies which deal with parents.

It seems likely that this fragile theory of human personality resulted from the limited sample observed by analysts and other psychiatrists; they see only those who seem to have been damaged by their experiences and this sample is seldom matched against one from the general population. It may well be true, for example, that for every adult sex deviate who had certain experiences as a child that there is also an adult who had the same set of experiences but did not become a deviate.

There is a revealing example of this sort of research problem in the literature on unmarried mothers. Several years ago Leontine Young published a book on unmarried mothers in which she concluded that these girls had almost invariably come from homes in which the mother was dominant.[32] But a few years later Clark Vincent matched a group

---

[30] Leo Rosten, who has a Ph.D. in social science from the University of Chicago as well as being an editor of *Look* magazine and a writer of Hollywood films, puts this point as follows: "There is the myth that you can explain neurotic behavior by attributing it to an unhappy childhood. But *all* childhood is unhappy; all childhood is charged with uncertainty and fear, with conflict and frustration, with unbearable rage and unattainable desire. It makes little sense to talk about unhappy childhoods unless we ask why some people emerge from childhood with their productive capacities enriched, while others remain paralyzed by unresolved and infantile dilemmas." Leo Rosten, *The Many Worlds of Leo Rosten* (New York: Harper & Row, 1964), p. 207.

[31] Orlansky, *op. cit.* Benjamin Spock, *Baby and Child Care* (New York: Pocket Books, Inc., 1963 ed.).

[32] Leontine R. Young, *Out of Wedlock* (New York: McGraw-Hill Book Co., 1954). Her data are based on interviews with unmarried mothers but she does not compare this group with a control group from the general population. Thus her findings may well be true of the unmarried mothers she interviewed but the same characteristics might be found in a matched sample from the general population.

of unmarried mothers with a group of girls who were not unmarried mothers and he could not determine any significant difference in the family dynamics of the two groups.[33] He also could not isolate any particular personality pattern that would distinguish the unmarried mothers from the matched sample from the general population.

The art of sampling is relatively new in behavioral science and probably even newer in psychoanalysis and related psychiatric disciplines. Yet almost anything can be proven and believed if the sample is sufficiently unrepresentative.[34]

One of the replies usually given by the psychiatric profession to this sort of argument is that "no two human beings ever have identically the same experiences." This is obviously true, but on the same grounds it follows that no scientific or professional body of knowledge can be built on unique experience: science and professional knowledge presuppose generalization from known cases to new cases. And this always requires that some of the unique factors be considered as if they did not exist. For example, there are no two identical marriages, yet all persons who work with maladjusted married couples know that many of them have similar problems. If they didn't, how could one develop a body of knowledge that would be of any value in treating new cases?

Another reply given by the psychiatric profession to the above discussion is that the so-called normal people *are* sick; they just haven't come in for treatment. This is, indeed, a gloomy view of human nature and lends itself to the argument that what man needs is not more psychiatrists but a new society—or perhaps different organic ancestors.

Regardless of how one views the above argument, it seems reasonably clear that Freudian theory resulted in a massive amount of responsibility being assigned to modern parents.

5. *Freudian theory took some of the romance out of parenthood.* Since the Freudian picture of the child is a realistic one,[35] it almost inevitably makes parenthood a more grim proposition. In other words, some price has to be paid for realism. One can't have the illusions inherent in a romantic version of the child (God's little angels, for example) if he accepts the Freudian view of personality development. Indeed, any parent who knows the Freudian conceptual system very well must approach his parental role with some foreboding, knowing that even with the best of luck the most he can hope to produce is a "mild neurotic."

---

[33] See Clark E. Vincent, "Psychological and Familial Factors," *Unmarried Mothers* (New York: The Free Press, 1961), Pt. III.

[34] The classic example of poor sampling that produced totally misleading findings was the famous poll taken by the now defunct *Literary Digest* which predicted that a man named Alf Landon would defeat Franklin D. Roosevelt in the 1936 Presidential election. Landon carried two states.

[35] Realistic, but not entirely accurate in our opinion.

This same parent will also be frightened at times by what he sees in his children: behavior which would not arouse the slightest anxiety in a non-Freudian. As we said earlier, we believe that a realistic view of children is less damaging in the long run than a superficial romantic view,[36] but this doesn't alter the fact that some of the oldtime glow in being a parent disappeared with the development of the Freudian system of personality theory. It is, perhaps, similar to the psychological burden some moderns feel when they think of nuclear physics and the development of the hydrogen bomb: there is no way to erase the facts and yet they have changed the world forever. And perhaps not for the best.

It is impossible to determine objectively how helpful Freudian personality theory has been for parents and professional practitioners who work with them. It seems to the writer that Freud's theories were an improvement over the crude Watsonian psychology of the 1920's; they also have some advantages over the raw environmentalism put forth by some social scientists over the last several decades. The main reason why Freudian theory appeals to some professional practitioners is that it endows the organism with some drive and desires of its own, thus avoiding the carbon paper passivity inherent in the other theories. At the same time, as we have seen, there are serious faults in the Freudian theory of personality which need to be taken into account.

It seems clear that human behavior is the result of the interaction of at least three basic sets of variables: the organism and its genetic components, the cultural norms of the social world in which the person lives,[37] and the psychodynamic (the unique experience of any given person). There is also another factor which is seldom mentioned in books on personality but which parents talk about quite often—the unpredictable and improbable combination of events. This is what earlier generations of fathers and mothers called luck or fate. It is literally true that the best efforts of parents can sometimes be nullified by some rare circumstance in which several events combine that would normally occur separately and could be handled better in another sequence.

It is extremely difficult for any theory of personality to deal adequately with all of these variables. Sociologists and social anthropologists do quite well with the cultural variable; physicians and biologists do reasonably well with the organic factors (although relatively little is really known

---

[36] In an address to high school students a professor of psychiatry at the University of Wisconsin Medical School cautioned the young people not to be fooled by the romantic myth about family life. Home is the place to get mad and blow up when you need to, he said. Dr. Jack Westman, M.D., quoted in the *Wisconsin State Journal*, Madison, Wisc., October 3, 1968, pp. 1–2.

[37] In a complex and pluralistic society such as ours each individual is exposed to a variety of subcultural norms which may deviate somewhat from those of the larger society.

about human genetics); Freudians and other psychiatrists do well with the psychodynamic and idiosyncratic variables. Since parents are normally concerned with a particular child rather than children in general, it is understandable that they would find most useful a theory which can be applied to their specific child. This does not, however, prove the theory to be correct or adequate—it only establishes its popularity. It is entirely possible that a better theory of personality can be developed, one that would not only be helpful to parents but also one that would not be so threatening to them. As yet, however, such a theory has not made its appearance. If it exists, most parents are unaware of it.

It seems to the writer that some of the neo-Freudians such as Horney have done a good job of incorporating cultural factors into Freudian theory,[38] but this has not met all of the objections to Freud's system. The concept of sex, for example, remains ambiguous; the instinct concept still clouds the theory; the fragile, tentative view of psychosexual development remains, and so forth.[39]

Encouraging new developments in science which may help parents

We wish to end this somewhat gloomy chapter on a positive note. It is our firm belief that eventually the social and behavioral scientists will produce findings that will be more helpful to parents than has been true in the past. Let us review briefly some of the encouraging developments.

The relatively new specialty in biology, ethology, seems to be making progress in sorting out behavior patterns which man has inherited from his organic predecessors—built-in or preprogrammed behavior sets which reflect the hundreds of thousands of years in which present men evolved. This is not the crude instinct theory which social scientists found inadequate decades ago: it is more sophisticated analysis based on cross-species research.[40] Social anthropologists have proven what insight about human behavior could be obtained with cross-cultural research;[41] and

---

[38] The writer has recently taken the trouble to reread *The Neurotic Personality of Our Time* by Karen Horney (New York: W. W. Norton, 1937) and was surprised to find how relevant her adaptation of Freudian theory to the American scene still is.

[39] A critique of Freudian theory may be found in Clinard, *op. cit.*, pp. 133–136. See also Hall and Lindzey, *op. cit.*, pp. 64–72.

[40] A classic in this field is *On Aggression* by Konrad Lorenz (New York: Harcourt, Brace & World, 1963); for more popular treatments, see Robert Ardrey, *The Territorial Imperative* (New York: Atheneum Press, 1966), and Desmond Morris, *The Naked Ape* (New York: McGraw-Hill Book Co., 1967). We are aware that some social scientists have been critical of these studies, but they do seem to have some value in establishing a biological base from which to analyze social behavior.

[41] See *Mirror for Man* by the late Clyde Kluckhohn (New York: McGraw-Hill Book Co., 1949). This volume won an award when it was first published for revealing the vast range of human behavior in different societies as well as some of the similarities.

now the biologists seem to be shedding light on our behavior by cross-species research: comparing man's behavior to that of other mammals, for example.

Biological perspective of this sort will not eliminate cultural or personality variables as determinants of behavior, but the way in which people behave will be seen in greater perspective.

There are also signs that human genetics may be reaching the point at which it will be more helpful to parents.[42] A new profession of "genetic counseling" seems to be emerging for fathers and mothers who have reason to be concerned about their future offspring.[43]

In the field of family counseling a major breakthrough seems to have been achieved by the Palo Alto family research group in their use of communication theory to diagnose family dysfunctioning.[44] The works of Jackson, Haley, and Satir are having wide impact on social work, psychiatry, and the other counseling professions. An interesting part of this development has been the insistence of this group that *total* families be seen in the counseling process, not just individuals.

The writer does not despair about social and behavioral science; he only hopes that parents will see its limitations as well as its possibilities.

Summary and conclusion

In this chapter we have attempted to analyze the impact of the behavioral sciences on the modern American parent. While the value of scientific research is granted, the results to date in the area of parenthood have not been too impressive. There is an infinite variety of parent and child in any modern pluralistic society such as America and it is not easy to generalize about them on the basis of limited research, inadequate samples, lack of control groups, and poor research design.

It is true that the better professionals recognize these limitations in the data and urge their application with some caution. But it is also true that the less well-trained professionals are not that modest in their consultation with parents. The most serious problem, however, in the opinion of the writer, develops when the research findings are written up for popular consumption by the general public. Newspapers, magazines, and

---

[42] For a brief review of the developments since 1950 see Gerald E. McClearn, "Genetics and Behavior Development," in Martin L. Hoffman and Lois W. Hoffman (eds.), *Review of Child Development Research* (New York: Russell Sage Foundation, 1964), Vol. 1.

[43] This statement is based on interviews with members of the medical school staff at the University of Wisconsin.

[44] See Jay Haley, *Strategies of Psychotherapy* (New York: Grune & Stratton, 1963); also Virginia Satir, *Conjoint Family Therapy* (Palo Alto: Science and Behavior Books, 1964); and D. D. Jackson (ed.), *Communication, Family, and Marriage* (Palo Alto: Science and Behavior Books, 1968).

other forms of mass media in the United States are not noted for being reluctant to arouse public interest by rather sensational methods, and this tendency is compounded by the fact that journalists and other writers for the mass media have usually had no professional training which would equip them to recognize limitations in research method or design.[45] This places great responsibility on professional researchers in the family field to make sure that their findings cannot easily be misunderstood. This is not easy in the mass society.

The chapter closed with some encouraging developments in the sciences of human behavior.

---

[45] The University of Wisconsin School of Journalism now has a grant to bring newspaper journalists to the campus to improve their understanding of social science and thus to upgrade their reporting on the developments in this field. This program is supported by the Russell Sage Foundation. For an interesting analysis of the problems of science reporting for the general public, see Hillier Kriegbaum, *Science and the Mass Media* (New York: New York University Press, 1967). He writes: "If there is a major expansion in science reporting in the decade or two ahead, much of this should take place in improved coverage of our social problems and the scientific attempts to overcome them." (p. 192.)

chapter
four

Role analysis
of parenthood

The use of role analysis

IN recent years a body of knowledge known as "role theory" has come to be widely used by social scientists and some members of the various helping professions.[1] While there are different things that one can do with this approach, one of the most useful is that role analysis can be utilized to dissect small social systems so that we can see how each part is supposed to function and how it is related to the rest of the system. For example: in marriage counseling one can analyze the role of wife in its various subroles, identify those producing problems, and proceed to find out the source of the problems—is the husband complaining about his wife's failure as a sexual companion or is it the housekeeping subrole that bothers him? Using this approach such a complex interaction system as a marriage can be broken down into parts that can be analyzed separately.

Essentially, a role is a task that some person is supposed to perform.[2] Roles have to be defined, assigned, perceived, performed, and integrated with other role tasks. Every role carries with it a position in the interaction system that relates to status and prestige. In a well-organized family the major roles have been identified, assigned, and performed with some degree of competence. Where this does not occur the family

---

[1] The definitive source for role theory is Bruce J. Biddle and Edwin J. Thomas (eds.), *Role Theory: Concepts and Research* (New York: John Wiley & Sons, 1966). See also Robin Williams, *American Society* (rev. ed.; New York: Alfred A. Knopf, 1960), pp. 55–73.

[2] Biddle and Thomas, *op. cit.*, have found over 250 different concepts used by role analysts. See their chap. 1, "The Nature and History of Role Theory," pp. 3–19.

For a good brief introduction to role analysis, see Edwin J. Thomas (ed.), *Behavioral Science for Social Workers* (New York: The Free Press, 1967), pp. 15–50.

may be said to be disorganized to a certain extent. Minor roles may be ignored or performed indifferently without producing too much difficulty but major roles (such as care of young children) require constant and at least adequate role performance.

In the modern American family male and female roles have been shifted and reorganized extensively since about 1920, and some families appear to be disorganized in that nobody seems to know who is supposed to do what. An analogy can be made here to bureaucratic theory: a business firm or an academic department may be said to be disorganized when major tasks have not been properly assigned or are not being performed adequately.

In this chapter we seek to apply role theory and role analysis to modern parents. We feel that this approach is helpful in understanding the problems that many American fathers and mothers seem to have.

Our procedure will be to state the major points and to comment on them briefly. More extensive analysis will be given some of the points later in this chapter and other points will be elaborated on in other chapters.

Role analysis of modern parenthood

1. The role of parent in modern America is not well defined. It is often ambiguous and hard to pin down.
2. The role is not adequately delimited. Parents are expected to succeed where even the professionals fail.
3. Modern parents are not well prepared for their role as fathers and mothers. Brim demonstrates this rather conclusively in a study conducted for the Russell Sage Foundation.[3]
4. There is a romantic complex about parenthood. The writer has published a paper on this and Lerner discusses it at some length.[4] In some ways the romantic complex surrounding parenthood is even deeper and more unrealistic than that relating to marriage.
5. Modern parents are in the unenviable position of having complete responsibility for their offspring but only partial authority over them. Our thesis on this point is that parental authority has been eroded gradually over the past several decades without an equivalent reduction of parental responsibility.[5]

---

[3] Orville G. Brim, Jr., *Education for Child Rearing* (New York: Russell Sage Foundation, 1959), various chapters.

[4] E. E. LeMasters, "Parenthood as Crisis," *Marriage and Family Living*, 19 (1957), pp. 352–355. See also Max Lerner, *America as a Civilization* (New York: Simon and Schuster, 1957), pp. 560–570.

[5] See J. M. Mogey, "A Century of Declining Paternal Authority," *Marriage and Family Living*, 19 (1957), pp. 234–239.

6. The standards of role performance imposed on modern parents are too high. This arises from the fact that modern fathers and mothers are judged largely by professional practitioners such as psychiatrists and social workers rather than by their peers—other parents who are "amateurs" and not professionals.

7. Parents are the victims of inadequate behavioral science—as was discussed in the previous chapter. They have been told repeatedly by psychiatrists, social workers, sociologists, ministers, and others that nothing determines what the child will be like but the influence of the parents. As Brim makes clear, this is obviously not true.[6] It is a form of Watsonian environmentalism made so popular in the 1920's and later repudiated by many students of personality. Freudians have had a hand in this deception also.

8. Parents do not choose their children, unless they are adoptive parents.[7] Thus they have the responsibility for children whether they find them congenial or not. This, of course, is nothing new in parenthood the world over, but the expectations of role performance for modern American parents are such that the nature of the child can impose severe strain. Middle-class college graduate parents, for example, are supposed to get their children through college regardless of the child's intellectual interest or desire for learning. In an earlier America college attendance was less compulsive and such children could be apprenticed to the local banker or placed in some business operated by one of the relatives. This sort of parental maneuvering is becoming harder and harder. Fortunately, a new type of college which specializes in the delicate task of giving college diplomas to students who don't want them is beginning to emerge.[8] There is every reason to think that their future is bright.

9. There is no traditional model for modern parents to follow in rearing their children. The old model has been riddled by critical studies, yet no new model that is adequate has developed. Instead we have had a series of fads and fashions in child rearing based on the research of the moment. Wolfenstein has an interesting paper on this.[9] Brim,

---

[6] Brim, op. cit., chap. 2, "The Influence of Parent on Child." See also Dennis H. Wrong, "The Over Socialized Conception of Man in Sociology," *American Sociological Review*, 26 (1961), pp. 183–193.

[7] In a significant but unknown percentage of cases the parents did not even choose to be parents: the conception was unplanned. One estimate is that about 12 percent of all children born in the 1960's in the United States were unplanned— and perhaps unwanted. See *Marriage and Family Living*, 30 (1968), pp. 236–245.

[8] We do not wish to identify any of these colleges—the reader can supply his own names.

[9] See Martha Wolfenstein, "Trends in Infant Care," *American Journal of Orthopsychiatry*, 33 (1953), pp. 120–130.

in a very careful survey of the literature, concludes that parent educators have been unconsciously presenting their middle-class values
for all parents to emulate.[10] This has not been much help to parents
who probably need the most help—parents from low income groups.

10. Contrary to what some may think, parenthood as a role does not
enjoy the priority one would expect in modern America. The needs
of the economic system in particular come first as can be seen in
the frequency with which large firms transfer young managers and
their families around the country. One college girl interviewed by
the writer said that her family had moved 16 times in the first 18
years of her life. The armed forces and their manpower needs often
frustrate the efforts of modern fathers and mothers. Hours of employment in many retail businesses involving work at night and on
Sunday sometimes defeat the best efforts of parents to maintain close
family ties. Employed mothers as well as fathers face this problem.
Many tax laws are unfair to families and in particular to the woman
who works outside of the home. School hours and school vacations
often do not coincide with the needs of parents. All of this reflects
the fact that we do not have a national policy on the family in the
United States—various social institutions formulate their own policies.

11. Other new roles have been assumed by modern parents since World
War I that are not always completely compatible with the role of
parent.[11] The clearest and most striking example of this would be
the occupational roles assumed by millions of American mothers. And
for those who regard these women as frivolous it might help to remember that our schools, our social service agencies, and our hospitals could simply not be operated without these employed mothers.
Yet they are usually given little sympathy or public support if anything happens to their children. The Nye and Hoffman book makes
all of this very clear.[12]

12. The parental role is one of the few important roles in contemporary
America that one cannot honorably withdraw from. Most of us can
escape from our jobs if they are too frustrating; many of us escape
from our parents when we marry; and a considerable number of
husbands and wives manage to withdraw with some honor from
marriages that they no longer find enchanting. But it is harder to pull

---

[10] Brim, op. cit., chaps. 4 and 5.

[11] See Biddle and Thomas, op. cit., for a discussion of role conflict, pp. 273–310,
also Talcott Parsons, The Social System (New York: The Free Press, 1951), pp.
280–283; also Arnold W. Green, "The Middle-Class Male Child and Neurosis,"
American Sociological Review, 11 (1946), pp. 31–41.

[12] F. Ivan Nye and Lois Wladis Hoffman (eds.), The Employed Mother in
America (Chicago: Rand McNally & Co., 1963).

out of parenthood, especially for mothers, even when the parent knows he or she is failing. This is a difficult spot to be in and not an enviable one.

13. And last but not least, it is not enough for modern parents to produce children in their own image: the children have to be reared to be not only different from their fathers and mothers but also *better*. This point is commented on at some length later in the chapter.

Summary

We have presented 13 characteristics of the role of parent in our society that we feel merit some attention. A few of them may be obvious but others are less obvious if not new to some readers. All of the above observations are based on discussion groups with parents. They all create trouble for some parents—but not all. One finds a certain American parent who goes blithely about his or her way not reading Dr. Spock or going to PTA and happy about the whole process of being a parent. Whether this happy and hardy breed is in the majority or the minority the writer does not know and doubts that anybody else knows either. In their study of parents Miller and Swanson reported the majority of their parents found the parental role pleasant and satisfying.[13] The writer is skeptical of conclusions of this nature. In the same way one can get similar results by polling veterans of the armed forces, yet on any given day *while in the service* most men and women would have gladly accepted an honorable discharge and gone home. The writer is convinced that most parents have much the same attitude: looking back on the experience they would not have missed it for the world, but on a great many days (and nights) they would gladly have accepted an honorable discharge. This chapter is written from this point of view.

It may not be possible to discuss all 13 points in further detail but some of them demand expansion at this point and will be considered in the rest of this chapter. Others will be commented on in other chapters.

The role is poorly defined, ambiguous, and not adequately delimited

It is impossible to interview modern parents without concluding that large numbers of them are confused, frustrated, and discouraged. They have been robbed of the traditional ways of rearing children without having an adequate substitute; they feel that they cannot achieve what they are expected to achieve; the standards for child rearing are

---

[13] Daniel R. Miller and Guy E. Swanson, *The Changing American Parent* (New York: John Wiley & Sons, 1958), p. 216. It needs to be remembered that these mothers (fathers were not interviewed) were looking *back* at the early years of child rearing from the vantage point of the future.

too high; the authority of parents has been undermined by mass media, school officials, courts, social workers, and the adolescent peer group.

When should children be punished? Is it legitimate to use physical punishment anymore? Has fear been outlawed as a tool to be used by fathers and mothers when it seems appropriate? What is meant by "harsh" child rearing methods? Should fathers try to assume more authority with their children or less? Do parents have a right to defy public authorities when they are convinced the authorities are wrong? What rights do parents actually have in modern America? Is it true that there are no bad children, only bad parents? It it true that the first few years determine what an adult will be like 30 years later? Is it true that the violence so common on television has no negative effect on children? Is it true that modern parents are largely responsible for the increase in juvenile deliquency in the United States? Are parents responsible for the new type of violence and sadism characteristic of juvenile crimes today? Are parents the main cause of the increase in premarital sexual relations reported by some studies? Is it true that mothers who work outside of the home are virtually sentencing their children to juvenile delinquency or mental illness or both? Is the American mother as bad as the best sellers say she is? Do psychiatrists know as much about people as they think they do? Do parents ever have the right to be different whether society or the child's peer group likes it or not?

The writer submits that few, if any, of the above questions can be answered with any degree of certainty in modern America. Parents have been made the bad guy in the drama of modern living and have been blamed for the failures of all of the other basic social institutions in our society—the school, the church, the government, the mass media, the economic system, the armed forces, and so forth.

In 1967 a psychiatrist read a paper at a meeting in Chicago in which he concluded that sexual deviants are "acting out" subconsciously the sexual conflicts of their parents.[14] The sample on which he based his findings consisted of *seven* cases he had analyzed—not randomly selected, not matched with a control group, and with no independent review of his data. In other words, this so-called scientific study was the most unscientific piece of work one could imagine.

But a few days later a mother who has a boy who is a sexual deviant told us she had read the article and was upset by it—did we think she and her husband were the cause of their son being a sexual deviant?

---

[14] News story in *Milwaukee Journal*, October 12, 1967. In a story on sexual deviation in *Time*, December 30, 1957, pp. 37–38, the reporter states: "The psychiatrist agreed that the problem can be laid at the parent's doorstep." It may be that the news reporters did not give the complete analysis in these papers, but this is the sort of material that parents read in the daily press and their national magazines.

She pointed out that her two other sons were not sexual deviants, nor was her daughter. In fact, she had been unable to discover any previous case of sexual deviation either in her family or that of her husband.

Our reply was that the paper she referred to was without any scientific value and that probably nobody really knew what caused sexual deviation. It seems to vary from one society to another, from one historical period to another, from one occupation to another, and so on. There may well be genetic and biological factors as well as psychological and sociocultural factors. Who can determine in any given case the exact etiology? The state of knowledge about sexual deviation, we said, was analogous to that about alcoholism: no one really knows the cause, yet we do know something about treatment.

It seems to us that modern parents are beset by problems of the above nature—inadequate knowledge which focuses the blame on parents but offers them no security that what they do with the next child will turn out any better.

We believe that industrial executives forced to work under such conditions would quit. But then, of course, parents can't quit.

Responsibility without authority

In American industry one of the cardinal principles of management is that responsibility should be tied in with authority. In other words, a person in a position of responsibility should be given the authority to carry out his (or her) assignment. This is not true of modern parenthood.

In his history of the family in Western society, Zimmerman of Harvard University points out that the father in Roman society during the golden era of the Roman empire was absolute lord and master of his children as well as his wife.[15] We will not dwell in this book on the delicate subject of the relationship of husbands and wives in modern America, but it would be a crude joke (or travesty) to suggest that the modern father is any lord or master over his children—indeed, he is lucky if they are not lord and master over him.

It is easy, of course, to blame this condition on the modern American male but the matter is not that simple. American society in almost every respect has become feminine—even sports, to some observers[16]—and the reasons are not entirely clear. From the outside toilet in the dead of winter to the two-bathroom home is a long stretch, but Americans have

---

[15] Carle C. Zimmerman, *Family and Civilization* (New York: Harper & Brothers, 1947).

[16] When the writer played semiprofessional baseball in the 1930's, the players chewed tobacco. Today many of them chew bubble gum. See the discussion "Notes on the Femininization of Society," by Myron Brenton in *The American Male* (New York: Coward-McCann, 1966), chap. 3.

made it in little short of a century—and plumbers have done even better than that. Automobiles have been designed for women, saloons have given way to cocktail lounges, and so on. How would fathers escape such a massive assault on masculine dominance?

On a more sober note, it seems clear that the rights of fathers and mothers over their children have been seriously proscribed in the past several decades. Parents in Wisconsin, for example, are no longer permitted to prepare their infants for burial in the event of death—yet their ancestors were allowed to do so.[17] And in states such as Minnesota even university professors are not considered qualified to educate their children at home unless the state education department says so.[18] Parents who oppose medical procedures on the basis of religious faith have consistently had their pleas denied by the courts; parents who punish their children physically are often called into court to answer for their behavior. There seems little doubt that parents today are as responsible as ever—and even more so—for their children but have much less authority over them. And what power has not been usurped by the formal society has been grabbed by the informal society of the child's peer group, especially at the adolescent level.

We do not wish to belabor the point. But in our own family we have the distinct feeling that many agencies (including the church) are anxious to influence our children but that none of them wish to assume any final responsibility for them. That delightful bit is reserved for parents.

The best illustration of all of this is provided by those guardians of the public morals, the owners of the mass media in modern America: the magazines, the movies, radio, and television. Whenever some public agency questions the content of the mass media these groups always cry that they don't influence children—they only entertain them. And yet many parents are shocked when they take the time to examine the nature of the material their children are exposed to by these groups. If advertisers have reason to believe that the mass media influences adults, what reason is there to believe that it doesn't also influence children?

---

[17] In 1964 a married couple of low income was prosecuted in Wisconsin for burying an infant without employing a mortuary. News story in the *Wisconsin State Journal*, April 10, 1964. Ancestors of the writer living in rural Ohio always buried their own dead without consulting authorities of any kind—unless a minister was called in to help with the burial rites.

[18] In the 1960's a celebrated case in Minnesota resulted in a court order requiring that a University professor enroll his child in either a public or private elementary school approved by the state. The parents in this case had argued that they could give their child a superior education at home. We have lost the news story citations on this case but it was widely publicized nationally. Compare this with the era of the poet, Robert Frost, who sent his children to school only when he felt like it—see Lawrence Thompson, *Robert Frost* (New York: Holt, Rinehart, and Winston, 1966).

The usual reply is that good parents don't permit their children to see or read or hear such stuff—but on the same grounds why prohibit the sale of marijuana or the sale of alcoholic beverages to minors? Isn't it true that in the same sense good parents would make it impossible for their children to use such services?

The answer is that even conscientious and capable parents can not rear their children properly in an evil environment—and the basic solution is to make the society fit for children to be reared in.

Urban parents can never hope for the control and authority over their children that rural parents had. But at least they can hope that the urban neighborhood and the metropolitan community can be made a decent world in which to bring up children. And any person or any group which makes this impossible should be made to shoulder at least *some* of the responsibility for what happens to young Americans. Parents should not always have to be the bad guys in the modern world.

Judgment by professionals—not your peers

It is a basic principle in Anglo-Saxon law that persons charged with some offense are entitled to be judged by their peers, and especially so when the charge is serious. Parents in modern society, however, are seldom given this consideration: they are judged by professional practitioners. As a rule these professionals represent fields such as psychiatry, clinical psychology, social work, the teaching profession, or the law. In the opinion of the writer, this is one of the reasons why parents in modern America feel so threatened and insecure.

If one analyzes the situations in which parents in trouble find themselves it seems clear that they are usually facing one or more of the above professional groups. If the problem relates to school work, the teachers, the school guidance counselors, and/or the school administrators will be sitting in judgment.

Often the problem will involve either some public welfare agency or a juvenile court, in which case a professional social worker or a judge will be evaluating the parental effort.

In metropolitan areas a child guidance clinic or a mental health facility will be involved in the assessment of parental role functioning.

Regardless of the professional agency involved, the father and mother will be judged against the professional norms of the practitioners. In few instances are the parents evaluated by other parents. And yet this is the essence of the law of our land.

The writer has been impressed with this matter in listening to professional workers discuss parents and their failures. Very often some specialized knowledge of the practitioner is advanced to show what the parents should have or should not have done with some particular child.

And often it seems to be assumed that modern parents have no right to be amateurs: they should practice parenthood as if it were a profession.

It might be argued that parenthood is becoming professionalized. The writer would argue just the reverse: parents today are just as confused (if not more so) than ever, and their preparation for parenthood is just as poor as ever, but they are being *judged* by professionals. And this is an uncomfortable position at best.

One can argue, of course, that this has always been the case, but the fact is that parents in the 18th and 19th centuries were closer to public officials in terms of values and background than they are today—social work, psychiatry, juvenile courts, and schools in modern America reflect professional subcultures much more today than they did yesterday. Schoolteachers in 1900, for example, had only a high school diploma or at best one or two years of college education, but when the writer is summoned to the local school to discuss his children the guidance counselor is a specialist, the teacher is often a specialist, and even the school principal has had fairly elaborate training in child development, school guidance, and related matters.

It is easy to overlook changes of this nature in thinking about parents in modern society, and yet they are very real. And for some parents they are quite frustrating and threatening.

One parent interviewed by the writer said their son had come home from school with a note that he needed to have his eyes examined. The school nurse had given all of the pupils a vision test and this particular child had scored below the acceptable norm. A visit to the local oculist resulted in glasses being prescribed at a total cost of approximately $50. The parents were glad that the vision problem of their child had been identified but at the moment they didn't have the money to pay for the glasses. When the child appeared in class two weeks later without them a note was sent home from the school asking why the corrective work had not been taken care of. The mother finally went to a small loan company and borrowed the money for the glasses.

One can appreciate the fact that school nurses are trying to be helpful to parents, but it is not always possible for fathers and mothers to take the action recommended by the school.

It might be pointed out that in some Western societies the school would not only have identified the vision problem in this case but would also have corrected it through a school eye clinic.[19]

If the parents in this case had been receiving public welfare the glasses could have been provided at public expense, but they fell into that economic no man's land in which they didn't qualify for public

---

[19] A professor from Sweden told the writer that in his country the school not only identified vision problems but provided the glasses at a very nominal charge to the parent.

assistance but at the same time could not afford good medical care for themselves and their children.

In a sense parents in the above bind are caught in a mass affluent society in which fathers and mothers at all economic levels are held to the same standards but are not given the means to live up to the standards. As Harrington says, it is more painful to be poor in a wealthy society than in a poor one.[20]

Ethically, it is cruel to call such matters to the attention of parents unless the school or some other social agency is prepared to help correct the situation.[21]

One could illustrate endlessly the ways in which modern parents are judged by professional practitioners, but perhaps the point has been made.

No margin for error

In most areas of life there is some margin for error—even those of us who have never had a serious automobile accident will admit that at times we have been lucky, or that the other driver made it possible to avoid a serious collision.

One certainly feels in a profession such as teaching that some students will simply not learn—or at least they will learn very little. Yet if most (or even some) of the students learn, the average teacher or professor will find it not too hard to rationalize his failure to make the material meaningful to all of his students.

This same philosophical acceptance of some defeat is certainly found in medicine, law, the ministry, nursing, and social work. Nobody expects these professionals to save everybody who presents himself at their office. It is recognized and accepted that some people are "too sick" or "too maladjusted" to make effective use of the service provided. Parents, however, are expected to succeed with every child. This is disturbing to some parents. The writer talked with one mother who put it this way: "I am scared to death when I think that what happens to my children rests on my shoulders—it makes me feel so inadequate."

One factor has been the smaller family. It is one thing to fail with one or two children if you have five or six, but failure in the smaller family is more absolute. As an only child put it to us in a college class, "My parents only have one child and if I fail them *all* of their children will have failed them." She went on to say that this was a frightening spot

---

[20] Michael Harrington, *The Other America* (New York: The Macmillan Co., 1963).

[21] In some ways this situation reflects the odd mixture of the welfare state and the free enterprise system in modern America: the free clinic identifies the problem but one has to turn to the private medical fraternity to correct the problem.

to be in and that she herself hoped to have several children when she married.[22]

It is probably true that the higher birth rate since World War II has taken some of this "preciousness" out of the parental role, but one has the impression that a considerable amount is still lurking about.[23]

The late President Kennedy once said that the most awful thing about a possible nuclear war is that a single mistake could be fatal to millions and millions of people—if not a whole nation. He[24] went on to say that this was not true in earlier wars: commanders could (and did) make grievous errors with only moderate losses of men and material—a luxury no longer permitted by nuclear weapons.

It is inhuman not to permit modern parents some margin for error. And yet that seems to be the attitude of some of the professionals who evaluate parental failure. The writer for one rejects the thesis that only the professionals can make mistakes. Amateurs have this right also.

Parents can't quit

Many of us in our lives find ourselves in roles that are not congenial: occupational roles, religious roles, military service roles, community volunteer roles, kinship roles, even marital roles—and one of the comfortable features of living in an urban, pluralistic society is the mobility available to us. If we don't like our home town or our home state we move on somewhere else. As Mead says, Americans love their home towns as long as they don't have to live there.[25] One could even go further and say: Americans love their relatives as long as they don't have to live near or with them.

Some roles, however, even in our fluid society, are hard to escape if they are not comfortable. One of these is the military service role for men in certain age and status categories, but even here conscientious objectors and persons not suited for military duty are usually given special consideration.

Some of our kinship and family roles are not always comfortable but the mobility of modern America makes it possible as a rule to reduce these to manageable levels. A daughter leaves the small town of birth where most of her family and other relatives live and moves to the

---

[22] The writer has never found an only child who wanted to repeat the experience in their own marriage: they always want more children than one. And this is in spite of the feeling they have for their own parents.

[23] But in 1967 and 1968 the birthrate was declining again and was near the level of the 1930's.

[24] This was during the famous crisis with the Soviet Union over the Russian nuclear missiles being installed in Cuba.

[25] Margaret Mead, *And Keep Your Powder Dry* (New York: William Morrow & Co., 1942).

great city or its suburbs; a son migrates from Ohio to California; married couples often live far from all of their in-laws, and sometimes by design.

Most of us find it possible to try on for size and comfort many occupational roles before settling into one for life. In an earlier America, where most people were farmers, this was harder to manage. It is still true that some Americans get trapped in jobs not exactly tailored to their fit, but this usually represents a series of decisions that did not turn out well.

It is even true that modern Americans can withdraw from their marital role if it is too uncomfortable, and the statistics show that an increasing number of men and women have been availing themselves of this new role flexibility since the end of World War I.[26] Many persons do not approve of this newfound freedom to try again but it is now legal in all 50 states and is to be found in some of the best families.[27]

It is the writer's impression that the role of parent is one of the hardest to give up in our society once it has been assumed. And this is especially true for mothers.

The law in most states says that natural and adoptive parents are responsible for their children until the children attain legal adulthood in that state.[28] A considerable number of American fathers take this obligation somewhat lightly, judging by divorce, desertion, and separation statistics, but the vast majority of American mothers stick it out, for better or worse. Some observers, such as Ashley Montagu, believe that mothers in all of the mammals and primates are more reliable parents than are the fathers, and it certainly is true at the human level.[29] In the sense of being a permanent parent the old saying is true: the woman pays and pays and goes on paying until the child is no more.

Even among fathers, however, there is a lot of reluctance to desert or abandon children and undoubtedly many American men preserve their marriages and homes for the sole purpose of "doing what is right for the children." Whether their sacrifice really benefits the children may be debated but their intentions are clear: they feel obligated to do what they can to provide their children with a stable home. American wives, of course, feel this even more strongly and often continue their marriages for the above reason.

26 For an interesting study of the gradual shift in attitudes toward divorce in our society see William L. O'Neill, *Divorce in the Progressive Era* (New Haven: Yale University Press, 1967).

27 This list now includes the Henry Ford II family, the Franklin D. Roosevelt family, the Rockefeller family, and the Kennedy family.

28 For a review of the legal framework within which parents in our society operate, see Alfred Kadushin, *Child Welfare Services* (New York: The Macmillan Co., 1967), chap. 6. See also Helen Clarke, *Social Legislation* (rev. ed.; New York: Appleton-Century-Crofts, 1957).

29 Ashley Montagu, *The Natural Superiority of Women* (New York: The Macmillan Co., 1968 ed.).

In a sense it is a sobering thought to find you are going to be a parent and that for the next 18 to 25 years you will have a large responsibility for another human being. And the period of responsibility seems to be lengthening in spite of the trend toward earlier marriage. The reason is that marriage for young couples today no longer symbolizes complete severance from the silver cord or the family checkbook: it means partial independence but not absolute.

It is interesting to see this difference in the writer's family. Our father left home at 15 and never lived at home or received any steady support from his family after that. Our mother was married at 16 and was independent from that day on. In the next generation, the one we grew up in, our oldest brother quit school in the eighth grade and was essentially on his own after that. The next son left school in the second year of high school and was relatively independent after that. An older sister attended college for one year and was responsible for herself after that. The youngest of the four children, the writer, went to college for nine years in obtaining a doctor's degree but was essentially on his own after the age of 23. At this time it is hard to determine how long the writer's two sons will need financial support and some form of aid before they complete their preparation for adult life. One has the impression that they will be somewhere in their mid-twenties at least.

This longer period of dependency has been written about by various observers[30] and undoubtedly places a strain on both parents and children. In reading over 1,000 term papers written by college students about their family life the writer has been much impressed by their frequent reference to this long period of dependency. Parents are not reluctant to discuss it either.

It is a truism that the human infant has by far the longest period of dependency of any of the so-called higher animals but the fact remains that the period has been getting even longer in modern America. The age of marriage was later in earlier centuries in the United States—especially for men—but the period of dependence was shorter. And the frontier offered avenues of escape not available to modern young Americans.

It is not true, of course, that modern parents can never quit because some of them do, but the fact remains that public disapproval of child neglect is probably as strong as that for any kind of deviance in our society—and the courts symbolize this by their attitude toward parents who do not fulfill their obligations as fathers and mothers.

One point usually made in discussing this matter is that "after all they didn't have to have children. Nobody forced it on them." Well,

---

[30] Evelyn Millis Duvall, *Family Development* (Philadelphia: J. B. Lippincott Co., 1957), chap. 12.

maybe not, but in the same sense the writer doesn't have to contribute to the March of Dimes when the neighbor lady comes knocking on the door—but we always do. There is a very thin line between "voluntary" and "involuntary" behavior at the human level—and the line seems to be getting even thinner in the mass homogenized society.

We are not sure what good research on the point would show, but one might hazard a guess that a considerable proportion of parenthood in this or any other society is not voluntary in the best sense of the word.[31] It has some of the ring of the word *volunteer* as used in the armed forces: someone who got trapped. Some modern parents feel this way, and with some reason.

Modern parents are expected to rear children that are not only different from the parents but *better*

Probably the title of this subsection makes the point as well as it can be made. Both Riesman and Lerner, as well as Brim, point out that it is not enough for modern parents to simply produce children who will replace them in the larger society, one reason being that the larger society is changing so rapidly that the old models will no longer suffice.[32]

This point is aptly demonstrated by the dilemma facing rural parents today: rural society as the parents know it is disappearing from modern America—there is no place in rural America for the majority of the children growing up there. Modern agriculture is becoming big business. The capital investment, the managerial skills, and the technology required today to succeed in almost any phase of farm production are beyond the reach of most of the children growing up in rural communities.[33] This means that these rural fathers and mothers are rearing their children for a world the parents have never lived in: the urban world of commerce and industry, the world of the city and the suburb.

Even urban parents face some of the same problems. It will not be enough if the children go through junior high school and perhaps part of high school. The minimum educational requirement in the future for almost any type of decent job will be a high school diploma, if not more. The parents, the schools, and the children will have to be better than

---

[31] At least 85 percent of American married couples attempt to "plan" their families but not all of them are entirely successful in their "planning." See Ronald Freedman et al., *Family Planning, Sterility and Population Growth* (New York: McGraw-Hill Book Co., 1959).

[32] Brim and Lerner were cited earlier in the chapter. See also David Riesman et al., *The Lonely Crowd* (New Haven: Yale University Press, 1961 ed.), pp. 37–65.

[33] See chap. 11, "Parents and Social Change" in this volume for further discussion of the problems of rural parents.

they have been in the past if the children are going to have a chance to compete.

This is a sobering thought. It will not be enough for the parents to produce carbon copies of themselves; they will have to do what some of the new copying machines are supposed to do—turn out copies better than the originals.

It would seem that this is one of the reasons why modern parents feel so inadequate. They are not sure they are able to do what is required. And their children are not sure either.

To some extent, of course, American parents have always faced this problem, at least the immigrant groups did. But the country was expanding then, the frontier was still open, and individual ability rather than formal education was probably the main ingredient required for economic and personal success. One has the distinct impression that this era in American history is over.

It is possible that parents will not be able to meet this challenge and that some social institution other than the family will have to assume more of the burden. In the recent effort of the federal government to strengthen local school programs, especially in low income areas, there is emerging a strategy of helping parents in these areas give their children a better chance.[34] Perhaps the function of the family in urban-industrial society will be delimited even more than it has to date, with the government and the school becoming more dominant in the socialization of children and their preparation for adult life. Some of the programs designed to enrich the lives of preschool children from deprived families seem to represent this approach to the problem.

There is a truism in political sociology that societies undergoing major social revolutions almost always (if not always) de-emphasize the family and its influence on the next generation until the major changes sought in the revolution have been achieved. Russia did this in the 1920's, Nazi Germany did this in the 1930's, and Red China is doing this today.[35] To the extent that America is now in another socioeconomic revolution, perhaps the same strategy will be employed here—at least for a generation or so. And maybe the results will be better than some expect—the family, after all, is basically a conservative, if not a reactionary, type of group. It prepares much better for the past than it does for the future.

---

[34] Some of these possibilities are explored in Peter Schrag's study, *Village School Downtown* (Boston: Beacon Press, 1967); see also Benjamin Fine, *Underachievers: How They Can Be Helped* (New York: E. P. Dutton & Co., 1967), chap. 11. There are also some interesting illustrations of new school programs in an earlier study by James Conant, *Slums and Suburbs* (New York: McGraw-Hill Book Co., 1961).

[35] For a discussion of this point see William J. Goode, *World Revolution and Family Patterns* (New York: The Free Press, 1963).

In a society oriented toward the future, as is the United States, this inevitably produces certain problems. Perhaps some of these can be resolved or reduced by strengthening other social institutions rather than the family itself. To the extent that parents are relieved of some of their parental responsibility the results may be therapeutic for all concerned.

Role theory and parenthood

With the arrival of the first child, the married couple assume a brand new role—that of father and mother. Even though most of them have looked forward to having a child, a significant proportion of them will find that they are poorly prepared for this new role, and some of them will even find that they are unable to function adequately as a parent.

Some of the difficulty experienced by many new parents will be related to what Wright calls "the discrepancy of expectations"—the role of parent will not be exactly as they had imagined it to be.[36] For some of them being a father or mother will be more satisfying than they had anticipated, while for others parenthood will be more frustrating than they could have imagined.

One source of difficulty related to the arrival of the first child is the fact that all through courtship and the childless years of marriage the young couple have functioned in a two-person (dyad) group, but now with the beginning of parenthood they find themselves in a three-person group (the triad). There is an old bit of folklore in our society which says that "two is company but three is a crowd"—the point being that a triad is infinitely more complex than a dyad.[37]

In a three-person group there is always the possibility that the group will subdivide. Two persons will form a subgroup and leave the third person more or less stranded.[38] The young wife, for example, may be so enamoured of her new role as mother that she begins to neglect her role as wife. If this happens the husband-father may feel left out of the charmed circle.

---

[36] See Beatrice A. Wright, "Disability and Discrepancy of Expectations," Biddle and Thomas, op. cit., pp. 159–164.

[37] For a discussion of the dyad and triad types of groups see Theodore Caplow, Two Against One: Coalitions in Triads (Englewood Cliffs, N.J.: Prentice-Hall, Inc., 1968). He writes: "In the primary triad of father, mother, and child, the formation of a coalition may undermine paternal authority before the child is out of the cradle." Preface, p. vi.

[38] While serving as a Dean of Students the writer was impressed with the number of complaints received from students assigned to three-person rooms. Quite often two of the occupants would gang up on the third person and that student would request a new room assignment. This appeared to happen much less often in two-person rooms.

It is quite easy for an American mother to overload her parental role and become a mommy—a woman who always gives priority to her children over her husband. This is a problem of "role balance"—dividing one's time and energy between the various roles that make claims on fathers and mothers.

In family counseling one gets the impression that role balance for American husbands is most often jeopardized by their occupation, their male peer group, or some hobby such as fishing or golf. When this happens the wife feels neglected.

With American wives it seems that role balance is often upset by their becoming a mother. The baby is so small and helpless, and its needs are so great, that the husband loses all of the priority he formerly enjoyed with his wife. Whether it is sex or social companionship, he may begin to feel neglected and be jealous of the new child.

Benson has this sort of syndrome in mind when he comments: "There is no evidence to suggest that having children improves or enhances a couple's ability to handle marriage problems.[39] He then goes on to cite a study by Koos which concluded that in the sample *twice* as many of the conflicts reported involved the parent role rather than the marriage role.[40]

It is literally true that children destroy some marriages but the proportion is difficult to determine. It is also true that children save some marriages, but here again the precise proportion is not known.

Arnold Green has argued that there are basic conflicts between the role of parent and other basic roles at the middle and upper class levels in our society.[41] The parent's drive for occupational mobility is often frustrated, Green thinks, by the presence of children. Green believes that parents at these class levels develop a deep ambivalence about their roles as mothers and fathers.[42]

Unfortunately, feelings of this nature are not uncovered in the house-to-house surveys of parents so often published in professional journals.[43]

---

[39] Leonard Benson, *Fatherhood* (New York: Random House, 1968), p. 113.

[40] *Ibid.*, p. 114.

[41] Green, *op. cit.* See also David F. Aberle and Kaspar D. Naegele, "Middle-class Fathers' Occupational Role and Attitudes toward Children," *American Journal of Orthopsychiatry*, 22 (April, 1952), pp. 366–378.

[42] It would seem that young fathers in the middle class are especially prone to role conflicts in that they are attempting to establish themselves in their occupational role at the very moment when their wives and children need them most. One can see this clearly on the college campus in talking with the wives of junior faculty members.

[43] We have reference to the material on parents found in survey studies such as *Husbands and Wives* by Robert O. Blood, Jr. and Donald M. Wolfe (New York: The Free Press, 1960). This is a valuable study but it does not delve into the depths of parental feelings and conflicts.

Being a parent is a sacred trust, one of life's deepest experiences, and persons do not readily admit the full range of their parental feelings. One mother said to us: "I love all of them and yet on certain days I felt like killing each and every one of them." The amazing thing about this statement is that this mother is actually a very competent parent—she has reared five children with what appears to be above-average results.

It may be that the stress of becoming a parent in our society is related to the fact that parenthood (not marriage) actually represents the last step in the long process of becoming an adult in American society. This may seem obvious but the writer has the distinct impression that many young Americans feel that marriage itself is the last step into the adult world. This may indeed be the case legally but is certainly is not true psychologically or socially. If this line of reasoning is sound it would mean that the role of parent would present somewhat of a surprise to many young married couples—they may think they are fully grown up when in fact they have to prove it all over again when they become parents.

In the paper by Green cited earlier he argues that the father's occupational role is often in conflict with his parental role. If this is true a similar conflict would be found among employed mothers who still have children at home. We discuss this matter elsewhere[44] and do not want to consider it here at any length, but it certainly seems to be true that economic efficiency is given so much priority in our society that it is difficult to imagine an American father neglecting his job (or refusing a promotion) out of deference to the needs of his children. Mothers undoubtedly do this, at great sacrifice to their occupational success, but fathers who did so would have to be regarded as deviants.

We do not wish to romanticize the farm family, but some observers have felt that the farm father has had an advantage over urban-industrial fathers in that his parental role is easier to integrate with his occupational role. This may be true, but farm parents have other problems in modern America that are analyzed in Chapter 11.

Summary and conclusion

In this chapter the position has been taken that the parental role in modern America is poorly defined, not well delimited, and that most fathers and mothers have had inadequate preparation for the role.

It was also suggested that parental authority has been eroded in our society over a period of several decades without any reduction in parental responsibility. This development apparently reflects the "rights

---

[44] See chaps. 7 and 8 on the American mother and the American father.

of children" movement since World War I and has resulted in some confusion as to the rights of parents.

Another major point developed in the chapter was the idea that the parental role in our society is harder to withdraw from than other major roles. The best illustration of this is the new right of Americans to discontinue marriages that they no longer find congenial. There has been no comparable development for parents.

The chapter closed with a consideration of role theory and its application to the analysis of parenthood.

chapter
five

Parents and
social class

IN the past several decades American social scientists have produced a mass of research on the behavior of the various socioeconomic levels in our society.[1] It is not implied in this material that all individuals or families at a given social level are identical in their beliefs and overt behavior, but simply that they tend to reflect a subculture or way of life evolved by the group over time. Some persons may be marginal members of their social class and reflect only partially its subculture. There may also be subcultures within subcultures: dentists and physicians, for example, are both members of the upper middle class in our society but they each also have unique group behavior patterns related to the different nature of their occupations. Dentists have regular hours, to cite one difference, while most physicians do not.

It should be understood clearly that while the terms *upper* and *lower* are used to designate positions in the American social class structure that these are not meant by social scientists to reflect value judgments—they designate, for the most part, power and prestige, not moral worth.

Some levels of the social class structure have been studied more intensively than others: the middle class, for example, tends to be overrepresented in much research, while the upper class is often missing

---

[1] See Donald Gilbert McKinley, *Social Class and Family Life* (New York: The Free Press, 1964), also Ruth Shonle Cavan, *The American Family* (3d. ed.; New York: Thomas Y. Crowell, 1965), chaps. 4–7 inc.

For a general analysis of the American social stratification system see Robin Williams, *American Society* (rev. ed.; New York: Alfred A. Knopf, 1960), chap. 5.

Herbert Gans has an extensive analysis of social class subcultures and family life in his study, *The Urban Villagers* (New York: The Free Press, 1962), especially chaps. 11 and 12.

entirely in many studies. In recent years special efforts have been made to reach low income groups and to record their way of life.[2]

To the extent that American society is becoming a mass or homogenized society the social class differences considered in this chapter may be diminishing, but at the moment this is a difficult matter to assess. Rural subculture, for example, may be disappearing, but at the same time other and new subcultures related to social class position may be evolving.[3] The reader needs to keep this in mind in considering the material presented in this chapter.

We will begin with the parents on the bottom of the system, the so-called lower class.

Parental problems at the lower class level

The average American is not well informed about lower-class people.[4] Most college students have never met such a person. In the affluent society the lower-class person is actually a deviant. He shouldn't really exist—but he does. And in great numbers. Most of the estimates by government and private research groups as of the 1960's placed about one fifth of all Americans below the poverty line of $3,000 annual income per family per year.[5] This is an improvement over what Franklin D. Roosevelt saw in the 1930's—"one-third of the nation ill fed, ill housed, and ill clothed." At least 40 million fathers, mothers, and their children must be considered to be at the lower class level in our society as of the late 1960's. If one assumes that at best rearing children in modern America is the most difficult role that most adults ever have, then it follows that lower class fathers and mothers have an almost impossible task in rearing their children.

The lower class has often been romanticized in our society. The bum who doesn't have to worry about tomorrow, as the folklore goes, or the

---

[2] The work of Oscar Lewis, even though the families were not American, illustrates this effort. See his *Five Families* (New York: Basic Books, 1959). Lewis' thesis is that the culture of poverty cuts across societal lines and is more or less the same in all societies.

[3] The black nationalist group illustrates a new type of subculture. See Stokely Carmichael and Charles V. Hamilton, *Black Power* (New York: Alfred A. Knopf, 1967).

[4] Some students of social class, such as Warner, use the term *lower lower class* to designate the group on the bottom in our society. The writer prefers to simply designate this group as the *lower class*. For a summary of the Warner social class system, see W. Lloyd Warner, *American Life: Dream and Reality* (Chicago: University of Chicago Press, 1953).

[5] A good discussion of this may be found in the book that is credited with inspiring the war on poverty: Michael Harrington, *The Other America* (New York: The Macmillan Co., 1962). For a comparison with the 1930's, see David A. Shannon, *The Great Depression* (Englewood Cliffs, N.J.: Prentice-Hall, Inc., 1960).

happy-go-lucky black family of the urban slums that hasn't a care in the world because it has nothing to care about—these are portraits painted by persons who have never been poor, who have never lived in slums, who have never been on the bottom of the social order. As Max Lerner puts it in his study, *America as a Civilization:* "One image that we shall have to discard after studying the recent divorce figures is the romantic image of the lower lower class family as stable, integrated, and happy, while the middle-class family is divorce-ridden and neurotic."[6]

A mass of data can be cited to contradict the romantic folklore image of the lower class family—we cite only a few representative studies. In his classic analysis of divorce in Detroit after World War II Goode found divorce highest in the low-income groups, and higher among black poor people than white people of the same income level.[7] In their study of mental illness and social class Hollingshead and Redlich found psychosis rates higher in lower class families than in the middle or upper class.[8] In his analysis of school dropouts, Conant found much higher rates among the lower class.[9] Except for embezzlement, almost all forms of crime in modern America are highest in low-income groups.[10] Studies of physical disease find most ailments more frequent among low-income groups—this is especially true of such outmoded diseases as tuberculosis.[11] Surveys of dental care report over half of low-income children and adults to suffer from serious dental neglect.[12] Alcoholism has always been common among low-income groups but in modern America it may be almost as common among middle and upper income groups.[13] Kinsey found premarital sexual experience to be highest among the lower class (persons who had not gone beyond the eighth grade in school).[14] Rejection rates for the armed forces are almost three times as high in the lower class

---

[6] Max Lerner, *America as a Civilization* (New York: Simon and Schuster, 1957), p. 558.

[7] See William J. Goode, *After Divorce* (New York: The Free Press, 1956), chap. 4.

[8] See August B. Hollingshead and Frederick C. Redlich, *Social Class and Mental Illness* (New York: John Wiley & Sons, 1958). See also the analysis of Paul M. Roman and Harrison M. Trice, *Schizophrenia and the Poor* (Ithaca, N.Y.: New York School of Industrial Relations, 1967).

[9] See James Conant, *Slums and Suburbs* (New York: McGraw-Hill Book Co., 1961).

[10] See Marshall B. Clinard, *Sociology of Deviant Behavior* (rev. ed.; New York: Rinehart & Co., 1968), chaps. 6–9 incl.

[11] This material is summarized in Alvin L. Schorr, *Slums and Social Insecurity* (Washington, D.C.: U.S. Government Printing Office, 1963), pp. 13–14.

[12] News release from Wisconsin Department of Public Health, Madison, Wisc., August 24, 1967.

[13] For an analysis of alcoholism and social class, see Harrison M. Trice, *Alcoholism in America* (New York: McGraw-Hill Book Co., 1966), pp. 21–24.

[14] Alfred C. Kinsey et al., *Sexual Behavior in the Human Male* (Philadelphia: W. B. Saunders Co., 1948), chap. 10; also Kinsey et al., *Sexual Behavior in the Human Female* (Philadelphia: W. B. Saunders Co., 1953), various chapters.

as they are for the middle and upper classes.[15] Public welfare recipient rates are, of course, highest among the lower class.[16]

This revised portrait of the lower class family is hardly in harmony with the folklore picture. A psychiatrist would probably say that those of us who have done better in the system don't want to really know how the lowest fifth lives: we need to cherish our fond image of these happy-go-lucky souls who don't have to worry about PTA meetings or that dent in their new car. Harrington takes this position in his best seller, *The Other America* cited earlier. Some observers say that white people in America need to feel that the black person is really happy and contented with his lot.

As we stated earlier, lower class persons in our affluent society are really deviants, and as such they experience the problems of any deviant group—one of which is lack of acceptance and understanding by the rest of the society.[17] Lower class people have to endure suspicion, discrimination, public attack, and avoidance. Nice people don't wish to associate with them or live near them. They also don't want their children going to the same schools or running around with lower class children, regardless of race. Some middle-class blacks, for example, don't want their children belonging to lower class peer groups, white, black, or yellow.

In addition to this pattern of isolation or avoidance lower class parents can be said to suffer from the following disadvantages in rearing children.

High birth rates

Lower class people have never been famous for their skill in birth control.[18] As Lee Rainwater makes clear in his study, *And the Poor Get Children*, the low-income groups know relatively little about contraception and don't even practice what they know most of the time.[19] It does not seem likely that poor people actually like children more than any other income group: they just have less success controlling the size of their families. The net result of all of this is that with all of their other disadvantages lower class parents have more than their share of children to rear.

---

[15] See Alvin L. Schorr, *Poor Kids* (New York: Basic Books, 1966).

[16] *Ibid.*

[17] For an excellent discussion of the deviant in our society, see Howard S. Becker, *Outsiders* (New York: The Free Press, 1963).

[18] For a review of birth rates in the lower class see Cavan, *op. cit.*, chap. 7.

[19] Lee Rainwater, *And the Poor Get Children* (Chicago: Quadrangle Books, 1960). One estimate concludes that perhaps 35 percent of all children born into poverty families in our society are unplanned and maybe unwanted. See *Journal of Marriage and the Family*, 30 (1968), pp. 236–245.

Slum neighborhoods

Studies have shown for a long time that certain behavior character-izes slum areas regardless of what group happens to be living in the area at any given time. In their study, *Beyond the Melting Pot*, Glazer and Moynihan document the various behavior difficulties that have been endemic in certain slum areas of New York City regardless of whether the area was inhabited by Italians, Negroes, Irish, or Puerto Ricans.[20] It may be true, as they seem to think, that Jews offer an exception to this generalization, but this may be because Jewish families have been living in urban ghettos in Europe for generations.

Middle-class parents are well aware of the importance of living in the "right" neighborhood in rearing children: many of us examine the schools in an area we are thinking of moving into before we look at the house or the apartment. We know the importance of good recreational facilities for our children—the availability of the YMCA, the distance to the church, the kind of people who live in the area, and so forth.

Lower class parents may or may not be aware of the importance of these things, but in any event they have little if any choice. They must enter the urban community at what the sociologists used to call "the point of least resistance." It is undoubtedly true that some lower class parents are very adept at getting the best out of their social environ-ment,[21] but the fact remains that rearing children in such a world is a challenge that most parents would be happy not to have to face.

Inferior employment

Lower class mothers are more likely to seek outside employment if it is available, and if they find it, the working hours, the wages, and the conditions of employment are apt to be less than ideal. Low-income black mothers in Chicago, for example, according to Drake and Cayton in their study, *Black Metropolis*, are likely to be domestic servants, com-

---

[20] Nathan Glazer and Daniel Patrick Moynihan, *Beyond the Melting Pot* (Cambridge, Mass.: Harvard University and M.I.T. Press, 1963).

[21] Pearl and Riessman argue that some lower class parents are superb in their capacity to cope with slum conditions. See Arthur Pearl and Frank Riessman (eds.), *New Careers for the Poor* (New York: The Free Press, 1965). In an interesting paper Kadushin argues that "Tables correlating fathers' work and health records with mothers' health records and the sizes of the families have shown that the struggle to bring up very large families on low incomes is a test that would break all but the most resourceful and capable personalities." See Alfred Kadushin, *The Introduction of New Models to Child Welfare Research*, mimeographed, School of Social Work, University of Wisconsin, Madison, Wisc., 1963.

muting long distances to the suburbs and working long hours, six days a week, with little or no vacation time off.[22]

These mothers face almost insuperable problems in rearing their children properly regardless of their devotion to them. The proper conditions for good parenthood are simply not available.[23] The three generation or extended family system, with a grandmother or other relative in the home, has probably been the best defense these mothers have had for coping with their parental problems. But the three generation or extended family system has never been very popular in urban America and this tends to mitigate against these mothers using this coping device.

If the lower class father is living with the family his employment is also likely to be sporadic and not of the best nature. His wages are relatively low, his skills are limited, and his unemployment rate is generally high.[24]

A majority of the poor white families live in poverty-stricken rural areas, such as Appalachia, which offer very few, if any, public welfare or health services that might help these parents with their children.[25] The urban poor, bad as the ghetto is, have at least some public and private agencies to help them with some of their parental problems.[26]

One concludes that it is not only the low income which poses problems for lower class parents: it is also the other conditions of employment or unemployment they have to contend with.

Inadequate education

These lower class parents do not usually have a high school education —if that is the right word for what American high schools have been giving their graduates since the 1920's. Many of them have not even completed the eighth grade. Some of them can not read or write. All of

---

[22] St. Clair Drake and Horace R. Cayton, *Black Metropolis* (New York: Harcourt Brace & Co., 1945).

[23] One problem facing these mothers is the lack of adequate day-care facilities for their preschool children. See *Report on Day Care* (Washington, D.C., Child Welfare Report No. 14, U.S. Government Printing Office, 1964). This report shows that in the 1960's for three million children under the age of six, whose mothers work outside of the home, there were only 185,000 places available in approved child care centers for preschool children.

[24] For an excellent study of lower class men, see Elliot Liebow, *Tally's Corner* (Boston: Little, Brown & Co., 1967).

[25] For a good summary of these problems, see Harry Caudill, "Appalachia: The Dismal Land," in *Poverty: Views from the Left*, edited by Jeremy Larner and Irving Howe (New York: William Morrow & Co., 1968), pp. 264–279.

[26] The writer is of the opinion that urban slums, bad as they are, offer some advantages over rural slums—chiefly in the superior welfare services offered in metropolitan areas. For an illustration of this see Camille Jeffers, *Living Poor* (Ann

this means that they face almost insuperable handicaps in trying to understand the world they and their children live in, to say nothing of trying to cope with that world.[27]

There is another dimension to this handicap: they find it difficult, if not impossible, to retain the respect of their children, most of whom have more formal schooling than their parents, and this discrepancy is made more devastating by the fact that these children are living in a world in which a high school diploma is taken for granted.

It is certainly true, as Handlin and others have pointed out, that most of the earlier immigrant groups in America had this same sort of problem,[28] but those immigrants and their children were living in a very different kind of world—a world in which poverty was taken for granted and formal education was unusual rather than typical. The world of the earlier immigrant and his children was also less dangerous and less complicated: there were fewer laws to violate, there was (apparently) less serious juvenile delinquency, and certainly the expectations applied to these immigrant parents were lower and less harsh than those applied today.

It is hard for those who have considerable schooling to understand what it is like not to have it. The writer happened to grow up in a family in which his mother had gone to the second grade and his father through the third grade. These parents faced all sorts of handicaps as they tried to help their children improve their lot: the parents did not understand school systems and how to deal with them; when the writer wanted to go to college his parents were at a loss to even understand what a college was, and they could be of no help in selecting a college or even talking about such things.[29] This was a world they never knew and it not only confused them but also frightened them: they had heard terrible things about wild college students and were inclined to believe what they had heard. And they were especially impressed by anything that appeared in print—"it has to be true if they print it, doesn't it?"

The world of the uneducated has always been a different world but it is even more different today. Lower class parents know this only too well. But do the rest of us know it?

Arbor: Ann Arbor Publishers, 1967)—a participant-observation study of life in an urban low-income housing project.

[27] Gans, op. cit., says the lower class views the outside world with suspicion and distrust. See chap. 11.

The median years of formal schooling completed by nonwhites in the United States as of 1966 was 9.2 years for persons over 25 years of age. See U.S. Book of Facts (Washington, D.C.: U.S. Government Printing Office, 1968), Table 158, p. 116.

[28] Oscar Handlin, The Uprooted (Boston: Little, Brown, & Co., 1952).

[29] The first time the writer's parents ever saw a college campus was when they drove their son down to begin his freshman year.

Poor health

With a few exceptions such as heart attacks, there seems to be overwhelming evidence that the lower class parent has more illness, both mental and physical, has less resistance to various diseases, has inferior medical and hospital care, and dies earlier than parents who hold a more favorable position in the class structure.[30]

Any person who has ever been a parent knows what it is like to try to take care of young children when the parent is not feeling well, and the situation is no different when trying to cope with an adolescent youngster under similar circumstances. In over a hundred parent discussion groups conducted by the writer in the past several years, ill health was one of the items most often cited by fathers and mothers for not being able to live up to their own standards of parental performance.[31]

In some types of illness, such as tuberculosis, the illness often results in the afflicted parent being out of the home for considerable periods of time. This might also be true of mental illness.

For financial reasons lower class parents often go to work when ill when other parents would stay home. For the same reasons they (and their children) often do not have medical attention when they should. These parents, because of their poor education and relatively low "social intelligence," are also preyed on by all sorts of medical quacks, such as patent medicine vendors, chiropractors, and witch doctors. The money they do have to spend on medical care is often poorly spent.

Unstable marriages

Goode has conclusively demonstrated that marital failure rates are highest among low-income groups.[32] This may not always be reflected in the official divorce rates because divorces cost money—and sometimes lower class parents were not married in the first place and don't need a divorce to dissolve their relationship. But if desertion and separation rates are added to divorce rates, there is no question that low-income groups have the highest rate of marital failure in our society.

Among the discussion groups referred to above, conducted by the writer in recent years, a good marriage was often cited by fathers and

---

[30] For an illustration of this, as found among American black families, see Thomas F. Pettigrew, *A Profile of the Negro American* (Princeton, N.J.: D. Van Nostrand Co., 1964).

[31] The other item mentioned most often was the one about rearing children with a husband (or wife) who does not agree with you about how to rear children.

[32] Goode, *op. cit.*, chap. 4.

mothers as the most important element making for successful parenthood. There is no reason why the relatively high rate of marital failure among the lower class would not create very grave problems for these parents, especially for the mothers who usually retain custody.[33] Some studies of such family units, primarily based on urban black samples, indicate that the father is such a shadowy figure that the family system really represents a matriarchal type. Since this typology will be considered in another chapter it need not be analyzed here.

The advantages of lower class position

Odd as it may seem there are probably some advantages in living at the lower class level. In a paper reported in the public press, Frank Riessman, of New York City, was quoted as citing the following advantages of lower class life: "The cooperativeness and mutual aid that mark the extended family; the avoidance of the strain accompanying competitiveness and individualism . . . the freedom from self-blame and parental overprotection . . . the enjoyment of music, games, sports, and cards.[34]

There are other features of lower class life in the affluent society that may offer some advantages for parents. These include: (1) less fear that they will lose status or position in the society. Being already on the bottom the only direction they can go is up. This is probably an oversimplification since there are various levels even in the lower class. A mother on Aid to Dependent Children (ADC), for example, may worry a great deal about whether her grant will be increased or not, or even whether it will be continued. Lower class people worry about what their landlord will do if the rent isn't paid—not all landlords operate with the same generosity or harshness. These people worry about their health or illness, but probably in different ways from those of the middle or upper class. And lower class parents worry about their children; what the school authorities will do, what the juvenile court will do, and so forth. They also worry about their heterosexual love life as the rest of us do. Judging from the Hollingshead and Redlich study of mental illness there seems reason not to push too far the notion that people on the bottom don't worry about what will happen to them.[35]

---

[33] For an extensive consideration of marital failure and parental problems at low-income levels, see Salvador Minuchin et al., *Families of the Slums* (New York: Basic Books, 1967).

On the contemporary black family in America see Andrew Billingsley, *Black Families in White America* (Englewood Cliffs, N. J.: Prentice-Hall, Inc., 1968).

[34] *Milwaukee Journal*, June 30, 1965. Riessman is a well-known student of low-income families.

[35] Hollingshead and Redlich, *op. cit.*

(2) Lower class parents are probably not haunted by the achievements of their ancestors in the way that middle-class and upper class parents are. They don't have the ghost of their distinguished parents and grandparents hovering over them as upper class people often do. And they don't have to worry about their children doing as well in school as the father or mother did in the way that some middle-class people do—college professors, for example.

(3) Lower class people don't have to go to all of those meetings: PTA and all the rest,[36] nor do they have to accept responsible positions in such organizations and worry about program speakers, fund drives, and so on. Some lower class parents may have more time with which to rear their children than anybody else, but they lack the preparation, the tools, and the values to use the time to advantage.

All in all the writer is somewhat skeptical about the advantages of life at the lower class level but this may reflect social class bias to some extent. It certainly seems to be true, however, as was indicated earlier in this chapter, that the systematic studies of lower class people in our society do not report any glamorous or romantic pattern of life at the bottom of the heap. But perhaps the researchers themselves are biased since they reflect middle-class and upper class values.[37]

The implications of these problems
for lower class parents

We are of the opinion that the above problems create insuperable obstacles for most lower class parents as they attempt to rear their large families. And the above list of handicaps is by no means exhaustive. If one accepts this conclusion, then it follows that some other social institution has to intervene if lower class children are to receive even the minimum preparation for life in modern America. Since the 1930's the main intervention system to help these families has been the county or city public welfare department—specifically, the Aid to Dependent Children (ADC) program which is supported by local, state, and federal funds.[38] There is every reason to believe that this approach has been inadequate for the enormous task it has had to face.[39] The ADC program

[36] In the 1968 jukebox hit, "Harper Valley PTA," there is expressed a considerable amount of hostility toward the middle class by the mother featured in the song.

[37] It is interesting to note that in his study of blue-collar workers Gans, *op. cit.*, takes the position that the "professional upper-middle class subculture is more desirable than all the rest." See chap. 12, "Evaluation of Class Subcultures," p. 264.

[38] In recent years the name of this program has been changed to Aid to Families with Dependent Children (AFDC).

[39] For a general evaluation of welfare programs and their ability to help lower class families, see Alvin L. Schorr, *op. cit.*; also S. M. Miller and Frank Riessman, *Social Class and Social Policy* (New York: Basic Books, 1969).

has used largely a case work or person to person counseling approach supplemented by monthly financial aid. As a rule staff problems have been severe with only a small percentage of the caseworkers having full professional training in social work. Staff turnover has been high in most areas of the country.[40]

In addition to staff problems only a few states have been willing or able to maintain financial support of these families at even minimal levels.[41]

The writer happens to believe that even at its best the case work approach used in ADC would not solve the problems of these families. It is our belief that the social world around these families has to be drastically changed, and case work is not known for changing social systems.

The federal government in the 1960's has been dedicated to the proposition that the public schools serving lower class families can be used as an effective instrument of social change if outside funds are made available, mostly from federal sources. This approach seems promising but it is too early to measure the results.

Other new attacks on the problems of lower class families include the youth job corps, vocational training programs for unemployed fathers and mothers, better planned parenthood services, and so forth.[42]

It is a truism in social planning that when a social institution cannot achieve its functions there are two possible means of intervention: (1) try to improve the social institution not functioning properly by direct intervention on that segment of the social system. This has been tried for about 30 years in the ADC program with results that are dubious at best. (2) Strengthen other social institutions which affect the people about which we are concerned. In this approach the family itself is not the direct target of the intervention. Schools, cities, churches, neighborhoods, and other features of the larger community are improved or reorganized with the hope that families will ultimately be enabled to function more effectively.

Essentially, this approach is aimed at societal reorganization rather than personality reorganization—although it is hoped that the persons affected by the social reorganization will change as individuals as their

---

[40] See Alfred Kadushin, *Child Welfare Services* (New York: The Macmillan Co., 1967), various chaps.

[41] *Ibid.*

[42] Various approaches to solving the problems of low-income families are considered in Arthur Pearl and Frank Riessman, *New Careers for the Poor* (New York: The Free Press, 1965), chap. 2.

For a critique of the war on poverty see Daniel P. Moynihan, *Maximum Feasible Misunderstanding* (New York: The Free Press, 1969).

social world is improved. Undoubtedly some of them will not be able to respond to improved living conditions and for them some sort of intensive case work would probably be required.

One might summarize this discussion by saying that there are really only three basic intervention systems available to help families in our society: (1) change the family; (2) help the family maneuver better in the social world around them; (3) change the social world itself. It would appear, at least to the writer, that the problems of lower class parents are so severe that only the third approach can have much impact.[43]

Blue-collar parents

Some writers, such as Gans, refer to this group as "the working class," but it seems to the writer that this term is rather unfortunate in that it implies that people in the other social classes don't work. For this reason we prefer the term "blue-collar."[44]

During and after World War II the skilled blue-collar workers in the United States made such dramatic improvement in their net earnings that many of them earn considerably more money than a great many white-collar workers. In the writer's community, for example, qualified plumbers average $10,000 to $12,000 a year whereas school teachers average about $7,500.

As a rule the blue-collar worker's job requires him to perform some manual skill. Thus he is usually not required to have elaborate formal education—a high school diploma would suffice today but only a few years ago even this was not required in most apprentice programs.

Physical health is crucial to the blue-collar worker: you can not lay bricks with a serious heart condition.

One great advantage blue-collar workers have over many white-collar employees is their protection by powerful trade unions. Seniority rights protect them against persons below them in the hierarchy; fringe benefits pay for their medical expenses; and dismissal must be for very specific violations of work conditions.

There is almost unbelievable social distance between blue-collar workers in modern America. A carpenter earning $12,000 a year can afford to live quite differently from a school custodian earning $5,000 a year. The term "blue-collar aristocracy" is sometimes used to designate

---

[43] This was the basic conclusion of Minuchin et al., *op cit.*

[44] A useful source book on blue-collar Americans is *Blue-Collar World* edited by Arthur B. Shostak and William Gomberg (Englewood Cliffs, N. J.: Prentice-Hall, Inc., 1964); see also Mirra Komarovsky, *Blue-Collar Marriage* (New York: Random House, 1964); most of the Gans book cited earlier deals with blue-collar workers and their families.

the elite of the blue-collar world: electricians, plumbers, and other highly skilled operators.

Let us look at some of the special problems of blue-collar parents.

Special problems of blue-collar parents

It was indicated earlier that there is considerable range of income, status, and security in the blue-collar world in contemporary America. The following discussion will have to be read with this in mind.

Some of the special problems of blue-collar parents are the following.

1. *The declining proportion of this segment of the population.* America is becoming increasingly a white-collar world. This is forcing the sons and daughters of these parents to move into white-collar occupations, which are increasing. Unions such as the steel workers' have actually lost membership since World War II as the steel mills have been automated. The same situation prevails among printers, dock workers, and many other blue-collar work groups.[45] This means that the father may not be able to get his son into his union or into an apprenticeship; it also means that the blue-collar fathers and mothers are not as able to guide their children as the children move into a white-collar world. Such parents don't know as much about colleges, and they often don't push their children as hard in elementary or secondary school. It is simply harder for blue-collar parents to launch their children into the white-collar world than it was to help them get into a trade at the blue-collar level. Basically, such parents face the same problems farm parents face: most farm children will not be able to find a niche in agriculture, yet both they and their parents have grown up in a rural world.

2. *The percentage of mothers employed outside of the home tends to be somewhat higher at the blue-collar level.* Nye and Hoffman point out that this differential is not as pronounced as it was before World War II, but the fact remains that blue-collar mothers work outside of the home considerably more often than do mothers at some of the middle-class levels.[46] There is not much difference at the lower middle-class level.

Blue-collar mothers have some compensating factors to offset their outside employment, however: they do not belong to as many voluntary

[45] For a brief summary of these trends, see George Meany, *Labor Looks at Capitalism* (Washington, D.C.: AFL–CIO Publication No. 139, 1966).

In 1956 the number of white-collar jobs exceeded blue-collar jobs for the first time in the United States. See Michael Harrington, "The Politics of Poverty," in *Poverty: Views from the Left,* edited by Jeremy Larner and Irving Howe (New York: William Morrow & Co., 1968), p. 18.

[46] These data are reviewed in F. Ivan Nye and Lois Wladis Hoffman, *The Employed Mother in America* (Chicago: Rand McNally & Co., 1963), pp. 7–16.

organizations as do middle-class women and when they do belong they don't carry as much responsibility.

3. *Blue-collar parents have some social distance problems with their children.* All American parents have this problem to some extent because of rapid change and the vast amount of social mobility in the United States. But blue-collar parents suffer more from this situation due to the fact that their children are being forced to move into the white-collar world. This is quite different from the lower class where vertical social mobility is relatively rare.

4. *Blue-collar parents are not portrayed by the mass media.* The self-image of these parents and that of their children is affected negatively to some extent by the fact that their world does not exist for the television program directors or for most advertising executives. There has never, to this writer's knowledge, been a nationwide television series based on any honest portrayal of the blue-collar worker's world. The soap operas, even in the days of radio, have always zeroed in on the upper middle-class and upper class worlds. It is true that advertisers in recent years have featured the blue-collar aristocracy to some extent,[47] but the rest of television and radio are strictly white-collar worlds. This is also true of the mass magazines.

It may well be that carpenters and plumbers don't give a damn whether Madison Avenue knows they exist or not, but black parents have complained that the self-image of themselves and their children has been negatively affected by their portrayal in movies and on television, and this may well be true also of the blue-colar parent and his children. As their proportion of the U. S. population shrinks they become more and more a member of a minority group—as farm parents have become—and in the process they face some of the problems of all minority group parents.

The lower middle-class parent

The lower middle class is the fastest growing social class in America; the people who work largely to distribute goods and perform services. The woman who checks out your groceries at the supermarket, the man who comes to repair your television set, the cosmetics saleslady who brings the latest shade of lipstick right to your door—these are all representative of the lower middle class. They are usually white-collar people with a high school education.

Some of these persons really represent a new type of occupation. The

[47] We have reference to the handsome range hands featured in the "Marlboro Country" commercials, plus other blue-collar elites seen once in a while in television spots, such as truck drivers.

television repairman, for example, comes out to fix your set, but he may also have a chance to sell you a new one, or at least get you to come down to the shop to see the new ones. This man has some mechanical training, yet he is not a mechanic in the old sense: he has to be able to handle people as well as things.[48]

These lower middle-class people often don't have unions to bargain for them or protect them, hence they are frequently subject to low wages, long hours, and job insecurity. To the extent that they can be unionized they represent one of the largest labor pools available to the mass trade unions.

Some observers of modern America, such as Max Lerner, regard the lower middle class to be one of the least enviable positions in the contemporary social class system.[49] These people lack the pride of the old blue-collar aristocracy; they make less money; they have less skill to sell; and they lack job security. At the same time they tend to identify with the more highly educated and prosperous white-collar groups above them.

Lower middle-class parents are apt to face some very real problems. The wife-mother often works full time in an attempt to achieve the standard of consumption the family aspires to.[50] The marital failure rate at this socioeconomic level is relatively high.[51] These fathers and mothers tend to be ambitious for their children, pushing them toward college even though the parents themselves are not usually college graduates. If the children succeed in climbing up the social class ladder the family ties often suffer from vertical social class mobility.[52] The ability of the parents to guide their mobile children is limited by the fact that the parents have never lived in the social world the children are moving into. As socialization for the child's new position proceeds, some of the ideas and values inculcated by the parents have to be discarded. This sometimes hurts the parents or the child or both. And in the process, sibling relationships are often weakened also.

---

[48] In one of the earliest studies of social class in America, the Lynds pointed out that as a rule the blue-collar worker handles *things*, whereas the white-collar employee handles *people*. See Robert S. Lynd and Helen Lynd, *Middletown* (New York: Harcourt, Brace & Co., 1929).

[49] Lerner, *op. cit.*, pp. 488–495.

[50] There is also a tendency for the father at this class level to moonlight (hold a second job) to achieve a decent standard of living.

[51] See Goode, *op. cit.*, chaps. 4 and 5.

[52] See E. E. LeMasters, "Social Class Mobility and Family Integration," *Marriage and Family Living*, 16 (1954), pp. 226–232. For a different version of this matter see Eugene Litwak, "Extended Kin Relations in an Industrial Society," in Ethel Shanas and Gordon F. Streib (eds.), *Social Structure and the Family* (Englewood Cliffs, N.J.: Prentice-Hall, Inc., 1965), pp. 290–323.

The lower middle class reflects its insecure social position in many ways: high rates of alcoholism, above average rates of marital failure, relatively high rates of mental illness.[53] They may use retail credit excessively and be chronically in debt.[54]

It is not clear, at least to the writer, as to how much juvenile delinquency develops in the lower middle class but one would certainly expect a wide range of adjustment problems in the children from these parents.

One seldom, if ever, sees this group portrayed in the mass media, either in mass magazines, radio, television, or advertising. On the contrary the middle-class families seen in the mass media are almost always upper middle class, business owners or professional people. Thus the lower middle-class parents and their children are constantly exposed to a model of living which is slightly similar to their way of life, yet essentially beyond their reach. It would seem that there must be considerable stress and frustration in such a situation.

Since this is the most rapidly growing group of parents in the United States it deserves more attention than it has yet received from students of family life.[55]

The middle middle-class parent

In the Warner social class system there is no middle middle class, yet in some communities such a category is essential to identify certain groups in the class system. A good example is a college town or university community—the professors do not fall into either the lower middle class or the upper middle class. Except for the president, a few deans, or some very famous faculty members, the professors don't make enough money to belong to the upper middle class. They can't afford to live in upper middle-class neighborhoods, belong to country clubs, and so on. In one college town of 30,000 known to the writer, only one professor out of eighty lived in the major upper middle-class suburb.[56] It is true,

---

[53] The social class variations in mental illness rates are reviewed in August B. Hollingshead and Frederick C. Redlich, op. cit. See also Roman and Trice, op. cit.

[54] This pattern is considered in E. E. LeMasters, Modern Courtship and Marriage (New York: The Macmillan Co., 1957), chap. 20.

[55] There is some analysis of the lower middle-class life in Herbert J. Gans, The Levittowners (New York: Random House, 1967). See especially chap. 10, "Family and Individual Adaptation."

[56] The observations in the following pages are based on seven years of participant-observation in a private liberal arts college in the Middle-West located in an industrial community of about 30,000. The period covered is the 1950's.

For the details of the Warner stratification system see W. Lloyd Warner and Paul S. Lunt, The Social Life of a Modern Community (New Haven: Yale University Press, 1941).

however, that private means (not faculty salary) made it possible for a few other professors in this community to live in upper middle-class style but most of these preferred to live out in the country or in remodeled older homes close to the campus.

Only one faculty member in this college town belonged to the country club, and this person was a member of the athletic coaching staff. There undoubtedly were other faculty members whose private means would have permitted them to pay the country club dues but whose values did not run in that direction.

If professors don't belong to the upper middle class, they certainly don't fit into the lower middle class. For one thing they have too much formal education to be comfortable in the lower middle class. They also have a different set of values: they spend less money on cars, more on travel, more on education for their children, less on clothes, and so on.

It is our impression that they use consumer credit much less than does the lower middle class; their wives are employed less often; and their marriages are more stable.

If one accepts the proposition that there is a middle middle class in some communities, what are the problems and advantages of parents in this socioeconomic position? It is the writer's belief that fathers and mothers in this group do rather well with their children. Of the 80 faculty members in the college community being discussed here, 74 were married and had 210 children at the time the writer was able to observe the group. Of these children only one was overtly identified as a juvenile delinquent (had been placed on probation for a juvenile offense). Several had apparently received some attention from a child psychiatrist but the exact number was not available. Two boys had been placed in expensive boarding schools by affluent faculty members who felt that their children would be safer and better educated if they did not attend the local public high school.

Only two faculty divorces occurred in the six years the writer was on this particular campus. Only three wives held full-time jobs outside of the home but several others had some part-time employment.

These couples tend to hold relatively nonmaterialistic values, which helps them avoid the consumer debt pattern so common at the lower middle-class level. This was apparent in the faculty of this particular college. If they owed a large sum of money other than that of their house mortgage it was apt to be related to foreign travel for the entire family. Late model or expensive cars were conspicuous by their absence. Television sets were either not visible in the homes or of very modest size. FM radios and good record playing systems were more numerous.

Historically, these parents have had rather modest birthrates, although this has tended to change since World War II. But until recently they had small families and this, combined with relatively secure income, gave these parents a good chance to spend considerable time with each child, to individualize the child, and to work on whatever problems developed. We were often impressed in informal discussion with these fathers and mothers at their capacity to see each child as a unique human being.

The extensive formal education of these parents (mothers as well as fathers) gives them a real advantage in helping their children succeed in the school system. These parents belong to PTA, go to meetings religiously, often hold office in such an organization, and in general work closely with teachers and school administrators in developing their child's intellectual capacity. Children who lack their parents' academic aptitude are often enabled to cope with the school system by the efforts of the parents, and at the college level schools are found that seem appropriate for such a child. This is the sort of guidance which parents at lower socioeconomic levels are unable to give their children.

Of the faculty children of college age during the seven-year period the writer was on this campus, only one youngster did not go on to college with reasonable success—and this one deviant was apprenticed to an artist. This is a remarkable academic record when it is remembered that children in this group, as in any other group, vary considerably in native intellectual capacity.

The stable marriages in this group give the parents a great advantage in rearing children, as does the relatively short and flexible working day of the father. The long summer vacations, the relatively low pressure nature of the job—all these factors would seem to be aids in helping these parents in rearing their children.

On the negative side one might list the following: (1) These parents are a sort of minority group in American society. They may not own a television set, for example, or a decent car. Their children are often not given as much spending money as other children. Political and religious beliefs may be unconventional. In other words, the values of these parents are often in some conflict with those of the larger society. Insofar as these parents can inculcate their somewhat deviant values into their children family peace is maintained. But once a child is fully socialized into the value system of the community some friction is apt to occur.

(2) These parents hold rather high educational achievement levels for their children which means that sometimes the parents are at odds with ordinary teachers and ordinary school systems. In fact they often move because of what they consider to be serious school deficiencies. Their children may be regarded as eggheads by their fellow students, and the parents may be so labeled themselves. To the extent that the children resemble their parents—that is, if the whole family is egghead—no problem exists. But this is not always the case.

(3) The children are not always bright enough to measure up to their

parents' scholastic expectations, which put the child, the school, and the parents in a difficult spot.

(4) It is quite common for college or university professors' children to associate with children of the upper middle class—physicians, dentists, business owners and business executives—whose parents have substantially higher incomes. This affinity results from the fact that all of these youngsters are headed for college educations and perhaps graduate school as well. The difference in incomes poses some problems but they do not seem to be severe.

All in all it is the writer's belief that middle middle-class parents are in a relatively favorable position in our society for performing their parental role and it is our impression that they do a better than average job as fathers and mothers.[57]

The upper middle-class parent

The following analysis is based on 560 case studies of upper middle-class families conducted while the writer was teaching at a private liberal arts college which catered largely to an upper middle-class clientele.[58]

By upper middle class the writer refers to the families of physicians, dentists, successful attorneys, business executives, the owners of small but profitable businesses, and a few clergymen. These people are almost invariably college graduates, very often with advanced degrees. They are frequently self-employed, and in a considerable proportion of the sample studied by the writer the family had been in the upper middle class for two or three generations.

It can be argued with some logic that this is the most comfortable position in the American social class system.[59] These people are economically secure, either owning their own business or having skills which are readily marketable. Their income in the 1950's, when the writer's study was made, ranged from $15,000 to $40,000 depending on the size of the community. They live in comfortable homes in nice neighborhoods or good suburbs. They have enough money to do most of the things they want to do. They educate their children, help them get established in the competitive society, and look forward to their role as grandparents. Their marriages are relatively stable; less than 5 percent of the sample studied by the writer had experienced divorce.

---

[57] The writer is, of course, open to the charge of social class bias or ethnocentrism on this point. Based on his sample, however, the statement seems justified.

[58] Elaborate analyses of student families were required as part of a senior course in the family. The detailed outline for this paper is reproduced in E. E. LeMasters, *Modern Courtship and Marriage* (New York: The Macmillan Co., 1957), pp. 601–605.

[59] Gans does argue this in *The Urban Villagers*, p. 264.

For a more pessimistic view of the upper middle class see Peggy Haroff and John F. Cuber, *The Significant Americans* (New York: Appleton-Century, 1965).

Perhaps the nicest feature of the upper middle-class position is the fact that they have all the money and social status they need, yet they are not conspicuous enough in the community to be under great pressure. As a rule their children are comfortable and relaxed. Some faculty members at this particular college would have used the word *smug* to describe the general attitude of these students and their parents.

Some alcoholism and mental illness appeared in the sample but the vast majority of the families appeared to be basically sound and well organized. Over 90 percent of the students in the study felt that their parents were happily married and that they had done a good job as parents.

Contrary to what some observers have reported, the writer found no striving pattern among these college students from the upper middle class: they were quite content to live as their parents did. This was actually a problem from the faculty point of view in that the students were not given to prolonged probing of life and its meaning. What they had seen in their own homes seemed good to them and most of them merely wished to continue living as they always had.[60]

The parents in these families seemed to operate quite democratically, with the father and mother sharing basic decisions and the children participating in less crucial choices. Since most of the marriages were stable the parents were able to help each other.

Many (or most) of these families were characterized by social class continuity, which meant that to a large extent the social world of the child was quite similar to that of the parent. Over 30 percent, for example, of these families had an alumnus from this particular college, sometimes a grandparent but still an alumnus. Since almost all of the parents were college graduates themselves it was possible for them to give their youngster considerable guidance in the public school system as well as in the college or university system. In fact one could identify students who obviously would not have been admitted to this particular college if their parents had not worked hard through elementary and secondary school to help them prepare and qualify for college.

It was obvious that medical and dental care had been excellent in these families, often of a type that helped to avoid adjustment problems for the student—surgery, for example, which had corrected birth defects, or elaborate orthodontic treatment to make the teeth more attractive.

There were certain problems which these parents faced, however. These might be summarized as follows:

1. The parents did not have enough wealth, as the upper class parent often has, to guarantee the child's continued social status. This meant, really, that each child had to achieve again the status of the parents.

---

[60] This picture has changed somewhat in the 1960's as the hippy revolt spread into the Midwest.

In the case of girls this was not too difficult. By living in the right suburb and the right high school district, and by sending the daughter to the right college, it was almost assured that the daughter would make a marital choice that would place her in the upper middle class if not higher. It seemed obvious that most of these girls, regardless of their intellectual ability (which was higher than that of the boys in this particular college) had come to college to get a good husband.

The problem was somewhat more complicated in the case of sons. Since the families usually owned no large businesses they could not guarantee a good position for their son regardless of his native ability. In the case of physicians, for example, the father could not pass the premed courses for his son or guarantee him admission to a medical school. All of these parents did have some social, professional, or business contacts that could be useful to a young man but this was not always enough. Several dramatic cases involved the sons of physicians who flunked out of the premed program by the end of the sophomore year.[61]

2. Another problem was that of occupational pressure on the fathers. One male student, whose father was an obstetrician, put it this way: "My father is a wonderful man, but when I was a small boy he was always at the office or the hospital—we seldom saw him. Mother reared us practically alone. But now that I am older I go hunting with my father and even help him at the office sometimes. Now we are quite close."

A woman student whose father managed a factory reported that his job was so demanding that she had scarcely known him as a child. For all practical purposes she had only one parent during her childhood: her mother.

3. There were rather basic value conflicts between some of these upper middle-class college students and their parents. The parents were more apt to be materialistic in their values, conservative in their politics, and in general less "bohemian" than their sons and daughters. Some of this difference was simply a reflection of age and responsibility, but some of it was more basic than that. Curiously enough, this difference was a reflection to some extent of the good high schools and colleges these parents had been able to send their children to: the sons and daughters had better educations and had become more intellectual and more open-minded than their parents. This is, of course, the age-old story of the poor immigrant in America who struggles to send his children to school and then finds that he no longer understands them or perhaps even approves of them.

---

[61] This sometimes produced rather tragic situations. In one case, the father had always hoped that his only son would someday join him in his medical practice, but by the end of the freshman year it was clear that the boy would never qualify for medical school and his career plans had to be changed. The father was very disappointed.

It was the writer's impression that this value conflict between parents and their college children was most apparent when the family was first-generation upper middle class; in other words, they had only held this social position since World War II. These fathers and mothers were less apt to be college graduates and were still fresh from the hard climb up the ladder. Being new to their social position they were not too secure and were afraid that their children might slip back into the middle middle or lower middle class. They were not willing for their children to be different from themselves for fear this would jeopardize their sons' and daughters' chances of success.

But in the families that had been doctors and dentists and lawyers for two or three generations—where there was social class continuity—one was much less likely to find value conflicts between parent and child. These parents were themselves relatively well educated; they might be conservative politically but not reactionary; they appreciated books, good music, and intelligent discussion of social problems; they were likely to be liberal on racial issues (while living in a segregated suburb, of course); they liked to drink, as did their children. It seemed to the writer that these parents had had their social position long enough to realize that money is not everything and that their sons and daughters could legitimately consider other ways of spending their lives if they wanted to. A daughter could aspire to be an actress, for example, if she showed any talent, and a son might decide to enter the ministry rather than law or medicine or a business career.

4. There is a certain *smugness* about the upper middle-class way of life that produced problems for some of these parents and their children: the parents were so satisfied with their patterns of living that they could not understand why some of their children wanted to be different. This discrepancy was quite apparent to many of the faculty in this old private liberal arts college: the parents had put up the money to pay for a good education for their children but when they found that such an education might question all that the parents put their faith in they were somewhat appalled—perhaps dismayed would be a better word.

Actually many of these parents would have been happier if they had sent their children to a college that was less rigorous in its liberal arts approach to life. But parents from this social class value good schools and good colleges highly (some of these students had come from the best high schools in America) and it would have been difficult, if not impossible, for them to have deliberately sent a child to a second-rate college. This would have been tantamount to sending him to a second-rate physician.

Many of these sons and daughters seemed to lack any real ambition or drive. You might have described them as "overadjusted"—life had always been good to them and they saw no reason why it wouldn't always be that way. As the baseball managers like to say, "these kids are not *hungry.*"

Lower upper class parents

In the Warner social class system the upper class is divided into two groups, the lower upper and the upper upper. In the original study of Yankee City (Newburyport, Massachusetts),[62] the upper class was represented by the old, original settlers who had made their money a long time ago—much of it in either the Revolutionary War or the Civil War. These people have had their wealth for several generations and know what to do with it. They live in lovely old mansions up on the hill in Yankee City, in the most fashionable area of the city where the last lots were sold before the lower upper class made their money. The houses of the upper upper class are furnished with valuable antiques handed down from parent to child, while the lower upper class has to buy its antiques from the dealers in Boston. The upper upper class runs all the old, high status social clubs, send their sons to Harvard, and their children intermarry.

The lower upper class made its money in World War I or World War II. They have not had their money long enough, in most cases, to consolidate their social position; they may not yet live on the right street or belong to the right clubs. Furthermore, their values have not distilled to pure upper class: they may drive the wrong cars, send their children to the wrong colleges, or decorate their houses in the wrong style. They often belong to the wrong church and their ancestors are buried in the wrong cemeteries.

There were a few lower upper class families in the college students studied by the writer in the research referred to earlier. These parents have many advantages, of course: they can afford good medical and psychiatric care, good neighborhoods, good schools, good colleges, foreign travel, and plenty of domestic help. Their children usually receive preferential treatment in the community if they get into trouble—both the schools and law enforcement agencies are sensitive to pressure from these families.[63] The marriages are relatively stable but not necessarily good. Divorce is an expensive proposition for the fathers in this income bracket.

These lower upper class parents are by no means without their troubles, however. Their children occupy a marginal status in the social system of the community: they are too wealthy to fit into the upper

---

[62] See Warner and Lunt, *op. cit.*

[63] For data on this see August B. Hollingshead, *Elmtown's Youth* (New York: John Wiley & Sons, 1949).

middle class, yet they are not really accepted by the children of the upper upper class.

These newly rich parents are much more prone to spoil their children —"I don't want them to go through what I went through"—than is the upper upper class parent. These latter have seen what harm too much money can do.

The value systems are often confused in these lower upper class families, with money and materialism predominant. People are judged by how much money they have and things are judged by how much they cost. The upper upper class parents are likely to be above this sort of thinking, having had their money long enough to know its limitations.

Another problem in these lower upper class families is the tendency for the children to feel superior to their parents: they go to the best prep schools, the best colleges, the best resorts, and so forth. By degrees they assimilate the values and the way of life of the upper upper class, thus creating a social gulf between themselves and their fathers and mothers. This process is so common that it has become a major theme in American novels.[64] Another problem in these families is the fact that the sons often do not have anything like the ability of their fathers, the self-made men who fought their way to the top. Fortunately, there is usually enough money to go around, and any son who is at all reasonable can be fitted into one of the family enterprises someplace. But some of the sons (and daughters) are not reasonable and reject the values and way of life of their parents completely. These children usually leave the home community and become artists, college professors, and so on.[65]

The writer has had several long interviews with male college students whose fathers got rich during World War II. These sons felt themselves to be in difficult positions. They usually had no real interest in the family business, yet their fathers assumed the sons would follow in the fathers' footsteps once they had gotten a good education—something the father never had, of course. The sons had to go to a good college, naturally, which is often the beginning of trouble: the liberal arts professors pound away at materialism, capitalism, the Republicans, until the son decides he wants no part of the business world He then decides on medicine, law, literature, philosophy, social science, art, or something of that sort.[66]

Down underneath, of course, there is the ever-present fear that he

---

64 For an example see the novel by Herbert Gold, *Fathers* (New York: Random House, 1966).

65 A student known to the writer rejected a chance to become a full partner in his father's prosperous fur business and became a high school music teacher.

66 The writer interviewed many of these students while serving as a Dean of Students in New York in a state college. The fathers were often self-made men in the garment or fur industry of New York City who wanted their sons to go to a good college before entering the family business. Most of these families were Jewish.

couldn't possibly compete with his father. This, actually, is not necessary, since the family business is now well established, but the son
usually doesn't realize this.

Often these sons are like their mothers rather than their fathers: they
are gentle rather than aggressive, moral rather than ruthless, feminine
instead of masculine.

All in all it is the writer's impression that lower upper class parents
have more child rearing problems than upper middle class parents have.

The upper upper class parent

We have now come to the elite group in the Warner social class
system—those families at the very top. In essence these are the people
who settled in the region first and have had their money the longest.[67]

Several characteristics of the upper upper class parent may be identified.

1. These people are not confused about their values. They take
money and luxuries for granted, of course, but they don't talk about
such things. Why talk about something you have had as long as you can
remember? These families don't have to flaunt their wealth to impress
anybody; everybody *knows* they have the money.

These families have had money long enough not to be too impressed by
it, which means that they place high value on things and qualities other
than money, such as brains, creative ability, beauty, breeding, loyalty,
and stability. Their children seem more likely to grow up with a sound
set of values than are the children of the newly rich.

2. The children in these families do not move into a social world
much different from that of their parents. If the son goes to Harvard,
for example, the chances are that his father went there too (and perhaps
his grandfather as well). If a daughter matriculates at Vassar, it is not
unlikely that other women in the family would have preceded her. To
use a sociological concept, these families are characterized by *social
class continuity*. Not too many American families can make this claim.
This intergeneration stability of social position should give upper upper
class parents a real advantage in rearing their sons and daughters.

3. Another pattern that can be observed in upper upper class parents
is their willingness to permit sons to enter fields other than business. The
various enterprises of these families are usually so well established that
it really doesn't matter very much whether the sons choose to join one

---

[67] For a summary of these characteristics, see Cavan, *op. cit.*, chap. 5.

An interesting analysis of several generations of an upper upper class family may be
found in John D. Davis, *The Bouviers* (New York: Farrar, Straus & Giroux, 1969). This
is the family of the widow of John F. Kennedy.

of the family's firms or not. After all, managers can always be hired to keep the store open, as the saying goes.

The Rockefeller family illustrates this pattern quite well. The grandfather devoted his life to financial affairs and established the family fortune.[68] His son, John D., Jr., went into the business for a few years and then decided he wanted to devote his life to other things—mostly to philantropy.[69] By the time the grandsons came along they were free to do anything decent that interested them, such as politics, farming, or banking. At this third generation level there is no necessity to revolt against business as a way of life—you can do as you please.

There are, of course, some problems which confront upper upper class parents. As Cleveland Amory sees them in his study of wealthy families in the United States these might be summarized as follows:[70]

a) The sons are often besieged by beautiful and ambitious girls who only wish to marry them for social and economic purposes. Divorces come high at this level as the third generation Rockefellers have discovered.

b) It is difficult to motivate children who already have everything that money can buy. In an effort to overcome this these parents often send their sons to Spartan boarding schools which feature extremely simple living arrangements and enforce strict discipline.[71] The English upper class has always done this and the pattern seems to have carried over to the United States. Franklin D. Roosevelt's boyhood letters from his boarding school reflect this way of life.[72] John D. Rockefeller, Jr.'s letters from college to his father tell how and on what he spent his modest weekly allowance.[73] These upper upper class parents seem to try hard not to spoil their children but their social position makes this quite difficult.

---

[68] On the founder of the fortune, see Jules Abels, *The Rockefeller Billions* (New York: The Macmillan Co., 1965).

[69] See Raymond B. Fosdick, *John D. Rockefeller, Jr.* (New York: Harper & Brothers, 1956).

[70] Portraits of upper class families in our society are found in Cleveland Amory: *The Proper Bostonians* (New York: E. P. Dutton, 1947); and by the same author, *Who Killed Society?* (New York: Harper & Brothers, 1960).

[71] See, for example, the types of boarding schools they are sending the future King of England to in Geoffrey Wakeford's study, *The Heir Apparent* (New York: A. S. Barnes & Co., 1967).

[72] On Franklin D. Roosevelt's early years see John Gunther, *Roosevelt in Perspective* (New York: Harper & Brothers, 1950). For the youthful letters, see Elliott Roosevelt, *FDR: His Personal Letters* (New York: Duell, 1947). An interesting discussion of how upper class parents educate their children may be found in George G. Kirstein, *The Rich: Are They Different?* (Boston: Houghton Mifflin Co., 1968). See especially chap. 5, "The Education of the Rich," pp. 77–93.

[73] Fosdick, *op. cit.*

c) These parents often do not find it possible to spend much time with their children because of the demands of their social position. This is especially true of the fathers but also common among the mothers. Mrs. Franklin D. Roosevelt has been quoted as saying that this was one of the problems she and the late President had to contend with in rearing their children.[74] The Duke of Windsor reports that when he was being reared to succeed to the English crown that he was only permitted to see his father and mother an hour a day—late in the afternoon before the King and Queen departed for their evening events.[75] The rest of the time the Prince of Wales spent with tutor, governesses, nurses, and maids.

It is clear that upper upper class people in all societies rely heavily on employees to rear their children, including all sorts of boarding schools and camps.[76] The old Southern black mammy of the cotton aristocracy was a good example of this sort of substitute parent.

d) The children of these elite families are always in public view, especially when they get into trouble. Even minor scrapes are apt to produce newspaper headlines.[77] The resulting publicity is not always good for these sons and daughters. The late President and Mrs. Kennedy became concerned about the vast interest displayed by the mass media in their young daughter Caroline.[78] They reached the point where they found it necessary to shelter their daughter from the public spotlight.

Summary and conclusion

In this chapter parental roles have been examined in terms of social class position. It is recognized that some Americans are hostile toward the social class concept but sociologists seem to find it useful.

It is also recognized that social class patterns vary widely in different regions and in different communities in the United States, but this is not to say that such patterns do not exist or that they can be ignored. It only means that the concept of social class has to be used with some intelligence and some discrimination.

---

[74] Eleanor Roosevelt, *This Is My Story* (New York: Harper & Brothers, 1937).

[75] See Edward VIII, *A King's Story* (New York: G. P. Putnam's Sons, 1951).

[76] There are pathetic letters from Winston Churchill to his upper upper class parents begging to be allowed to spend Christmas at home instead of having to travel to France with his tutor. See Randolph S. Churchill, *Winston S. Churchill: Youth 1874–1900* (Boston: Houghton Mifflin Co., 1966).

[77] One of the writer's students was the daughter of the state governor; her father was also prominent in many other ways in the state. She related how a minor incident involving an automobile accident was played up by newspapers who opposed her father's political program.

[78] This material is found in Theodore C. Sorenson, *Kennedy* (New York: Harper & Row, 1965), p. 381.

Insofar as social class position involves a subculture or way of life it would seem to affect parental performance in a variety of ways. Some of these have been described in this chapter. The writer is of the opinion that the social class concept merits more attention than it has received from the students of American parents.[79]

---

[79] The late James Bossard of the University of Pennsylvania was an exception in this respect. See *The Sociology of Child Development* (New York: Harper & Brothers, 1948).

chapter
six

Minority group
parents

G OD knows how I ever raised them kids in that hell-hole," one black mother said to us, "but somehow I got 'em raised and none of them turned out too bad."[1]

This woman had migrated to the Middle West after her husband had died in Mississippi. Friends and relatives helped her finance the move (no furniture—just herself and her three children and a few personal possessions).

She was fortunate in that she hit the North during World War II when labor was scarce and she obtained immediate employment as cook and baby-sitter for a wealthy white family. This family became fond of her and through them the two sons obtained employment when they completed high school. A daughter is now married to a career man in the armed forces. Thus, in one generation, this family moved up from the rural South to the urban North and achieved solid blue-collar status.

The hell-hole referred to by the mother was the urban ghetto in which she was forced to rear her children. While her actual living quarters were not too bad, by her account, the neighborhood itself was dilapidated and dangerous. She felt that in some ways it was harder to rear children in the urban North than in the rural South, and yet she did not regret making the move.

To a certain extent this mother's story is typical of all minority group parents: they move because conditions were not good where they were before, and then they find that the situation in the new community is far

---

[1] Statement by a woman who migrated from rural Mississippi to Wisconsin during World War II.

from ideal also. Some of them, such as a great many Puerto Rican parents, decide that the move was a mistake and return to their former home.[2] But the vast majority stay and make the best of it in the new community.

For some, the move is disastrous. For others, if they can survive the first "culture shock," the move may prove eventually to have been a wise decision.[3]

In this chapter we wish to explore some of the problems that all minority group parents have to struggle with in American society. In addition, attention will be given to the specific problems presented to the parents of particular minority groups.

First, however, let us look at the concept of minority group as the sociologists use it.

The concept of minority group

The main thing about minority group status is that it always involves prejudice and discrimination.[4] Whether the parent is a Jew, a Roman Catholic, an American Indian, a Puerto Rican, an Afro-American—no matter what minority group a person belongs to, prejudice and discrimination are always involved.

Statistically, a minority group may actually constitute a majority of the population, as blacks do in many counties of the South (and as they now do in Washington, D.C.).

In terms of power the minority group is always at a disadvantage. The dominant group controls the economic system, the political system, the police force, and so forth.

The basic image of the minority group projected by the dominant group is always one of inferiority, worthlessness, and potential violence.

And lastly, the dominant group always feels morally superior. It is not that they have ever mistreated the minority group. On the contrary, they have always been good to the minority group and cannot understand why these people are not grateful.

With this background let us look at the generic problems experienced by all minority group parents. This will be followed by a discussion of

---

[2] Oscar Lewis in *La Vida* (New York: Random House, 1965) reports that in 1960 there were perhaps a million moves by Puerto Ricans to and from the United States with a net in-migration of about 20,000. See the "Introduction."

[3] In a beautiful book about an Italian village during World War II there are several descriptions of peasants who had immigrated to the United States and then had returned to their village for one reason or another. Most of these people regretted not staying in America. See Carlo Levi, *Christ Stopped at Eboli* (New York: Farrar, Strauss & Co., 1947).

[4] For an analysis of the concept of minority group see J. Milton Yinger, *A Minority Group in American Society* (New York: McGraw-Hill Book Co., 1965), chap. 3, "Minority Groups, Castes, and Classes."

some of the relatively unique situations faced by parents in specific minority groups.

Generic problems of minority group parents

All minority groups have problems, but they are not always the same problems. Jews in modern America, for example, do not usually suffer from lack of money or education, yet they face overt and covert prejudice and discrimination that take many forms—Jewish quotas in some of the better private colleges; restrictive deeds that in the past (and perhaps even today) have excluded them from desirable suburbs; anti-Semitic clauses in fraternity and sorority membership requirements that have forced Jewish students to form their own campus fraternal groups; country clubs that deny membership to Jews; private dining clubs that limit membership to Gentiles; resorts that are sold out if the person requesting reservations has a Jewish name; and even virtual exclusion from entire industries.[5] Jewish parents have to help their children cope with anti-Semitism as part of the process of growing up.

Briefly, what are the generic problems common to all minority group parents in our society? They seem to the writer to be: residential segregation, slum housing, poverty, inadequate schools, unemployment (or underemployment), poor health (mental as well as physical), loss of civil rights, prejudice, discrimination, and the problem of self-image.[6]

An exception to most of the above, as we indicated earlier, would be the American Jewish parents of today, but their predecessors in the United States had their full share of ghetto life and all that goes with it.[7]

Space does not permit the full discussion of these generic problems of minority group parents, but some of their dimensions will be dealt with as we look at the problems of specific groups.

The Afro-American parent

One scarcely needs to document the statement that black parents in the United States have faced severe problems in rearing their children

---

[5] For an excellent study of how Jewish persons are discriminated against, see Judith R. Kramer and Seymour Leventman, *Children of the Gilded Ghetto* (New Haven: Yale University Press, 1961).

[6] For a good analysis of the problems of minority groups in general, see Yinger, *op. cit.* An excellent discussion is also to be found in Nathan Glazer and Daniel Patrick Moynihan, *Beyond the Melting Pot* (Cambridge, Mass.: M.I.T. Press, 1963).

[7] The popular writer, Harry Golden, in various books, has described conditions faced by early Jewish immigrants on the lower East Side of New York City. See also the autobiography of Alfred Kazin, *Starting Out in the Thirties* (Boston: Little, Brown & Co., 1965).

since the day the first Afro-American walked ashore.[8] In the days of slavery these difficulties were largely those of the mother, since black marriage was not recognized under slave law and black fathers were not accorded the status of parent.[9]

American society and the position of black parents have changed drastically since slave days, but the stresses on these parents remain severe. It is the purpose of this section to make these explicit.

1. The generation gap between black parents and their children. What would it be like to have grown up in rural Mississippi and be rearing your children in New York City or Denver or Los Angeles?

What would it be like to spend all of your early life in a rigidly segregated society and then try to rear your children in a partially integrated society?

What would it be like to grow up in the so-called lower lower class and then help your children work their way up into the world of a college education and a middle-class position in the society?

Black parents can best answer the preceding questions for only they have lived through the racial revolution in the United States.

The so-called generation gap results from rapid and deep social change, which explains why the gap has been so prominent in the black family in our society since 1940.[10]

The "Uncle Tom" type of black parent who is afraid to insist on his rights as an American citizen can no longer retain the respect of his children; he must either join the revolt or be cast on the pile of discarded elders. It is not easy for parents to change their outlook on life, nor is it easy to watch your children man the barricades. These dilemmas are part of the social gulf that separates the generations in the American black community.

2. Geographical migration. In the past several decades several million Afro-Americans have moved—but not in the same way that most of us

---

[8] For historical perspective on the problems of the black family in America see E. Franklin Frazier, *The Negro Family in the United States* (New York: The Dryden Press, 1966 ed.). Afro-Americans are by far the largest minority in the United States with approximately 10 or 11 percent of the population as of the 1960's.

[9] For an excellent discussion of the conditions under slavery in the United States see Frank Tannenbaum, *Slave and Citizen* (New York: Alfred A. Knopf, 1946). The problems of the black father are considered in William H. Grier and Price M. Cobbs, *Black Rage* (New York: Basic Books, 1968). See especially chap. 4, "Acquiring Manhood."

[10] Some idea of the progress made by blacks in the United States since 1940 may be found in Thomas F. Pettigrew, *A Profile of the Negro American* (Princeton, N.J.: D. Van Nostrand Co., 1964), *passim*. See also Andrew Billingsley, *Black Families in White America* (Englewood Cliffs, N.J.: Prentice-Hall, Inc., 1968). Billingsley argues that the black family has been amazingly stable in view of the conditions that black parents have had to cope with.

move. Many of these families went from the rural South to the urban ghettoes of the North and West—Washington, Philadelphia, New York, Boston, Chicago, Denver, Los Angeles, and Seattle.[11]

This constitutes one of the great migrations in the history of Western society. Beginning in World War I it reached a peak during and after World War II.

Some of these parents had been urbanized in the South, but observers seem to think that it is still a long jump from Nashville or Birmingham to Chicago or Denver.[12]

In certain aspects these migratory families are similar to the great waves of immigrants who moved to the United States from Europe during the era 1870 to 1920.[13] They are similar in that they tear up their roots and seek a new life in a new place. They are similar in that the parents grew up one place and the children will be growing up in the new place. They are also similar in that the migrant usually enters the social structure in the new home at the bottom—what the urban sociologists call the point of least resistance. This, of course, has always been the urban slum.

But the big difference between these black migrants and their white predecessors is that these people originally came from Africa, not Europe, and for this reason their reception in the new community was less than enthusiastic.

It is true, of course, that the black Americans were not the only new arrivals in American cities to meet with a cool reception. The "yellow" Chinese and Japanese were not exactly met by cheering crowds when they arrived on the West Coast and eventually moved inland, nor was the "red man" (the American Indian) ever greeted with any emotion except distrust and suspicion.

It is also true that the "swarthy" immigrants from Italy met with great hostility—partly because they were Roman Catholics but also because they were from southern Europe rather than northern Europe.[14]

But the black parents *were* unique in that their ancestors had been

---

[11] The net migration of blacks from the South to other parts of the United States is estimated to have been about 5 million from 1910 through 1966. See the *U.S. Riot Commission Report* (New York: Bantam Books, 1968), p. 240.

[12] Some material on the complicated move from the South to a city such as Chicago may be found in St. Clair Drake and Horace R. Cayton, *Black Metropolis* (New York: Harcourt, Brace & Co., 1945).

[13] Some of these problems are looked at in Oscar Handlin, *The Uprooted* (Boston: Little, Brown, & Co., 1952).

[14] On Italians in the United States see Glazer and Moynihan, *op. cit.*; on the American Indian see William A. Brophy and Sophie D. Aberle, *The Indian: America's Unfinished Business* (Norman, Okla.: University of Oklahoma Press, 1966); on the Japanese-Americans a good discussion is available in Albert Q. Maisel, *They All Chose America* (New York: Thomas Nelson & Sons, 1957); on the Chinese-Americans see B. L. Sung, *Mountain of Gold* (New York: The Macmillan Co., 1967); also Gunther Barth, *Bitter Strength* (Cambridge, Mass.: Harvard University Press, 1964).

slaves, and part of the terrible price of slavery was that the black person's cultural heritage from Africa was literally obliterated. This was not true of the Italians or the Indians or the Chinese or the Japanese—all of whom could pass on to their children the glory that had once been theirs. The black father or mother could not do this; all they knew was that they had once been slaves.[15]

3. *A negative self-image.* Afro-American parents, as we have just indicated, were not in a position to help their children achieve a positive self-image. In the United States they had only slavery to remember, and of their ancestral achievements in Africa they knew nothing.[16] Modern psychotherapy has demonstrated that a positive self-image is one of the prerequisites of mental health.[17] This was a gift that few black parents could give their children.

4. *A matriarchal family system.* Under slavery the Afro-American family was inevitably matriarchal. The father was not recognized biologically, legally, or socially.[18]

To some extent this mother-centered system has continued into modern America, partly because it has been easier for the black woman to find employment, partly because of the percentage of unmarried mothers, and also because of the American public welfare system that favors mothers who do not have a man in the house.[19]

Goode and Moynihan claim that blacks in the United States have an unusually high proportion of broken families characterized by illegitimacy, divorce, desertion, separation, or the death of a parent.[20]

All parents know how difficult it is to rear children when both parents are present—and black parents have this advantage less often than the rest of us.

According to a study by Liebow, one reason why the lower class black

---

[15] Another crucial difference is that the Afro-Americans did not choose to come to the United States; they were forced to come, while the other immigrants chose to come. Since the American Indian was already here and then had the land taken from him, his situation is different from all of the other minority groups.

[16] Pettigrew, *op. cit.*, discusses the problem of the black's self-image in a number of places. See *self-esteem* in his Index.

[17] For an extensive discussion of the self-image and its relationship to personality adjustment, see Calvin S. Hall and Gardner Lindzey, *Theories of Personality* (New York: John Wiley & Sons, 1957), chap. 12, "Rogers' Self Theory." See also Lee Rainwater, "Crucible of Identity," in *Daedalus*, 95 (1965), pp. 172–216.

[18] Glazer and Moynihan, *op. cit.*, chap. 1, "The Negroes," have a discussion of the matriarchal family system; see also Frazier, *op. cit.*

[19] See Alvin L. Schorr, *Poor Kids* (New York: Basic Books, 1966), *passim*, for an excellent analysis of the impact of the American public welfare system on low-income families. See also the *U.S. Riot Commission Report*, chap. 7, "Unemployment, Family Structure, and Social Disorganization."

[20] On black divorce rates see William J. Goode, *After Divorce* (New York: The Free Press, 1956), pp. 48–52; see also *The Negro Family* (Washington, D.C.: U.S. Department of Labor, 1965). This has come to be known as "The Moynihan Report."

man leaves his family is a feeling that his wife and children will be better off (at least economically) if he is not in the home.[21] His intermittent employment does not really meet the family's financial needs; it only serves to complicate their eligibility for public welfare.

As the result of all of the factors that produced the matricentric family system it has been extremely difficult for the low-income black father to assume his parental role. This is not true, however, of the middle or upper class Afro-American father.

It is often assumed that the one-parent family system (usually headed by a woman) is inherently pathological, but a 1968 paper by Kadushin raised serious doubts about this assumption.[22]

5. *Residence in urban ghetto or rural South.* Relatively few black parents in America have ever enjoyed the privilege (or the advantage) of rearing their children in well-organized communities, with good housing, good schools, adequate recreation facilities, efficient police protection, and so forth.[23] Only a parent who has attempted to function in either a rural slum or an urban ghetto can testify to the heroic efforts required of fathers and mothers to prevail against such odds.

6. *Outside employment of mothers.* In the United States about one family out of three has both parents in the labor force. In black families, however, the percentage is much higher, from 70 to 80 percent in the lower socioeconomic levels.[24]

This, of course, does not mean that such mothers necessarily neglect their children, but it certainly does mean that these mothers have to juggle a complex set of roles to fully discharge their parental responsibilities.

7. *Social welfare support.* American black families are overrepresented on the welfare rolls in the various states.[25] This not only means that they are in the so-called poverty group (about 40 percent, twice the national average),[26] it also means that they are forced to live (or exist) at

---

21 For a very insightful participant-observation study of the lower class black man see Elliot Liebow, *Tally's Corner* (Boston: Little, Brown & Co., 1967).

22 A massive review of the data available on the one-parent family is to be found in an unpublished paper, "Single Parent Adoptions: An Overview and Some Relevant Research," by Alfred Kadushin, May, 1968. Available in mimeographed form from School of Social Work, University of Wisconsin.

23 One of the best studies of the impact of slum housing on family life may be found in Alvin L. Schorr, *Slums and Social Insecurity* (Washington, D.C.: U.S. Government Printing Office, 1963).

24 This estimate is from *The Negro Family* (The Moynihan Report), *op. cit.*

25 In addition to Schorr's study, *Poor Kids*, see M. Elaine Burgess and Daniel O. Price, *An American Dependency Challenge* (Chicago, Ill.: American Public Welfare Assn., 1963), for an analysis of public welfare and low-income families.

26 *The Negro Family* (The Moynihan Report) *op. cit.*, estimates 40 percent of American black families to be in the so-called poverty group. For an analysis of the attacks on the Moynihan Report, see Lee Rainwater and William Yancey (eds.), *The Moynihan Report and the Politics of Controversy* (Cambridge, Mass.: M.I.T. Press, 1967); also Billingsley, *op. cit.*, pp. 199–202.

a level well below the poverty line.[27] This, of course, has all sorts of ramifications in terms of medical care, dental care, housing, educational opportunities, and so on.

It is not only that welfare budgets are too low to begin with—most states in the 1960's were not even paying what their budgets called for.[28]

8. *Social class mobility.* Almost all American immigrant parents suffered the experience of their children surpassing them in educational and socioeconomic achievement.[29] This, of course, is why the parents migrated in the first place—so their children could enjoy a better world— but at the same time parent-child stress is often generated as the child moves up the social ladder.[30] It becomes more difficult for the parent to understand the child and vice versa. It is not that they no longer love each other; it is only that the child is now different.[31]

These, then, are some of the special problems of black parents in America. Faced with these obstacles it is almost a miracle that any of these parents at the lower income levels ever succeed in fulfilling their parental responsibilities, and yet many of them do, one way or another.

The Puerto Rican parent

Background. The Puerto Ricans are relatively unique among American minority groups in that most of them entered the United States as *citizens* (citizenship was conferred on all Puerto Rican residents in 1917).[32] Thus they are different from the Afro-Americans, most of whom entered America as slaves, and also from the American Indian, who was conquered and not granted citizenship until 1924.[33]

Minority groups such as the American Chinese or the American

---

[27] On the standard of living made possible by our public welfare grants see Schorr, *Poor Kids*, chap. 3, "The Family Cycle and Income Development."

[28] A thorough review of welfare grants to families with dependent children may be found in Alfred Kadushin, *Child Welfare Services* (New York: The Macmillan Co., 1967), chap. 5, "Income Maintenance."

[29] In his book, Handlin, *op. cit.*, discusses how the European immigrants felt as their children became "Americanized" and displayed feelings of superiority to their parents. See chap. 9, "Generations."

[30] For a discussion of the impact of vertical social mobility on families see E. E. LeMasters, "Social Class Mobility and Family Integration," *Marriage and Family Living*, 16 (1954).

[31] For a study of urban kinship that reaches somewhat different conclusions from those of LeMasters, see Bert H. Adams, *Kinship in An Urban Setting* (Chicago: Markham Publishing Co., 1968).

[32] On the citizenship status of the Puerto Ricans and other relevant data about them see the following: Glazer and Moynihan, *op. cit.*, chap. 2; O. Lewis, *op. cit.*, the lengthy "Introduction;" Clarence Senior, *The Puerto Ricans* (Chicago: Quadrangle Books, 1965); and Oscar Handlin, *The Newcomers* (Cambridge, Mass.: Harvard University Press, 1959).

[33] For a discussion of the citizenship status of the American Indian, see Brophy and Aberle, *op. cit.*, p. 16.

Japanese had difficulty getting into the United States because of anti-Asian immigration laws, while the Puerto Ricans, being citizens, could enter and leave as they wished.

The American Indian had no choice about living in America since he was already here when the European whites got off the boats. The American blacks also had no choice because they were enslaved and transported to wherever the slave market was active.[34]

Tannenbaum makes an interesting point that the Indian in North America was never enslaved, at least not in large numbers.[35]

Puerto Ricans enjoyed two advantages when they migrated to the mainland, not only were they citizens on arrival, they also were accepted as *whites*, thus avoiding the racial caste barrier that has always plagued the Afro-American and the American Indian.[36]

Actually, some Puerto Ricans are a mixture of three different biological stocks—European, Indian, and African. But for the most part they are accepted as whites by the average American.

It is difficult to state exactly how many Puerto Ricans are in the United States at any given time due to the tendency for families to return to the island when economic conditions deteriorate in the United States. As of the 1960's the estimate was about one million.[37]

Puerto Ricans have never been evenly distributed over America but have been concentrated in a few urban centers such as New York City.[38] This uneven distribution has produced two effects: (1) a feeling in the areas of concentration that the Puerto Ricans were invading the country, and (2) almost complete ignorance of the rest of the country as to what a Puerto Rican is like.[39] This sort of situation tends to produce not only fear but widespread ignorance and misinformation.

Problems of Puerto Rican parents

1. Language.   With a native language derived from Spanish, the Puerto Rican parent faces his first handicap. He can not help his child

---

[34] Persons with very little knowledge of the slave trade and the conditions it imposed on blacks might find the following books useful: Daniel P. Mannix and Malcolm Cowley, *Black Cargoes: A History of the Atlantic Slave Trade* (New York: The Viking Press, 1962); also James Pope-Hennessy, *Sins of the Fathers* (New York: Alfred A. Knopf, 1968).

[35] For a discussion of the fact that Indians were seldom enslaved in the Americas, see Tannenbaum, *op. cit.*, p. 41.

[36] Senior, *op. cit.*, p. 46, reports that about 80 percent of the Puerto Ricans in the United States are classified as white by the Bureau of the Census.

[37] Lewis, in the "Introduction" of *La Vida*, estimates that there are about one million Puerto Ricans in the United States as of the 1960's.

[38] Lewis says that approximately 600,000 of the Puerto Ricans reside in New York City. See Lewis, *op. cit.*, the "Introduction."

[39] See Senior, *op. cit.*, pp. 37–40, for a discussion of this point.

learn English (or American) because he does not speak the language himself. This puts the child at a serious disadvantage in the school system and perhaps in the labor market.

The language barrier also creates problems for the father or mother. They have difficulty communicating with the school officials, the public welfare workers, the police, and so on. Language problems have always plagued immigrant parents in America and the Puerto Ricans are no exception.

2. *Matriarchal family system.* Oscar Lewis reports that among low-income Puerto Rican families the mother is the stable, dominant parent.[40]

There is nothing inherently wrong with a mother-centered family system, but with the father absent and the mother employed outside of the home this family system can be extremely vulnerable. This possibility is accentuated in the United States by the absence of the extended kin network found in Puerto Rico itself.[41]

Among middle or upper class Puerto Ricans, of course, the family system is patriarchal. But these are relatively rare in the United States.

Poverty

Puerto Rican families in the United States are often at or near the poverty level.[42] This is nothing new to most of these parents because they were also poor in Puerto Rico—that was the main reason for migrating to America.

But being poor in your native land, surrounded by friends and relatives, is quite different from being poor in Spanish Harlem in New York City or the slum areas of Chicago.

It hardly needs to be repeated here that poverty symbolizes a host of related problems for parents, such as poor housing, inadequate schools, deteriorated neighborhoods, marginal jobs, less than average health, and skimpy police protection. Parents who can cope successfully with this list of problems deserve some sort of medal.

Excessive fertility

Most minority groups in the United States have higher than average birthrates.[43] In view of the setting in which these parents operate, the

---

[40] Lewis reports that 26 percent of the sample he studied in New York City had households headed by a woman. About half of the marriages in his New York sample were of the consensual or "free union" type. See the "Introduction" to *La Vida*.

[41] A comparison of the kin network and its functions in Puerto Rico versus that in New York City may be found in Lewis, *op. cit.*

[42] Senior, *op. cit.*, p. 97, reports that Puerto Ricans in New York City are over-represented in the poverty group about two and a half times.

[43] The low-income birthrate of American blacks is about 30 percent higher than that of comparable whites according to Kingsley Davis. See his paper, "Some Demo-

rearing of large families poses extremely difficult problems for Puerto Rican parents. Being Roman Catholics these fathers and mothers lack the support of their church in using modern contraceptives, but some observers report a failure of Puerto Ricans to observe the Church's teaching on birth control.[44]

There is every reason to believe that Puerto Rican parents in the United States do a good job in view of the negative factors they have to cope with.

American Indian parents

As a group American Indian parents probably face the most difficult situation of any parents in the United States. In some areas as many as 90 percent of the Indian families are reported to be dependent on public welfare.[45] The infant mortality rate is several times the national average, depending on the particular disease.[46] School dropout rates, illiteracy rates, marital instability rates—all are greatly in excess of the national average.[47] Longevity is substantially lower than that of the Afro-Americans.[48]

Conditions vary, of course, from one tribe to another, but even the relatively well-to-do tribes, such as the Menominee in Wisconsin and the Navaho in the Southwest, are reported to be suffering from hunger and severe poverty.[49]

The American Indian has never been accepted as an equal by other

---

graphic Aspects of Poverty in the United States," in Margaret S. Gordon (ed.), *Poverty in America* (San Francisco: Chandler Publishing Co., 1965), pp. 299–319. Brophy and Aberle, *op. cit.*, pp. 162–163, say that the American Indian birthrate is about double that of the general population. Handlin, *op. cit.*, pp. 57–58, says that the birthrate of the Puerto Rican in America is "high."

[44] Senior, *op. cit.*, pp. 108–109, says that while Puerto Ricans in America are largely Roman Catholic, that only about 25 percent attend church—hence their attitude toward birth control does not necessarily reflect that of the church.

[45] Brophy and Aberle, *op. cit.*, pp. 70–72, report that for the period 1959–1960 three times as many Indian families were dependent on public welfare as compared with the rest of the nation.

[46] Brophy and Aberle, *op. cit.*, p. 163, report that in 1944 infant mortality among American Indians was three times that of the national average; by 1957–1959 the rate had dropped to about twice the national average.

[47] For a general review of the current status of the American Indian, see Brophy and Aberle, *op. cit.* This is the final report of the "Commission on the Rights, Liberties, and Responsibilities of the American Indian."

[48] Pettigrew, *op. cit.*, p. 99, reports that in 1900 average nonwhites in the United States had a life expectancy of 32–35 years. But by 1960 this had increased to 61–66 years, which is still 6–8 years less than that of whites. Indian longevity lags behind that of American blacks, however.

[49] On the precarious condition of the Menominee, reported to be one of the more affluent tribes, see Joyce M. Erdman, *Wisconsin Indians* (Madison, Wisc.: Governor's Commission on Human Rights, 1966); some of the problems of the Navaho are discussed in Brophy and Aberle, *op. cit.*, in various chapters.

Americans. He was not even granted full citizenship until 1924—seven years after Puerto Ricans were given their citizenship and over a half century after the blacks in America had been granted citizenship.

Tragically, the American Indian found, as did the Afro-American, that legal rights and actual rights are far from being the same thing.

The following problems would seem to face Indian fathers and mothers as they try to accept their parental responsibilities in modern America.

1. Language problems. The children often learn a language at home that is not used at school or in the larger society. As Brophy and Aberle point out, the Indian languages view the world in ways quite foreign to most Americans, and this greatly complicates the adjustment of the Indian child in the public school system.[50]

Language problems have always plagued new arrivals in America, except for the English-speaking settlers of the colonial era. But most of these other groups learned English (or American) rather rapidly because they had to in order to survive in the open society. The Indian, however, the first to arrive on these shores, wasn't forced to learn the language of the invaders because he was shunted off to isolated reservations where he continued to use his own language. This may have helped to preserve some small part of his cultural heritage but it also complicated his dealings with the outside world.

2. The reservation system. Of the estimated 600,000 to 800,000 Indians in the United States in the 1960's, a majority still live on tribal reservations.[51] This has resulted in the Indian not becoming a full member of the larger society, and at the same time it has not succeeded in helping the Indian to preserve a healthy subsociety of his own. In essence, then, the Indian parent is torn between two desires, to see his child continue as an Indian but also to see him become an American. This puts both the parent and the child in a difficult position: if you assimilate you lose your self-identify but if you don't you lose your chance to share in the economic abundance of the affluent society.

Most observers seem to regard the reservation system as a failure viewed from the point of view of the Indian.[52] But from the very first the primary function of the reservation system was to get the Indian out of the way, and it would be difficult to argue that this purpose was not achieved.

---

[50] The language problems of Indian school children are reviewed in Brophy and Aberle, *op. cit., passim.* See also William T. Hagan, *American Indians* (Chicago: University of Chicago Press, 1961).

[51] Exact population figures on the American Indian are difficult to compile because of the various definitions of the term *Indian.* See Brophy and Aberle, *op. cit.,* pp. 11–16, for a discussion of this problem. As of the 1960 U.S. Census the official count was about 500,000.

[52] On the failure of the reservation system see Dale Van Every, *Disinherited* (New York: William Morrow & Co., 1966); also Brophy and Aberle, *op. cit., passim.* See

3. *Culture conflict.* Among the hundreds of Indian tribes in the United States there are innumerable conflicts between the historic culture of the tribes and that of the larger society.[53] These include not only language but also marriage and family systems, child rearing practices, property ownership, religious faith, and so on.

Parents face the difficult task of living in and rearing their children for two different worlds. The more the child learns about his tribal culture the stranger the outside world appears to be. Some minority groups in the United States, such as the Jews, seem to be able to preserve their own subculture while competing successfully in the larger society. To date few American Indians have been able to do this.

4. *Poverty.* About 20 percent of all Americans were considered to be in the so-called poverty group as of the 1960's.[54] For Indians the percentage is probably closer to 80 percent.[55] If so they probably are the most economically deprived of all the minority groups in our society. This is a sad end for a once proud people who originally owned every foot of soil in North America.

Only poor parents really know what it is like to rear children in modern America without an adequate income. The society seems to be founded on money; something the poor don't have.

It is not only the inconvenience and the embarrassment of not having money—it is also the self-degradation. As Harrington makes clear, the day of the "honest and deserving poor" has long since departed in the United States.[56] Poverty today has a moral tone it did not have in an earlier America. Only the hippies, it seems, can live at the poverty level in our society and feel superior, but this is partly because they came from affluent homes. It is extremely difficult to laugh at money if you have never had much of it.

Poverty affects all phases of Indian life, such as housing, food, medical and dental care, education, and clothes.[57] Welfare programs help Indian parents meet some of these needs, but only at a bare subsistence level.

4. *Self-image.* Psychotherapists tell us that a negative self-image is

Stan Steiner, *The New Indians* (New York: Harper & Row, 1968), for a survey of how the new generation of Indian youth view their problems.

[53] For a discussion of culture conflict between the Indian and the white invaders, see John Collier, *Indians of the Americas* (New York: Mentor Books, 1947), especially chap. 13, "The Final Struggle Commences and Prevails."

[54] The figure of 20 percent of American families being in the so-called poverty group was popularized by Michael Harrington in *The Other America* (New York: The Macmillan Co., 1962).

[55] The estimate of 80 percent of Indians being in the poverty group is taken from a Washington, D.C. news release published in the *Milwaukee Journal*, April 5, 1968.

[56] One of Harrington's main points in *The Other America* is that being poor in our society is no longer respectable.

[57] Recent surveys of the Menominee in Wisconsin have revealed that at least 70 percent of the children of this "affluent" tribe are in need of immediate dental treatment—personal communication from the Wisconsin Department of Public Welfare,

one of the traits found in the emotionally disturbed person in our society.[58] In view of the Indian's position in modern America it would be odd if he did not have a self-image that was destructive.

The late Senator Robert Kennedy, in 1968, reported that in one Indian tribe in Idaho the suicide rate was 100 times the national average.[59] If true this is in sharp contrast to the suicide rate among Afro-Americans, which Pettigrew reports to be lower than that of whites.[60]

The American black community is in the process of rediscovering its African heritage and is using this to help restore self-respect and a sense of identity. It would seem that the American Indian needs very much to do this also.

5. *Excessive fertility.* It is reported that the birthrate of the American Indian in the 1960's was approximately double that of the general population.[61] It is difficult to see how Indian parents can hope to solve their problems at this fertility level. Perhaps new contraceptive methods and new attitudes toward planned parenthood will help to solve this problem.

6. *Smallness of group.* One problem of Indian parents is that there are so few of them—less than one percent of our population. This means a number of things; relatively few Americans, for example, have ever really known an American Indian. Their perception of this group is derived from television and the movies.

The smallness also results in lack of power. There aren't enough Indians for people to be afraid of.

This type of problem can only be solved by Indians forming a political alliance with other minority groups.

In the past, according to Van Every, Indian tribes have often failed to work together to solve their mutual problems.[62] In the future they will need not only to work together but also to align themselves politically with other deprived groups. As of 1968 there were some developments in that direction.[63]

1967. In the book by Erdman, *op. cit.*, p. 57, the statement is made: "Indian health is approximately a generation behind that of the non-Indian population in Wisconsin."

[58] For an interesting discussion of identity problems among American Indians see Erik H. Erikson, "Childhood in Two American Indian Tribes." *Childhood and Society* (2nd ed.; New York: W. W. Norton, 1963), Pt. 2.

[59] In the *Milwaukee Journal* news release, *op. cit.*, it was stated that the Indian suicide rate in Idaho is 100 times the national average. The writer has been unable to confirm this figure from other sources.

[60] Pettigrew, *op. cit.*, pp. 77–78, reports that for the period 1949–1951 the black suicide rate in the United States was only 42 percent that of the white.

[61] Brophy and Aberle, *op. cit.*, pp. 162–163, state that the Indian birthrate is at least twice that of the national average and perhaps higher.

[62] Van Every, *op. cit.*, in various chapters, documents the historical failure of the many Indian tribes to work together to resist the white man.

[63] The "poor people's march on Washington," in the summer of 1968, represented one of the first efforts of the American Indian to work with Afro-Americans to solve or alleviate their mutual problems. Steiner, *op. cit.*, chap. 19, has an extensive discussion of this matter.

Problems of American Jewish parents

1. Religion. Regardless of what other cultural differences they may have, most of the minority groups in America are nominally Christians. The society was founded and populated largely by Protestants and Catholics and these groups have shaped the basic institutions and are largely responsible for its tone.[64] Jews, no matter what their degree of orthodoxy, are thus a distinct religious minority. At one time or another Jews have been persecuted in almost every nation in Western society.

It is easy to underestimate the depth and strength of anti-Semitism in the modern world, but those who do have forgotten too soon the atrocities of World War II.

Jewish parents are not naive about their tenuous position in a civilization founded by the followers of Christ. Most of their ancestors suffered at one time or another at the hands of Christians who profess nothing but love for their fellowman.

The problem, then, for American Jewish parents is to somehow help their children preserve their own cultural heritage without seeming to feel odd in the society. One Jewish father said to the writer: "At times I am inclined to doubt that it is worth the trouble (and the potential danger) of preserving our Jewish subculture—I am tempted to join the Methodist church and not even have my boy circumcised."

It takes a nice balance and a gentle touch for American Jewish parents to help their children become not only good Americans but also good Jews. It is the perennial plight of the small religious minority that faces Jewish parents in our society.

2. Racism. The average American thinks of Jews as a separate race in the same way that Afro-Americans are considered to be a distinct race. Social scientists have argued for decades that Jews are a cultural group, not a separate and distinct race, but this message seems not to have filtered down to the average citizen.

Thus, in a very real sense, Jews in our society have suffered from racism as have the blacks and the American Indian.

All sorts of negative qualities have been attributed to Jews by racists, and Jewish parents have the problem of helping their children understand the nature of those Americans who hold such beliefs.

It is no accident that the Ku Klux Klan in the United States has always been bitterly anti-Semitic. This is part of the racist attack on minority groups.

---

[64] A good analysis of the three major religious groups in our society may be found in Will Herberg, *Protestant, Catholic, Jew* (New York: Doubleday & Co., 1956). A very useful recent book on Jews in America is the work of Sidney Goldstein and Calvin Goldscheider, *Jewish Americans* (Englewood Cliffs, N.J.: Prentice-Hall, Inc., 1968). See also Glazer and Moynihan, *op. cit.,* chap. 3, "The Jews."

3. The problem of too much success. American blacks, as well as the American Indian, have usually been accused of being lazy or lacking in ambition. Jews in our society are criticized for being just the opposite. They are condemned for being too aggressive, too clannish, and so forth.

In a sense the ability of the American Jew to compete in our society has been used against him. Although as a group they have one of the highest standards of living in the United States today, many Americans forget that the average Jewish immigrant entered our society at the bottom and that their affluence today often represents several generations of effort.[65]

4. Miscellaneous problems. Jewish children, as other minority group children, never know when they will run into prejudice and discrimination. When this happens the child is confused and hurt. Parents have to help their children understand such treatment and to respond appropriately.

The problem of interfaith marriage is a constant one for American Jewish parents. In some communities their children can simply not find suitable marriage partners of their own faith. One Jewish college girl put this to the writer in these words: "I come from the deep South. My father owns a beautiful clothing store in this town of 35,000 and we are the only Jewish family in that town. I was sent up here to meet 'a nice Jewish boy' and you know what happened? I fell in love with a Protestant boy whose parents don't have a dime. We are engaged and my mother is about to have a stroke."

These are real problems for any small minority, and parents have to be flexible and imaginative to cope with them.

The American Jewish community is by no means united or homogenous. There are wide variations in religious orthodoxy as well as vast differences in social class position. This heterogeneity within a relatively small minority poses its own problems for Jewish parents.

Problems of other minority group parents

It is an interesting and puzzling fact that Chinese and Japanese parents have done quite well in the United States in the face of extreme prejudice and discrimination.[66] It is true that these people did not enter the society

---

[65] Glazer and Moynihan, *op. cit.*, have a treatment of Jewish history in New York City; Goldstein and Goldscheider, *op. cit.*, have an analysis of three generations of Jews in Providence, Rhode Island. Kramer and Leventman, *op. cit.*, have a three-generation analysis of Jews in the St. Paul–Minneapolis metropolitan area.

[66] On the phenomenal success of the Japanese in the United States, see Maisel, *op. cit.*, chap. 9, "The Japanese." Maisel reports that in recent decades almost 50 percent of American-Japanese children of college age have been enrolled in college (p. 133). In their study of Jews in Providence, Rhode Island, Goldstein and Goldscheider, *op. cit.*, found that 41 percent of the Jews in this community had attended

as slaves, as the Afro-Americans did, but as Asiatics they suffered from the same racist attitudes that have plagued the American blacks and the American Indian. As late as World War II the Japanese-Americans were confined to what were essentially concentration camps no matter what the government called them.

Another minority group, the Mexican-Americans, have not done nearly as well, the bulk of them still being at the poverty level.[67]

Why have some minority group parents done so well while others have made relatively little progress? It seems to the writer that social scientists are not as yet prepared to answer this question but an analysis of the strategies employed by the successful minority parents may provide some clues.

Successful strategies for coping with problems

1. Reduction of family size. The minority group having the highest standard of living in the United States, the Jews, also have the lowest birthrate.[68] The four groups with the lowest standard of living—Negroes, Indians, Puerto Ricans, Mexican-Americans—all have relatively high birthrates.[69]

Middle-class blacks, in contrast, are reported to have birthrates below that of middle-class whites.[70]

In an urban society in which children are an economic liability, only the most capable parents seem to be able to rear large families with any

---

college compared with 13 percent of the general population in Providence (p. 65). In her study of the American-Chinese, Sung, *op. cit.*, p. 125, reports considerably above average educational attainment for this minority group—as of 1960 16.7 percent of the males in this group had completed four or more years of college, compared to 8.0 percent for American whites and 2.2 percent for American blacks.

[67] In the famous CBS television broadcast called "Hunger in America," June 16, 1968, the statement is made that in San Antonio, Texas, with a Mexican-American population of about 400,000, "A quarter of San Antonio's Mexican-Americans, 100,000 people, are hungry all the time." See p. 1 of the script released by CBS.

[68] Goldstein and Goldscheider, *op. cit.*, p. 118, report that Jews in America have consistently used contraceptives more widely and more efficiently than any other population group in the United States. They say: "Jews have the smallest families, marry later, expect and desire to have the smallest families, approve the use of contraception, are most likely to plan the number and spacing of all their children, and are most likely to use effective methods of contraception."

[69] Brophy and Aberle, *op. cit.*, were cited previously to the effect that American Indian birthrates are at least twice the national average; Davis, *op. cit.* reports that black birthrates in the United States are about 30 percent higher than that of whites at lower class levels. Maisel, *op. cit.*, pp. 172–184, discusses the relatively high birthrate of the Mexican-Americans. In *The Newcomers*, pp. 57–58, Handlin points out that both the Negroes and the Puerto Ricans in New York City have higher than average birthrates.

[70] American black families at the middle-class level do not have excessive birthrates. In fact they may average fewer children than white families of the same social class level—see Davis, *op. cit.*

degree of success. In a provocative book Schorr argues that four children seem to be the maximum number that most low-income American parents can manage—above that number problems seem to predominate.[71]

Religious affiliation may be a factor in the relatively high birthrates of the Puerto Rican or some American Indians, but this is not the case with most American blacks. It would seem that the relatively high fertility of this group reflects two basic factors: (1) recent migration from the rural South, and (2) lower class subculture.[72]

Whatever the causes of high birthrates for various minority groups, it seems unlikely that these parents can cope with their problems unless (and until) they have smaller families.

2. *Major stress on education.* As of 1955 about 62 percent of all Jewish children of college age were reported to be in college in the United States; this compares to 26 percent of the general population in college.[73] About the same time, the percentage of Chinese and Japanese children of college age actually attending college was estimated to be 40 to 50 percent.[74]

In recent years in the United States nonwhites have averaged only about 7.9 years of formal education.[75] There was a time in America when parents and their children did not need extensive schooling, but that time has long since passed.

It is true, of course, that Afro-Americans, Indians, and other minority groups have not found the American educational system well suited to their needs,[76] but unless they can work out some solution to their educational problems their competitive chances in the society do not appear very bright.

3. *Urban residence.* In the last 75 years the immigrant groups that have moved up into the mainstream of American society have found their opportunity in urban America. Once the frontier was closed and the free

---

[71] On family size and family disorganization at lower class levels, Schorr says: "There is a sprinkling of evidence that the fourth or fifth child represents a point of no return for poor families." (See *Poor Kids*, p. 38.) He goes on to point out that about seven out of every ten youths rejected for the Armed Forces come from families with four or more children.

[72] For a good study of birth control at lower class levels see Lee Rainwater, *And the Poor Get Children* (Chicago: Quadrangle Books, 1960).

[73] Maisel, *op. cit.*, p. 133.

[74] *Ibid.*

[75] Kenneth B. Clark and Talcott Parsons (eds.), *The Negro American* (Boston: Beacon Press, 1966), p. 84, report that in 1960 nonwhite males had an average of 7.9 years of schooling compared to 10.6 for whites.

On the inequalities in our educational system see James Coleman, *Coleman Report on Equality of Educational Opportunity* (Washington, D.C.: U.S. Office of Education, 1965).

[76] For an extensive analysis of the failure of the New York City public schools to meet the needs of minority group children, see David Rogers, *110 Livingston Street: Politics and Bureaucracy in the New York City School System* (New York: Random House, 1968).

land exhausted, there was relatively little opportunity for new arrivals in rural America.

Afro-Americans and American Indians are not, of course, new arrivals, but since World War II the Negro has become one of the most urbanized groups in the United States. The cities have not solved his problems but substantial improvement in his condition can be shown for the period since 1940—when the mass move to the city began.[77]

Groups that have done quite well in America, the Jews, Chinese, and Japanese, are all highly urbanized. In fact, nine out of ten Jewish families are reported to live in cities.[78]

It is an interesting fact that the minority group with the lowest standard of living in modern America—the Indians—are overwhelmingly rural in residence.[79]

Immigrants and migrants do not find the cities of America waiting with open arms, but if they can resist the initial culture shock they seem to move up within two or three generations. The Irish did it; the Italians did it; the Jews did it; so did the Chinese and Japanese. All of these groups were despised by the White Anglo-Saxon Protestants (WASPS) at one time, yet today hold a respected place in American society.

Perhaps the writer is too optimistic and underestimates the depth of racism in our society. Yet any one who lived through the anti-Catholic hatred of the 1920's, as the writer did,[80] can hardly believe the peaceful coexistence of Protestants and Roman Catholics today. And anybody who saw the hatred of the Japanese-American during World War II would find it difficult to see the position of this group in American society today.

With all of its faults the large city has been the most receptive community in our society for families that were different. It is to be hoped that this welcome has not worn out.

4. *Extended family system.* Some of the ethnic minorities, such as the Italians and the Jews, seem to have survived their first encounter with the large city by a process of doubling up—new arrivals moved in with relatives already established; mothers held outside jobs; older

---

[77] Pettigrew, *op. cit., passim,* has data on the progress made by American blacks since 1940.

[78] See Milton M. Gordon, *Assimilation in American Life* (New York: Oxford University Press, 1964), pp. 174–175, for a discussion of urbanization and American Jews.

[79] The evidence on the lack of urbanization among the American Indian may be found in various chapters of the Brophy and Aberle study, *op. cit.* About two thirds of the Indians still live on or near a reservation.

[80] The writer witnessed hatred of Catholics and violence toward them while growing up in a Ku Klux Klan home in Ohio in a small city in the 1920's. Returning to this community in the 1960's one finds that many of the children of these parents who hated each other have intermarried and the community itself reflects little tension between Protestants and Roman Catholics today.

brothers and sisters helped younger children to get a start.[81] This system of mutual aid seems to be extremely functional for low-income families. Resources are shared until each family can care for its own.

5. *Political power.* Some of the earlier minority groups, such as the Irish and the Italians, achieved power and respectability by means of political activity. They infiltrated the political machines of the metropolis and literally took over. Now that blacks are winning the right to vote and are becoming politically astute it would seem that they too could make themselves felt in the legislative halls and the city council chambers.[82] With a population of 10 or 11 percent of the total electorate (when they are all permitted to vote), the Afro-American is almost in the position of deciding who shall be President of the United States. The two major political parties are so equal in strength—outside of the South— that the black vote can make the difference.

The smaller minorities, such as the Indian, can only hope to exercise political influence by forming a coalition with other underprivileged groups. If such an alignment could ever be worked out it would constitute a formidable political force.[83]

Conclusion and summary

In this chapter an attempt was made to identify the generic problems of all minority group parents as well as those of specific groups.

To some extent these problems resemble those of all lower class parents, discussed in the previous chapter, but there are also differences. Frequent reference was made in this chapter to the struggles of earlier immigrant groups, such as the Italians, who in their day had to cope with suspicion, hostility, prejudice, and discrimination also.

The chapter closed with a review of some of the strategies that have been proven effective by minority group parents who are now firmly established in American society.

---

[81] In the work by Kazin, *op. cit.*, this doubling up process among early Jewish immigrants is described. See also the same extended family system as it worked in the home of Richard Wright, the black writer, as described by Constance Webb in *Richard Wright* (New York: G. P. Putnam's Sons, 1968).

[82] Kenneth Clark, in *Dark Ghetto* (New York: Harper & Row, 1965), pp. 154–68, analyzes the political possibilities and some of the related problems in the political efforts of blacks in the urban ghetto.

[83] Senior, *op. cit.*, p. 18, states that about one sixth of all Americans belong to one minority or another.

chapter
seven

The American
mother

I N this chapter we wish to examine the role of the mother in contemporary America. In doing this we shall examine some of the attacks on the American mother and attempt to explain the reasons for them. An evaluation of the data on which the attacks have been based will be made. A role analysis of the American mother will be followed by a brief defense of her record in recent decades. The chapter will close with a case study of a family drawn from the 1920's and the 1930's.

Background

Following World War II American mothers were subjected to an attack so vicious that one wonders why they were willing to go on bearing and rearing children. A famous psychiatrist, Strecker, accused them of almost causing the United States to lose World War II by emasculating their sons.[1] A popular writer, Philip Wylie, wrote an even more devastating book called *A Generation of Vipers* in which he charged American mothers with the psychological castration of their sons.[2] His reference to *Vipers* refers to the child rearing practices of the American mother by which she sucks the life blood out of her male children.

This is strong language and one might dismiss it as being merely the bitter reminiscences of an unhappy man except for the fact that the book became a runaway best seller—some 400,000 copies of the book were sold within the first few years of publication. It is difficult to imag-

---

[1] Edward A. Strecker, M.D., *Their Mothers' Sons* (New York: J. B. Lippincott Co., 1946).

[2] Philip Wylie, *A Generation of Vipers* (New York: Rinehart & Co., 1942).

118

ine a book of this nature selling well unless it met with a responsive chord in the minds and hearts of its readers. It would be interesting to know *who* bought the book—mothers? fathers? sons? daughters? Unfortunately, we do not know.[3]

In commenting on the Strecker book, Gorer, the English anthropologist, has this to say:

According to this book, Mom, the clinging, possessive mother, not only causes psychoneurosis, she is the main cause of every unpleasant phenomenon, from schizophrenia, through lynching to National Socialism and Japanese Emperor Worship! . . . reading it, one would almost think that Americans were produced by parthenogenesis, so vestigial is the role given to the father in forming his children's characters.[4]

Although Gorer's own critique of the American mother is more moderate and more humane than that of Strecker or Wylie, it is interesting that he labels this chapter, "Mother-Land."[5]

Vicious as the attacks by writers such as Strecker and Wylie were, they at least did not accuse American mothers of destroying *all* of their children—only their sons. More recent attacks, however, have been less charitable. In 1963 Friedan wrote a best seller called *The Feminine Mystique*, in which she accused the American mother of having retreated to the home with disastrous results for *everybody*—sons, daughters, husbands, the mothers themselves, and American society.[6] Here, again, it would be helpful to know who bought the book and who read it, but the writer has been unable to locate such information.

In 1964 the journal *Daedalus* devoted its entire Spring issue to "The Woman in America."[7] In a long and brilliant essay, Rossi condemns the American mother for dedicating her life to what Rossi calls "full-time motherhood."[8] Her theme is somewhat similar to that of Friedan but the analysis is more scholarly. One statement made by Rossi in this 1964 essay reminded the writer that the Strecker-Wylie tone of anti-motherism has not disappeared from the American scene. Rossi writes:

It is a short-sighted view indeed to consider the immature wife, dominating mother or interfering mother-in-law as a less serious problem to the larger

---

[3] The writer has been unable to locate any research on the readership of controversial books such as this.

[4] Geoffrey Gorer, *The American People* (rev. ed.; New York: W. W. Norton, 1964), p. 64.

[5] See chap. 2.

[6] Betty Friedan, *The Feminine Mystique* (New York: W. W. Norton, 1963).

[7] See "The Woman in America," *Daedalus*, Spring, 1964.

[8] Alice S. Rossi, "Equality between the Sexes," *Daedalus*, Spring, 1964, pp. 607–652.

society than the male homosexual, psychoneurotic soldier or ineffectual worker, for it is the failure of the mother which perpetuates the cycle from one generation to the next, *affecting sons and daughters alike.*[9]

Discussion of the attack on the American mother

We do not know how the average American reacts to these condemnations of the American mother but the writer finds them somewhat appalling—also somewhat unbelievable. This reaction has three sources:

1. As a son we do not feel that our mother was "smothering" or "castrating"—terms used by the critics to characterize the American mother. The writer's mother was a full-time mother, to use Rossi's phrase, but we do not recall the hovering or the smothering that is supposed to go along with full-time motherhood.[10] We recognize, of course, that one mother does not constitute a sample.

2. We don't remember over one or two mothers from our youth peer group who might fit the description of Strecker, Wylie, Friedan, Rossi, and others—and yet all of these were full-time mothers.[11] Furthermore, the adult records of these sons—the boys we grew up with—are good. With only one or two exceptions they have served honorably in the armed forces, have held responsible jobs, have married and reared families. Not one of them has ever been committed to a mental hospital or sentenced to a penal institution. One or two have been divorced, and a few of these men drink more than is good for them—but these behavior patterns reflect American society, not just mothers.

3. As an adult living in a community of about 6,000, we don't know any mothers who fit the description provided by the critics cited earlier. One or two mothers are considered to be too concerned about their children but this is readily spotted by the other natives and is regarded as an unfortunate aberration, a reflection of some neurosis. The point is that such mothers are easily identified as being "abnormal" or "peculiar" by the other fathers and mothers in this community.

As a husband and father the writer is convinced that his two sons are not being reared by a castrating or smothering mother—and their behavior to date (16 and 18 years of age) supports this belief.

Another source of disbelief about these attacks on the American mother is the fact that in the same generation when these mothers were supposed to be ruining their sons (and even their daughters), America

---

[9] Rossi, *op. cit.*, p. 621. Italics not in the original.

[10] For a discussion of the full-time mother, see Rossi, *op. cit.*, pp. 615–617.

[11] See also Ferdinand Lundberg and Marynia A. Farnham, *Modern Woman: The Lost Sex* (New York: Grosset and Dunlap, 1947). This is one of the most hysterical attacks on the American mother we have seen.

has reached the peak of its world power and prestige.[12] Could one argue, for example, that Russian mothers (or fathers) have been busy smothering their sons in the era since 1920 when Russia, along with the United States, has emerged as a leading nation in the contemporary world?

A family system cannot be evaluated apart from the society in which it functions. If American mothers are as devastating as their critics would have us believe, then it is difficult to see how the nation has survived. Lerner is making this point when he writes: "If the American family is sick, then the class system must also be sick, and the whole economy, the democratic idea, the passion for equality, the striving for happiness, and the belief that there can be free choice and a future of hope . . . the point is that the American family is part of the totality and reflects its virtues as well as weaknesses."[13]

It is interesting to note that criticisms have been made of the American mother that are dramatically the reverse of those leveled by Strecker, Wylie, Friedan, and Rossi—namely, that the modern mother in our society *neglects* her children. She is accused of holding down too many outside jobs, of engaging in too many community activities, and so forth.[14] The mothers known to the writer would seem to be too busy to smother their children; they just don't have enough time. One has the impression that these mothers are more vulnerable to the mother's rat race critique than they are to the smothering critique.

In the next section of this chapter the writer proposes to use the attack on the American mother as sociological data and to analyze it as such. What is the source of the attack? How adequate are the data on which the attack is based?

Sources of the attack

It seems to us that the steam (or the feeling) behind the attack on the American mother is related to the emancipation of women which began in the United States during World War I and probably reached its peak during the 1920's.[15] This was a period of massive social change— or revolution—in our society. The great wave of immigration from Europe

---

[12] As of 1968, when this is being written, the war in Vietnam and the Civil Rights riots have temporarily tarnished the American image at home and abroad, but since 1920 the United States has certainly gained in world power and stature.

[13] Max Lerner, *America as a Civilization* (New York: Simon and Schuster, 1957), p. 551.

[14] Many of these criticisms are reviewed by Ivan Nye and Lois Hoffman in *The Employed Mother in America* (Chicago: Rand McNally & Co., 1963).

[15] A readable analysis of social change in our society since 1900 may be found in Frederick Lewis Allen, *The Big Change* (New York: Harper & Brothers, 1952).

was dwindling to a trickle; millions of farmers and their children were moving into cities; the new jobs were industrial jobs; and women were invading not only the world of politics but other pockets of American society more or less closed to them before—colleges and universities, all sorts of community activities, industry and business, and even that male sanctuary, the saloon (known as a speakeasy during Prohibition). Out of all of this social explosion not only a new American woman emerged, but also a new American male and a new American family.

The new American male will be discussed in another chapter. Here we wish to concentrate on the new American woman and the new family system.

As we see it, the American father either abdicated or was pushed out of his position as head of the family during the process of female emancipation. In a sense he was kicked upstairs, as they say in industry, and was made Chairman of the Board.[16] As such he did not lose all of his power—he still had to be consulted on important decisions—but his wife emerged as the Executive Director or Manager of the enterprise which is called the family. The extent of this shift of responsibility can be seen in the wife-mother's new role or position as Director of the Family Budget. If there was any one symbol of the Victorian father's power and glory it was his complete control of family finances. In many Western societies prior to the modern era married women (mothers) could not even own property in their own name; if they worked their income belonged to their husband; and most of them were regarded as being too emotional to handle money.[17] Only big, strong men could do that.

Today, in modern America, the wife-mother is responsible for over 80 percent of the family's consumer expenditures—almost a complete revolution from the pre-1920 era.[18]

It is not clear whether the American father abdicated from his throne or was the victim of a palace revolution, but when the shooting and shouting of the 1920's and the 1930's were all over the Little Woman had emerged as the power behind the throne, so to speak.

At this point we are not concerned with an evaluation of this transformation but are merely trying to understand what happened.

By the beginning of World War II the American mother had become the bad guy in our family system. As the executive and administrator of

---

[16] For a discussion of how business kicks worn-out executives upstairs, see Alfred P. Sloan, Jr., *My Years with General Motors* (New York: Doubleday & Co., 1964); also Peter F. Drucker, *Concept of the Corporation* (Boston: Beacon Press, 1946).

[17] For a good brief summary of the changing position of women in American society, see Margaret Mead and Frances Balgley Kaplan, *American Women* (New York: Charles Scribner's Sons, 1965), pp. 78–95.

[18] For a detailed analysis of the role of the wife-mother in the economics of the modern American family, see Robert O. Blood, Jr. and Donald M. Wolfe, *Husbands and Wives* (New York: The Free Press, 1960), chap. 4, "The Economic Function."

the family she assumed more and more responsibility, made more and more decisions, and aroused more and more hostility.

This change can be seen in the psychiatric literature from 1890 to 1960.[19] In the early days of psychoanalytic theory it was the strong, patriarchal father who was the bad guy in the family system of Europe, the system inherited by the United States. It was the father that children feared; he made the crucial decisions; he handed out punishment; he dispensed money. Any hostility that was available could readily be focused on the old man. One can see this pattern in the play about his own family written by Eugene O'Neill.[20] The mother is sweet, loving, and forgiving, while the father is stern and forbidding.

In modern American psychoanalytic literature the typical father is seen as a passive dependent type—not very strong and not very sure of himself.[21] On television he looks even worse—pathetic and confused.

It is difficult to hate the current American father; he merits your sympathy and understanding. It is the American mother who draws the hostility; she is the one who hands out money and says yes or no.

When any group of human beings in a society battles its way out of an inferior social position hostility is always generated. This can be seen clearly in the current struggle of the American blacks for equality; white backlash is very apparent. It appears that a considerable amount of male backlash against women is still to be seen in American society.[22] Some men take the position, "OK, they wanted to wear the pants, now let them see what it is like." It is difficult to determine how widespread such an attitude is among American men but it is certainly not rare.

The foregoing analysis leaves many questions unanswered—some of which will be taken up in the chapter on the American father—but it seems to us that something of this nature must have taken place to explain the venom and the popularity of books such as Strecker's and Wylie's.

How does one explain the attacks on American mothers by women such as Friedan and Rossi? In some ways they represent the type of person who looks back at a social revolution and is bitter because its

---

[19] One has only to compare Freud's analysis of the father in Victorian society with that of Ackerman to see the startling change in the position of fathers since the 19th century. See footnote 21 for the Ackerman reference.

[20] See Eugene O'Neill, Long Day's Journey into Night (New Haven: Yale University Press, 1956). Other interesting material on O'Neill's parents may be found in O'Neill, the biography by Arthur and Barbara Gelb (New York: Harper & Brothers, 1962).

[21] See, for example, the description of the American father in Nathan Ackerman, The Psychodynamics of Family Life (New York: Basic Books, 1958), pp. 177–181.

[22] For discussions of the American male see Myron Brenton, The American Male (New York: Coward-McCann, 1966); Elaine Kendall, The Upper Hand (Boston: Little, Brown & Co., 1965); also Charles W. Ferguson, The Male Attitude (Boston: Little, Brown & Co., 1966).

basic goals were not achieved. Friedan and Rossi are *disenchanted* with the present plight of American women; they fought for their freedom, won it, and then didn't know what to do with it.

It is interesting to note that E. Franklin Frazier has accused the new American black middle class of the same error. They have won social equality, says Frazier, and all they can do with it is play bridge and drink martinis.[23]

It is quite possible that American mothers have achieved more equality than they really wanted. It seems clear that what was originally intended to be a 50-50 partnership in parenthood has turned out to be closer to 70-30 or even 80-20, with the American father having all the fun with the children and the mother all of the headaches.[24]

It seems clear that urbanization is related to many of the basic changes in the modern American family and it undoubtedly played a part in the shift of power from the American father to the American mother. Although theoretically the urban father had more time to spend with his children than the farm father had—because of the eight-hour day and the five-day week—the fact remains that the urban father's job was *away* from the home while the farmer's was not.

In the early days of the move to the city, before metropolitan areas became so dominant, city fathers could often go home for lunch, but this pattern rapidly disappeared as cities became larger.

It is our hypothesis that the assumption of power by the American mother took place between 1920 and 1940, an era that produced feminine equality but had not yet drawn women into jobs and the myriad of community roles they sustain today. This was actually the heyday of the full-time mother that Rossi writes about—a woman who no longer had a farm to distract her and had not yet gone to work in large numbers outside of the home. With her husband away at work all day, this mother had ample time and opportunity to pervade the lives of her children.[25] A portrait of such a family of the 1920's is presented at the end of this chapter.

It is our belief that this picture no longer fits the American mother— either she works outside of the home, engages in community activities, or serves as companion to her husband when he wants her to. In any event, she lives a rather busy, hectic life. One might say that the doting mother in American society has been replaced by the distraught mother.

Other socioeconomic changes were also involved in this shift of power. A woman who had as much education as her husband and had won legal and political equality was no longer content to be a second-class parent

---

23 E. Franklin Frazier, *Black Bourgeoisie* (New York: The Free Press, 1957).

24 The writer feels that his position in the family is much more that of the good guy than was true of his father.

25 A more extensive analysis of the impact of urbanization on parents will be presented in chap. 11, "Parents and Social Change."

at home. She wanted as much to say about money and children as her husband. If she held an outside job, not common for mothers in the 1920's or the 1930's, this was another reason for demanding equality in the home. And as the divorce rate increased, mothers increasingly served as both mother and father.

In so far as there ever was a possessive or smothering type of American mother, the lower birthrate of the 1920's and the 1930's might have been a factor—as families become smaller each child becomes statistically more precious.

The economic catastrophe of the 1930's, blandly referred to as the depression, apparently reduced the prestige and power of the American father, judging by the research of Cavan and others.[26] This, then, must have strengthened the position of the mother. Even in recent years the charge has been made that the nationwide ADC child welfare program has favored mothers over fathers in low-income families.[27]

The last socioeconomic force to be cited here is *war*. During the several decades under discussion here America fought two world wars. Millions of husbands and fathers were away from their wives and families for periods of two to five years. It seems only logical (and necessary) that while the men were away the women took over and did things that had to be done, not only in the home but in the community and larger society also.[28] And when wars end, things never entirely return to their prewar state.

We have now completed our attempt, inadequate as it may be, to explain the reasons for the bitter attacks on the American mother. Next we turn to an examination of some of the evidence used in these attacks.

The nature of the data used in the attack

A considerable proportion of the data used to condemn the modern mother has been taken from the clinical files of psychiatrists and psychiatric clinics. Strecker, for example, a psychiatrist, used data collected on men discharged from the Army for psychiatric reasons during World War II.[29]

---

[26] The basic research on the impact of the depression on families will be found in: Ruth Shonle Cavan and Katherine Howland Ranck, *The Family and the Depression* (Chicago: The University of Chicago Press, 1938); Mirra Komarovsky, *The Unemployed Man and His Family* (New York: The Dryden Press, 1940); Robert C. Angell, *The Family Encounters the Depression* (New York: Charles Scribner's Sons, 1936).

[27] See Alvin Schorr, *Poor Kids* (New York: Basic Books, 1966); also his more recent study of public welfare policy and its impact on low-income families: *Explorations in Social Policy* (New York: Basic Books, 1968).

[28] For an excellent discussion as to how mothers take over male roles when their husbands are in the armed forces, see the research reported in Reuben Hill, *Families under Stress* (New York: Harper & Brothers, 1949).

[29] See Strecker, *op. cit.*

In the attack by Lundberg and Farnham, the data were drawn from the files of a woman psychiatrist in private practice.[30] In a chapter on the American woman as mother, with the title of "Mother and Child: The Slaughter of the Innocents," the following statement is made: "The spawning ground of most neurosis in western civilization is the home. The basis for it is laid in childhood, although it emerges strongly later, usually from late adolescence until middle age, provoked by circumstances and conditions encountered in life. And as we have pointed out, the principal agent in laying the groundwork for it is the mother."[31]

On the surface there is nothing wrong with using psychiatric case material in analyzing American society. But unless the person doing the analysis has had good research training, a number of dangerous pitfalls will seriously damage the value of the findings. Some of these are as follows.

1. *The sample.* It should be remembered that psychiatric case material is drawn from a very limited and biased sample. The general population that copes with its problems is automatically excluded from the clinic or private practice sample. Furthermore, such samples are heavily biased in their social class composition, as Hollingshead and Redlich have demonstrated.[32]

The crucial error committed by the users of psychiatric data is to generalize from the clinic or private practice population to the general population in the society. A classic example of this would be the Lundberg and Farnham volume cited earlier.

2. *The failure to use a control group.* In social science research design a control group serves to check on our findings. Are the variables used to explain the behavior actually responsible for the behavior? If the Strecker book, for example, had utilized proper research design, a sample of soldiers who were *not* discharged from the Army for psychiatric reasons would have been matched with the cases Strecker was using. In this way it might have been determined whether or not there was a significant difference in maternal patterns between the men who broke down psychologically in the Army and those who did not. Without such a control group we really don't know what factors produced the psychiatric casualties.[33]

This may not impress the reader untrained in research methodology but some amazing results have been obtained when psychiatric data has

---

[30] Lundberg and Farnham, *op. cit.* Lundberg is a professional writer. Farnham is a psychoanalyst.

[31] Lundberg and Farnham, *op. cit.*, p. 303.

[32] For an extensive discussion of social class bias in clinic and private practice case records, see August B. Hollingshead and Frederick C. Redlich, *Social Class and Mental Illness* (New York: John Wiley & Sons, 1958).

[33] On the use of control groups, see Claire Sellitz et al., *Research Methods in Social Relations* (New York: Henry Holt and Co., 1959 ed.), pp. 114–122.

been subjected to control group analysis. In a study of unmarried mothers, for example, Vincent matched a group of girls who were *not* unmarried mothers with a group who were, in order to test the findings of an earlier study that had concluded that the unmarried mothers had suffered from a maternal syndrome that was relatively abnormal or unique.[34] The analysis of the control group revealed that these so-called normal girls reported a relationship with their mothers that was not significantly different from that reported by the unmarried mothers.[35]

3. *Failure to seek for other explanations of the behavior.* If you are convinced that the American mother is what's wrong with our society, then you do not need to look for other possible explanations of the problems under consideration. It seems that most of the critics of the mother in our society are guilty of this error. They simply do not grant the fact that forces other than mothers influence children and that it is extremely difficult to rear a healthy child in a sick society. The American value system itself—hardly created by mothers—may be one of the major factors producing personality disorganization in the United States.[36] Our highly competitive economic system subjects youth and parents alike to great stress. Conflicts in our culture related to sexual ethics, racial relations, or science versus religion, probably have some relationship to schizophrenia, the most common psychosis in our society.[37] But except for writers such as Lerner, Riesman, Erikson, or Brim, one seldom sees these other factors considered by the critics of the American mother.[38] Brim was struck by this anomaly when he wrote his classic analysis of the family education movement in the United States. He writes: "As a social scientist, one is struck by the fact that parent education seems to operate as if the parent existed in a social vacuum."[39] One certainly has this impression reading the attacks on the American mother.

4. *Failure to look for contrary data.* A basic principle of scientific

---

[34] For a dramatic illustration of the value of good research controls see how Clark Vincent's analysis of the unmarried mother in our society differs from that of Leontine Young. The two studies are Clark Vincent, *Unmarried Mothers* (New York: The Free Press, 1961) and Leontine Young, *Out of Wedlock* (New York: McGraw-Hill Book Co., 1954).

[35] A striking example of the value of a well-designed control group will be found in *Girls at Vocational High* by Henry J. Meyer, Edgar F. Borgatta, and Wyatt C. Jones (New York: Russell Sage Foundation, 1965).

[36] See Karen Horney, *The Neurotic Personality of Our Time* (New York: W. W. Norton, 1937), for a discussion of the interaction of culture conflict and personality conflict.

[37] A famous analysis of culture conflicts in American society is that of Robert S. Lynd, *Knowledge for What?* (Princeton: Princeton University Press, 1948), pp. 60–63.

[38] Lerner, *op. cit.*; Davis Riesman et al., *The Lonely Crowd* (New Haven: Yale University Press, 1961 ed.); Orville G. Brim, Jr., *Education for Child Rearing* (New York: Russell Sage Foundation, 1959).

[39] Brim, *op. cit.*, p. 68.

method is that every effort should be made to identify and assess data that might contradict your tentative conclusions. Even a single case that does not fit the theory may require a totally new approach to the analysis. Such niceties of scientific method do not bother the critics of the American mother. They simply ignore data that might contradict conclusions they have already reached. This may make exciting reading but it is hardly science.

This concludes our analysis of the evidence used against the American mother. If we were on a jury trying this case we would have to vote "not guilty." Most of the indictment is based on circumstantial evidence that will not bear careful scrutiny, in our opinion.

We now turn to a role analysis of the American mother with the hope that this will give the reader insight into some of the dilemmas faced by mothers in our society.

Role analysis of the American mother

It is our thesis that one of the problems of the contemporary American mother is that she is "overcommitted." Far from being the full-time mother that Rossi writes about, the American woman has expanded almost all of her roles since the end of World War I. Some observers even claim that today's mother puts in longer hours than her grandmother did.[40] It is certainly true that she is trying to do more things than her grandmother ever did—with no more hours available in the week.

It is true, of course, that modern appliances have lightened the burden of house cleaning and laundry, but as one woman said: "That machine doesn't take the diapers off of the baby and rinse them out. Nor does it put the diapers away or put them back on the baby. The machine *only* *washes* them."

It is also true that prepared foods have been a great boon to the American mother. But to balance the picture we wish to show in the next few pages how the role commitments of today's mother in our society have been expanded.

1. The role of wife. Being a wife today is not the same as being a wife in 1900. In the area of sex alone, today's wife is supposed to be a sexual *companion* for her husband; she is not supposed to just submit to him as the Victorian wife did. She is supposed to share her husband's enthusiasm for sex. This is part of the total partnership that modern American marriage is dedicated to.

In many other ways her role as companion to her husband has been expanded—bowling, golf, fishing, hunting, smoking, drinking—the mod-

---

[40] We have been unable to trace the study reported in the general press that mothers today may be putting in more hours than their grandmothers.

ern wife's place is not "in the home" but out in the world with her husband.[41]

It is true that this "togetherness" pattern is not found at lower class levels, as Gans and others have pointed out, but in so far as America is becoming increasingly a white-collar society the ideal of husband-wife togetherness would seem to be spreading.[42]

To the extent that the modern American wife-mother commits herself to being a companion to her husband she has expanded her role as wife. This will be illustrated in the case study at the end of this chapter.

2. *The role of mother.* We argued in an earlier chapter that modern American parents are operating under higher standards.[43] Mothers today are expected to be informed about new medical findings, such as new vaccines, and to make sure that their children receive them; they are supposed to be alert to new community programs for children, such as those available at the YMCA or some other community service agency, and to get their children interested and enrolled. Schools, PTA, Girl Scouts, Boy Scouts, Little League baseball—all of these child-centered organizations expect (and even demand) more from today's mothers than ever before in our society.

It is true, of course, that today's mother will not be criticized by her neighbors or her family if she buys a child's birthday cake at the supermarket—she has an advantage here over the mothers of yesterday. But it seems that she has paid dearly in time and serenity for such conveniences.

3. *Expansion of the home management role.* In taking over the family budget and the job of purchasing agent, the American mother got herself into more work than she bargained for. The writer's mother had her groceries delivered to her home daily, but today's woman has to go to the supermarket and bring the family groceries home herself. And if she wishes to shop economically she has to visit more than one store to take advantage of specials.

Mothers today shop for the men in the family as well as for their daughters and themselves.

It is not uncommon today to see an American mother mowing the lawn with the power mower, and even painting the house. But in an earlier America, at least in the cities, this was man's work.

---

41 It is recognized by the writer that lower income males do not usually subscribe to the cult of "togetherness." For an extensive discussion of working-class family subculture see Herbert Gans, *The Urban Villagers* (New York: The Free Press, 1962); also Mirra Komarovsky, *Blue-Collar Marriage* (New York: Random House, 1964).

42 For other studies of lower class family life see Lee Rainwater, *And the Poor Get Children* (Chicago: Quadrangle Books, 1960); also Elliot Liebow, *Tally's Corner* (Boston: Little, Brown & Co., 1967).

43 See chap. 4.

4. Expansion of the community role. In an interesting book called *The Gentle Legions,* Carter[44] has described the massive effort of American wives and mothers to raise funds for the voluntary health organizations. These efforts have often been lampooned by comedians but as Carter says, the triumph over polio was no joke.[45] The $160 million raised for these health organizations by American women is no joke either.[46]

Hill, of the Family Study Center at the University of Minnesota, points out that the American mother has taken on the "community liaison" role in our family system.[47] She is the major line of communication and contact with the schools, the welfare agencies, the youth organizations, the church, and the various health services.

This community role of the American mother is often taken lightly by her critics, but as one minister said: "Without the mothers this community would collapse." He may have been thinking of his own church but we feel that he had a point.

5. Expansion of her breadwinner role. Many critics of the American mother seem to forget that for the past several decades she has increasingly held an outside job while rearing her children. Nye and Hoffman, in their analysis of this revolution in our society, make this statement: "Few, if any, single changes in family life have as profoundly affected so many families in so few years as the movement of mothers into paid employment. Since 1940 there has been an estimated net increase of 10 million mothers in the labor force."[48] By 1955, according to Nye and Hoffman, over one third of mothers *with school-age children* were employed outside of the home.[49]

It is interesting to note that as of 1900 only one wife in 20 was in the labor force, but by 1950 the ratio was one out of five.[50] One has the impression that some of the critics who accuse American mothers of smothering their children have not read the U.S. labor statistics reports for several decades.

In view of the expansion of the contemporary American mother's basic roles we find it difficult to accept Rossi's description of these women as full-time mothers. This may have been partially true of the 1920's or the

---

[44] Richard Carter, *The Gentle Legions* (New York: Doubleday & Co., 1961).

[45] *Ibid.,* chap. 4, "The Polio Triumph."

[46] *Ibid.,* p. 21.

[47] "Sociological Frameworks for Family Study," paper presented by Reuben Hill of the University of Minnesota at a meeting sponsored by the Department of Psychiatry, School of Medicine, University of Wisconsin, December, 1967.

[48] Nye and Hoffman, *op. cit.,* p. 3.

[49] *Ibid.,* p. 6.

[50] U.S. Census Bureau News Release, *Wisconsin State Journal,* Madison, Wisc., August 29, 1968, Sect. 2, p. 14.

1930's, but beginning with 1940 the American wife-mother got herself involved in quite a rat race. And she is still running, it seems to us.

We now turn to a brief defense of the American mother.

In defense of the American mother

We believe that a good defense can be presented for the contemporary American mother. Some of that defense has been or will be discussed in detail in other chapters and need not be considered at length here.[51]

In our opinion the record of the American mother in recent decades needs to be judged against the following background.

1. The depression of the 1930's. America has seldom experienced a catastrophe more devastating to individuals and families than the economic disaster of the 1930's.[52] In a society dedicated to making and spending money, few things are more disturbing than unemployment. The studies of Cavan, Komarovsky, and Angell, cited earlier in this chapter, reveal some of the demoralizing effects of the depression on family life.

The magnitude of the depression is often forgotten—15 to 20 million people were unemployed at one time or another in the 1930's.

The writer was a social worker visiting families on relief during the period 1934 to 1936. In this capacity we had the opportunity to enter homes and interview hundreds of families suffering from unemployment. It was perfectly obvious to anyone but those unwilling to look or listen that the lives of these men, women, and children were being twisted out of shape by years of unemployment and economic deprivation.

Some of these children were the ones that Strecker found discharged from the Army for psychiatric reasons a decade later. Is it any wonder? Who was so naive as to think that a social disaster such as the depression would not exact its toll in human lives?

The writer saw firsthand the heroic efforts being made by mothers in the 1930's to hold their families together. But one seldom reads about these mothers; as a rule we hear about those that failed.

Parents do not operate in a social vacuum—they function in a world of reality. And when that world is as sick as it was in the United States in the 1930's, only the exceptional father or mother can function effectively. The critics of American parents would do well to remember this.

2. The increase in marital instability. America no longer has one marriage system, lifetime monogamy, but two: serial monogamy now

---

[51] In the sense that this book takes into account the conditions under which American parents operate, every chapter contains some defense of their record.

[52] A good source book on the depression of the 1930's is *The Great Depression*, edited by David A. Shannon (Englewood Cliffs, N.J.: Prentice-Hall, Inc., 1960).

involves at least one fourth of our married couples.[53] If one adds desertion, separation, and the chronically unhappy married couples to the divorce rate, the total marital failure rate exceeds one fourth.[54] Simon reports that 15 million Americans have now been divorced.[55]

No one questions that divorce and other forms of marital failure pose excruciating problems for parents.[56] Even though parents know that their children may be better off psychologically after the divorce, they often hesitate to separate because of their concern for their children.[57] In doing this they often damage themselves as adults.

In about 95 percent of the cases, it is the American mother who retains custody of the children after a marital failure and it is she who has to help the children through this crisis.[58]

In about 10 percent of American homes there is no father present.[59] This type of mother will be considered in a separate chapter, so it is only necessary to point out here that this woman is usually serving as *both* mother and father.

In some low-income groups, and among some minority groups, as many as 60 percent of the homes may have no father present.[60]

Simon points out there are seven million stepchildren in the United States—one child out of every nine has a stepparent.[61] The role of stepparent has historically been viewed as an unenviable job, and especially so for stepmothers.

The high rate of marital failure in the United States since the end of World War I has complicated the role of the mother in our society no end.

---

[53] The best empirical study of divorce to date in our society is that by William J. Goode, *After Divorce* (New York: The Free Press, 1956). Even this study, however, is marred by the fact that no husbands were interviewed. For a careful statistical analysis of divorce, see Paul H. Jacobson, *American Marriage and Divorce* (New York: Rinehart & Co., 1959).

[54] Marriages that have failed by any reasonable standards but have not been terminated are analyzed in a paper by the writer. See E. E. LeMasters, "Holy Deadlock: A Study of Unsuccessful Marriages," *Sociological Quarterly*, 21 (1959), pp. 86–91.

[55] Anne W. Simon, *Stepchild in the Family* (New York: Odyssey Press, 1964). These statistics are reviewed in chap. 4, "It's a New World," pp. 50–68.

[56] In addition to the studies of Goode and Simon, see also Morton M. Hunt, *The World of the Formerly Married* (New York: McGraw-Hill Book Co., 1966). A good history of divorce in America is that of William L. O'Neill, *Divorce in the Progressive Era* (New Haven: Yale University Press, 1967).

[57] Goode's divorced women felt that their children were better off emotionally after the divorce. See Goode, *op. cit.*, chap. 21, "The Children of Divorce."

[58] Hunt, *op. cit.*, pp. 260–261, has a discussion of parents after divorce.

[59] For a discussion of the American families with a female head see Alvin Schorr, *Poor Kids*, pp. 20–22.

[60] See the *U.S. Riot Commission Report* (New York: Bantam Books, 1968), chap. 7, "Unemployment, Family Structure, and Social Disorganization."

[61] See Simon, *op. cit.*, chap. 5, "The Child's World Changes," pp. 69–83.

3. The failure of the American father. Most of the data on personal disorganization indicates that the American male has a higher rate than the American female.[62] If one looks at data on crime, alcoholism, drug addiction, desertion, and so on, the male rates are significantly higher than those for the female. In reviewing the record of the two sexes, Montagu has concluded that females are superior to males at the human level.[63] While material of this nature is subject to various interpretations, the fact remains that men in modern America pose more problems for public authorities than women do.

One can argue that this male-female differential in social adjustment reflects dysfunctional child rearing methods, as the psychiatrists do; that it reflects genetic differences between the two sexes, as the ethologists do; or that it reflects greater cultural strain on the male, as sociologists usually do.[64]

More will be said about the American father in a separate chapter, but it does seem clear that he has failed quite often as a parent in our society in recent decades.[65]

4. The feminine revolution in the United States. In the preceding role analysis of the American mother an attempt was made to illustrate the expanded function of women in our society. We only wish to state here that American women have been involved in a social revolution since World War I and that this has inevitably complicated their parental role.[66] Once this revolution has been completed—and this may soon be the case—the maternal role in the United States should be less difficult.

5. The record of American mothers in recent decades is itself open to debate. The critics of the American mother would have us believe that we *lost* World War II. The fact is that most Americans performed well during the war and that the nation since then has gone on to become one of the most powerful in the history of the human race. It is recognized that the United States has innumerable domestic and international problems, but to say that American parents are failing to produce competent

---

[62] On social disorganization rates for men, see *Alcoholism in America* by Harrison M. Trice (New York: McGraw-Hill Book Co., 1966); also various chapters in Marshall B. Clinard, *Sociology of Deviant Behavior* (New York: Rinehart & Co., 1968 ed.).

[63] Ashley Montagu, *The Natural Superiority of Women* (New York: The Macmillan Co., 1968 ed.).

[64] Some of the psychiatric literature on this has been cited in this chapter. For the ethologists see Desmond Morris, *The Naked Ape* (New York: McGraw-Hill Book Co., 1967); also Robert Ardrey, *The Territorial Imperative* (New York: Atheneum Press, 1966); also Konrad Lorenz, *On Aggression* (New York: Harcourt, Brace & World, 1963).

[65] On the male in our society see footnote 22 of this chapter.

[66] On the emancipation of women in our society see Oscar Handlin, *The Americans* (Boston: Little, Brown & Co., 1963), pp. 362–367.

adults is to ignore the accomplishments of this society in the past few decades.

6. *Miscellaneous observations in defense of the American mother.* In the Strecker and Wylie books the major criticism of the American mother concerns her rearing of her sons. It is an interesting fact that upper class families in the United States, also in England, have never trusted mothers to rear sons—these have been sent away to boarding schools to be disciplined by stern male teachers and headmasters.[67] This may represent sound thinking, but most American mothers have had no choice in the matter; they have had to rear their sons for better or worse.

In many of the criticisms of the mother in our society it is implied that she is too easy on her children—that she smothers them with attention and caters to their every whim. But what about the traditional Jewish mother? She is usually represented as sentimental and gratifying, yet Jewish children in the United States have compiled an enviable record.[68]

The Italian mother resembles the Jewish mother in many respects and yet her children also seem to have done reasonably well in the relatively short time they have been in this country.[69]

This ends our rather brief defense of the American mother. We will close this chapter with a case study that illustrates many of the trends and many of the issues touched upon in this chapter.

Case study of an American mother

The writer grew up in the 1920's in an old-fashioned family that represented the Victorian model: the mother was in a subordinate position, not only in the family itself but also in the larger society, while the father played the role of the benevolent despot.[70]

---

[67] For descriptions of how English upper class boys are sent away to boarding schools see the autobiography of Harold Macmillan, *Winds of Change* (New York: Harper & Row, 1966); also *Winston S. Churchill* by Randolph S. Churchill (New York: Houghton Mifflin Co., 1966). This first volume deals with the childhood of Winston Churchill. For an account of how Franklin D. Roosevelt was saved from a doting mother see the account of his years at Groton in John Gunther, *Roosevelt in Retrospect* (New York: Harper & Brothers, 1950).

[68] On the Jewish mother see Martha Wolfenstein, "Two Types of Jewish Mothers," in *The Jews: Social Patterns of an American Group*, edited by M. Sklare (New York: The Free Press, 1958).

[69] On the Italian mom see Irving R. Levine, *Main Street, Italy* (New York: Doubleday & Co., 1963), p. 24. Levine, a foreign correspondent for one of the national television networks in the United States who is stationed in Rome, claims that no mothers anywhere spoil their sons as do the Italian mothers; for another treatment of the Italian mother, this one by an Italian, see Luigi Barzini, *The Italians* (New York: Atheneum Press, 1964), especially chap. 11, "The Power of the Family."

[70] This case study is taken from an unpublished book about this family by the writer. The locale is midwestern.

Both of the parents had grown up in rural America, the father on a farm and the mother in a rural village of about 400 population. This village had no industry. It was strictly a service station for the surrounding rural area.

The young couple were married in 1903, the husband being 21 years old and the bride 17. Neither had gone to school for more than three years.

After marriage the young husband operated a small farm for a few years on a rental basis. Not finding this very profitable he tried coal mining. When the mine workers went out on strike he found a job as a clerk in a grocery store at $12 a week.

By 1911, when the writer was born, there were four children in this family—three sons and a daughter. By this time the couple had joined the nationwide move to the city and were settled in a small city of about 12,000 population. The husband was now beginning what was to be a successful career as a salesman for wholesale candy and grocery firms.

In this family model from the 1900 era, there was never any doubt as to who was the head of the family. The husband-father earned the money, kept it in his wallet in cash, and doled it out to the mother and children as he saw fit. Except for purchasing groceries and meat, the wife-mother was never permitted to handle money. It was firmly believed in this family model that women were "too emotional" to manage money.

The usual line of communication in this family in matters concerning children was through the mother to the father and back the same route. "I have talked to your father and he says that we cannot afford a pair of roller skates this month. He will try to get them next month if possible."

Whatever influence or power the wife-mother had in this family model depended on how well she manipulated the husband-father. On the surface she had no power whatsoever. But unofficially she did influence decisions made by the husband and on some issues she prevailed.

In this particular marriage the husband was the stronger person and this buttressed his official position as head of the family. But in other families of that era known to the writer the wife was the stronger person and usually managed to dominate the family.

This mother never worked outside of the home after her marriage.[71] She had no great earning power and would have found it difficult to earn a living if she had ever left her husband—which she threatened to do periodically. Thus she was economically dependent on her husband.

When women were given the right to vote after World War I this woman refused to vote for several years. She once said that she felt men were better suited for politics than women. Later on she did vote, at her husband's request, in the great Republican drive which defeated

---

[71] In this generation the husband would have felt humiliated if his wife had had to help support the family. None of the sons has ever felt this way.

Al Smith in 1928. In the earlier 1920's, when the Republicans were sure of victory, her husband had not asked her to vote and she had not voted.

This wife-mother never drove an automobile, never smoked a cigarette, never had her hair bobbed, and never wrote a check. She had no community role—no PTA, no March of Dimes campaign to collect for, no Boy Scouts, or Girl Scouts. At various times she belonged to a church but even this membership was intermittent. She never held any office in her church and never belonged to any other organization in the community.

This woman represents what Rossi termed the full-time mother in the paper cited earlier in this chapter. She literally devoted all of her time to her children, her house, and her husband (and in about that order of priority). Compared to this woman the modern American mother is just a part-time mother.

It is interesting to see the decline in birthrates in this family as it moved from rural America to urban America, and as it moved up into the middle class.

Person	Number of Children
Maternal grandparents	14
Paternal grandparents	7
Father and mother	4
Oldest son	4
Daughter	2
Second son	2
Third son	2

In this case study we are trying to show the deep social revolution that mothers in America have gone through since 1900. In this family the Victorian family model came to an end with the parents' generation. The daughter in this family refused to accept a social position inferior to men and battled with the father all through the 1920's for the right to be a modern woman. She finally demanded and won the right to go to college (her father did not feel that girls needed that much education), the right to smoke, the right to have her hair cut short, the right to work in an office with men, the right to drive a car, and the right to have her own checking account.[72] And the first time the father tried to instruct his daughter whom to vote for she told him: "I'm just as smart as any man and you don't have to tell me whom to vote for." The feminine revolution was now complete in this house.

---

[72] It is interesting to note that this modern woman quit smoking once the father had conceded her right to smoke.

When she married in 1927 this daughter and her future husband had an understanding that theirs was to be a "modern marriage"—by this they meant a partnership with equal rights for husband and wife. Today, 40 years later, this daughter still feels the same way about equal rights for women.

It is an interesting fact that all of the three sons in this family married what might be called modern women—women who held outside jobs at various times, belonged to community organizations, drove cars, had their own checking accounts, smoked cigarettes if they felt like it, and took a drink if they wanted to. None of these women were willing to accept an inferior position in their households.

In this family, then, the Victorian mother and her world came to an end with the parents' generation. In some American families the feminine revolution came before the 1920's, and probably for some others it did not come until the 1930's or even the 1940's.[73] But by the end of World War II the American woman was a new person and American mothers must be viewed with this in mind.

Summary and conclusion

In this chapter we have considered some of the attacks on the American mother in recent decades. It has been our position that the evidence to support these attacks is dubious. The heavy sale of some of these books, however, makes one think that the new American mother, with her more powerful position in the family, has generated considerable hostility.

One of the hypotheses advanced in the chapter was that the American mother is really "overloaded" in her role commitments: she has taken on more jobs than she can handle. This increased responsibility poses even greater problems when her marriage is unstable—a problem we consider in a separate chapter.[74]

In the next chapter we will consider the American father.

---

[73] The feminine revolution came later for some of the immigrant groups who arrived in this country relatively late, such as the Italians. See Oscar Handlin (ed.), *Children of the Uprooted* (New York: George Braziller, 1966).

[74] See chap. 9.

The American
father

The neglect of the American father in family research

T HERE have been numerous best sellers written about American
women[1] but one has to look carefully to find the literature on the
American male, especially in his role as husband and/or father.[2] It is true
that novelists such as Ernest Hemingway, Norman Mailer, and others
have written extensively about what it is to be a man (or to fail to be a
man) but many of these works of literature focus on men in combat—not
family combat but military combat.[3]

Most of the behavioral and social scientists have simply ignored husbands and fathers in their empirical studies as we shall demonstrate later
in this chapter. One outstanding exception was the work of the late
Kinsey who scored his greatest publishing success with his first volume

---

[1] See chap. 7 for a review of this literature.

[2] In looking for books on the American male the writer came up with the following: Elaine Kendall, The Upper Hand (Boston: Little, Brown & Co., 1965); Myron
Brenton, The American Male (New York: Coward-McCann, 1966); Charles W.
Ferguson, The Male Attitude (Boston: Little, Brown, & Co., 1966); and Margaret
Mead, Male and Female (New York: William Morrow & Co., 1949). The Kendall
book is basically satirical but very insightful; the Brenton book is a survey of the
current "male crisis"; the Ferguson book is scholarly but historical; the Mead study
is cross-cultural. When this volume was nearly completed an excellent survey of the
literature on fathers appeared: Leonard Benson, Fatherhood: A Sociological Perspective (New York: Random House, 1968).

[3] The most widely read novel about World War I and its impact on men was
Ernest Hemingway's A Farewell to Arms (New York: Charles Scribner's Sons, 1929);
one of the most powerful novels of World War II and its horrible toll of human lives
and spirit was Norman Mailer's The Naked and the Dead (New York: Holt, Rinehart,
and Winston, 1948).

on the American male.[4] Another notable exception to this curtain of silence about males in the family can be found in the work of Pollak in his research on child guidance clinics and their treatment programs.[5]

This tendency to take the American male for granted is graphically illustrated in the work of Vincent on unmarried mothers: he found the ratio of studies on the girls as compared with the boys was 25 to 1.[6] In other words, there is considerable literature on unmarried mothers but hardly anything is known about unmarried fathers. This is understandable but hardly in the public interest. Unmarried mothers, after all, do not reproduce by budding; there has to be a partner to conceive (with perhaps one notable exception in Western history) and any well-organized attempt to control parenthood out of wedlock will have to take the unmarried father into account. As of now, however, practically nothing is known about him.

The writer has been amazed at the cavalier attitude researchers in the United States have taken toward the American husband-father. For example: in a famous study of 379 mothers a statement is made in the Foreword that the basic aim of the research was "to secure reliable information about the varieties of experience that many American children have had in their homes—with their parents—by the time they go to school."[7] Note the use of the word *parents* (not mothers), yet not a single father was interviewed in this elaborate research effort.

The subtitle of the report on this project is "A Report on Ways of Bringing Up Children," which might lead one to think that fathers had been consulted somewhere along the line. This is erroneous. The fathers' versions of child rearing were obtained through the mothers. As a father the writer would deny the validity of any attempt to get his version of parenthood from his wife, yet this has been standard practice in research on the American family.

In this same monograph this flat statement is made: "Since it was not feasible to interview the fathers, all the information we gained about their

---

[4] See Alfred Kinsey et al., *Sexual Behavior in the Human Male* (Philadelphia: W. B. Saunders Co., 1948). This large and technical work sold over 800,000 copies in the original edition.

[5] See Otto Pollak, *Integrating Sociological and Psychoanalytic Concepts* (New York: Russell Sage Foundation, 1956); also *Social Science and Psychotherapy for Children* (New York: Russell Sage Foundation, 1952). Pollak's point is that most of the child guidance clinic records examined by him more or less ignore the father of the child.

[6] Clark Vincent, *Unmarried Mothers* (New York: The Free Press, 1961), p. 3. In the writer's opinion this is the best study of unmarried mothers yet published.

[7] Robert R. Sears et al., *Patterns of Child Rearing* (Evanston, Ill.: Row, Peterson and Co., 1957), Foreword, p. vi.

It is interesting to note that in 1,140 pages, there are only five specific references to fathers in the *Handbook of Socialization Theory and Research* edited by David A. Goslin (Chicago: Rand McNally & Co., 1969).

child-rearing attitudes and practices we obtained from the mothers."[8] One immediately thinks that it was simply too difficult to visit homes when fathers might be available for interviews but this seems not to have been the real reason for their exclusion. In the Foreword this statement is made: "We wish to express warm thanks to our interviewers. They carried heavy recording equipment through icy streets, made evening calls when the mothers' busy schedules did not permit daytime interviews, and entered with tact and sympathy into a mutual exploration with the mothers of matters that were not always easy to talk about."[9]

Such dedication to science is to be appreciated but one finds it hard to believe that such intrepid field interviewers would not also have brought back some data on what fathers think of child rearing if anybody had considered it important enough to include fathers in the sample. Offhand one might think that instead of using 379 mothers, perhaps a better approach would have been to split the sample into male and female groups. It is hard to escape the conclusion that these researchers were guilty of what Pollak says child guidance clinics have been guilty of: they don't think fathers are very important.[10] They will go to any lengths to talk with mothers but fathers are considered to be not accessible.

In the Sears study there is not even an elaborate defense of the exclusion of fathers from the sample, yet other features of the sample are discussed at some length. The writer can only say that in his opinion *any* study of parents that excludes half of the parents (the fathers) has a poor sample no matter how carefully the mothers in the study group were selected.

In another famous study of parents, probably the most elaborate published in recent years, there were 582 interviews with mothers but not one interview with a father.[11] The published report, however, is titled *The Changing American Parent*. And in the report itself the word *parent* seems to be equated with *mother* most of the time. These behavioral scientists, both well known and both well qualified, go to elaborate lengths to describe how mothers were selected for the sample, but no elaborate defense of the exclusion of fathers is deemed to be necessary.

In what is probably the best empirical study of divorce we have in the United States, Goode and his staff went to endless trouble to locate and interview a representative sample of 425 divorced mothers in Detroit, but not one divorced father was included in the sampling design.[12]

---

8 Sears, *op. cit.*, pp. 18–19.

9 *Ibid.*, Foreword, p. vii.

10 Pollak makes this point several times in the two studies cited previously.

11 Daniel R. Miller and Guy E. Swanson, *The Changing American Parent* (New York: John Wiley & Sons, 1958), pp. 65–66.

12 William J. Goode, *After Divorce* (New York: *The Free Press*, 1956). See chap. 2 for a description of the sample. While Goode's study was not focused primarily on the parent role, this was part of the research design (see chap. 21).

In three studies of American parents published since World War II, those by Sears and his associates, Miller and Swanson, and Goode, a total of 1,386 American mothers were studied in detail, but not one father was interviewed in any of these major research projects.[13] It appears that "the American father" has replaced "the American Indian" as the forgotten man.

At some point one has to ask the question: are fathers that easily disposed of in studying American parents? Freud certainly wrote at length about the father's role in child rearing, and child welfare agencies historically in our society have considered fathers so important that they have refused to place children for adoption with women who didn't have a husband, regardless of the ability of the women seeking to adopt a child.[14]

There is one study which supports those of us who do not think that parenthood can be studied properly without including fathers—that is the study of parents in a Toronto suburb published in a book called *Crestwood Heights*.[15] This piece of research included fathers in the research design and concluded that fathers and mothers in this upper middle-class suburb have some very different ideas about child rearing and parental roles. For one thing the mothers have been exposed to a great deal of human development material and psychiatric theory via the women's magazines, child study groups, PTA lectures, and so on. Not only have the fathers not been a full partner in this educational process but have often been opposed to it. Many of them apparently feel that their wives are too permissive with the children and are spoiling them. The fathers often feel that their sons in particular are not being readied for the competition and strife of upper middle-class life in the marketplace.[16]

It is clear that upper class English men have always felt this way about the education of their sons and have packed them off at an early age to a Spartan boarding school run by men, thus taking the sons away from

[13] Another study of American families and of the parental role interviewed 909 wife-mothers but no husband-fathers. See Robert O. Blood, Jr. and Donald M. Wolfe, *Husbands and Wives* (New York: The Free Press, 1960). If this study is added to the three above we find that 2,295 wife-mothers were interviewed and not one husband-father. The writer finds this approach to sampling unacceptable.

[14] See Alfred Kadushin, *Child Welfare Services* (New York: The Macmillan Co., 1967), chap. 10.

[15] John R. Seeley et al., *Crestwood Heights* (New York: Basic Books, 1956).
On the importance of interviewing husbands, see David Heer, "Measurement and Basis of Family Power: An Overview," *Marriage and Family Living*, 25 (1963), 133–139.

[16] See Seeley et al., *op. cit.*, pp. 193–194. "For such a man, the child-rearing theories which his wife espouses may seem arrant nonsense; and the male experts from whom she derives her information frequently appear to him, unless they are doctors, as inadequate men who have 'not been able to make the grade in the *really* masculine world.'"

not only their mothers but *all* women during most of their developmental years.[17]

For those of us who have done family and/or marriage counseling it seems obvious that fathers and mothers very often disagree about ways of rearing children—in fact this may be more common than sex in marital disputes and conflicts.

It is still possible, of course, that one can accept the point of view that fathers are important in the child rearing process but that one can learn all one needs to know about them through their wives. We doubt this very much. So does Pollak. So do the people who did the research in Crestwood Heights. We are also convinced that fathers and mothers would very often have to be interviewed separately to obtain valid reports on their parental experience. It is easy to gloss over male and female differences in the glow of a joint interview with parents, but this often does not reveal the differences that lie beneath the surface of domestic tranquility.

Another reason why the writer believes that fathers need to be interviewed in studies of American parents lies in his conviction that there are substantial male and female subcultures in the American way of life and that these extend into the arena of child rearing.[18] It is known from empirical data that men and women differ in religious behavior in our society, in their sexual patterns, in their use of money, their use of alcohol, their political behavior, their willingness to desert children, and so forth.[19] On what basis can we assume that fathers and mothers do *not* differ on child rearing and parental roles?

Since mothers are much closer to children in our society than fathers are, it seems quite likely that they would view child rearing from a different point of view and that this could not always be obtained by interviewing the mother.

In a study of family life education which has become a classic, Brim found that the vast majority of such programs focused on mothers almost exclusively. He writes:

The failure of almost all parent education programs to assess the social setting into which they introduce their educational materials, the failure to recognize that the mothers who are primarily involved in such programs have husbands,

---

[17] The news media in recent years have consistently reported the various Spartan schools to which the current Prince of Wales has been sent. See the study by Geoffrey Wakeford, *The Heir Apparent* (New York: A. S. Barnes & Co., 1967).

[18] For a good discussion of sexual subcultures see Jessie Bernard, *The Sex Game* (Englewood Cliffs, N.J.: Prentice-Hall, Inc., 1968); also E. E. LeMasters, *Modern Courtship and Marriage* (New York: The Macmillan Co., 1957), chaps. 22 and 23.

[19] These data are reviewed in LeMasters, *op. cit.* See also Ashley Montagu, *The Natural Superiority of Women* (New York: The Macmillan Co., 1968 ed.).

parents, and neighbors with whom they must deal, is lamentable, since it is recognized that in many instances the net result of introducing change on the part of one member into the family system is to produce friction, resentment, and hostility between husband and wife, which in turn is probably detrimental to the child.[20]

This is the view of Pollak also. And it is the belief of this writer that the approach to parents must not only be broadened at the point of family life education or treatment but also at the point of research design. For the most part this has not been the case in America in recent decades.

Role analysis of the father in modern America

1. The parental role is a peripheral role for the American male. For the American mother the role of parent probably takes precedence over all other adult roles. For some women this may not be the case as they may choose to give priority to their role as wife or to an occupational role, but these women would seem to be in the minority in our child-centered society. Mrs. John F. Kennedy has been quoted as saying: "If you fail with your children, then I don't think anything else matters very much."[21]

For the American father the situation is quite different. Two roles in particular—that of his job and that of military service—almost always have to be given priority over his role as parent. Since 1940 between 15 and 20 million men in our society have had to go to the corners of the earth to discharge their military obligations, and the fact that they might be fathers does not entitle them to automatic deferment.

Nobody knows how many millions of American fathers have had their family lives disrupted by the long arm of the job but the total must be astronomical. In an unpublished study of blue-collar construction workers the writer was impressed by the frequency with which these men had to work out of town to maintain steady employment.[22] Almost all of these men agreed that such jobs posed real problems for them and their families.

When a man is transferred in our society, he often moves to the new community months before his family is able to join him. During this period his wife has to assume some responsibility with the children that normally would belong to the husband. Then, when the family is reunited, roles have to be redistributed again and lines of authority reestablished. In one research project during World War II Hill discovered

---

[20] Orville G. Brim, Jr., *Education for Child Rearing* (New York: Russell Sage Foundation, 1959), p. 70.

[21] See Theodore C. Sorensen, *Kennedy* (New York: Harper & Row, 1965), p. 381.

[22] This is an unpublished study of a tavern frequented by blue-collar construction workers.

that it was not always easy to "pick up where they left off" when the father returned from the armed forces.[23]

It seems to us that this peripheral nature of the parental role is often overlooked by critics of the American father. They judge him as if children were the center of his life in the way they are for American mothers. In our judgment this is not only unfair to the fathers but also unrealistic.

2. *There is no biological base or imprinting for the father role at the human level as there is for the mother.* In a famous book Davis puts this point as follows: "The weak link in the family group is the father-child bond. There is no necessary association and no easy means of identification between these two as there is between mother and child."[24] He goes on to point out that almost all human societies have evolved complex social devices for binding the father to his children.

Mead is making this same point when she says that the role of father at the human level is a "social invention"—strictly speaking, he could be dispensed with once conception had taken place.[25] Most societies have chosen not to let the male escape so easily, but to tie him to the child has required elaborate cultural arrangements, whereas these are not usually necessary for the mother.

All of this means that fathers in our society (or any other society) are almost entirely dependent on proper socialization and positive induction into the role of parent if they are to perform this responsibility adequately. This sets up the possibility that the father-child bond will not be as dependable as the mother-child bond. This certainly seems to be the case in our society.

3. *The human father is a mammal.* Among other things man is a mammal—and in the entire mammalian series there are only two fathers who assume major responsibility for their offspring. Most male mammals are present for the fertilization and are seldom seen after that. The wolf, oddly enough, is one of the exceptions, often helping to feed the young and baby-sitting with them while the mother is away from the den.[26]

Compared to other mammalian fathers the human father is a paragon of virtue. But he is still a mammal and some American fathers appear to function pretty much at that level. These are, however, only a small minority.

4. *The human father is also a primate.* In the literature on the monkeys and the great apes it appears that the father's role after procreation

---

[23] Reuben Hill, *Families Under Stress* (New York: Harper & Brothers, 1949).

[24] Kingsley Davis, *Human Society* (New York: The Macmillan Co., 1949), p. 400.

[25] Mead, *op. cit.*

[26] See Desmond Morris, *The Naked Ape* (New York: McGraw-Hill Book Co., 1967). On the wolf see Farley Mowat, *Never Cry Wolf* (Boston: Little, Brown & Co., 1963).

is to protect the female (or females) and their offspring, but with only one exception, already mentioned, does he ever assume any major responsibility for their daily care.[27] Here, again, the average human father makes the other primate fathers look bad.

5. *The father's parental role in the United States is peculiarly tied to the success or failure of the pair-bond between himself and his wife.* In a great many human societies a father can still be a good father even if his marriage leaves much to be desired: mistresses or women of some category other than wife are made available to him and he can still reside in his home and live with his wife and children.[28] This is usually not the case in our society. In modern America men are expected to be faithful to their wives or else leave the home and marry the other woman.

All of this means that if anything happens to the marriage of the American male he may find himself separated from his children and partially cut off from them—and this may happen in spite of his honest desires to be a good father. In other words it is difficult in our society to be a good father if you are not also a good husband. According to Lewis this has not been the case in societies such as Mexico.[29]

Other complications result if the marriage fails. Sooner or later the husband will find other feminine companionship, often with a woman who has children of her own, so that the man is now committed to two sets of children: his own offspring and those of his new love. In order to attract and hold a divorced woman or a widow with children, the male has to show a substantial interest in her children and their welfare—and in the process may neglect his own children.[30] Thus he may actually be doing a good job as a parent but with only one set of children, not necessarily his own.[31]

If we look at the figures on divorce, desertion, and separation we can see that marital failure is probably one of the major roadblocks to the American father who sincerely wants to be a good parent.[32] This is not the case with the American mother who retains custody of the minor

[27] See George B. Schaller, *The Mountain Gorilla* (Chicago: University of Chicago Press, 1963).

[28] George P. Murdock, *Social Structure* (New York: The Macmillan Co., 1949). In a survey of 250 human societies Murdock found that a majority of them permit a man to have more than one mate.

[29] See Oscar Lewis, *Five Families* (New York: Basic Books, 1959).

[30] In the tavern study referred to earlier the writer interviewed one man who was no longer close to his own children living in Indiana with their mother, but he was helping to care for three children who lived with the divorced woman he was then dating. Later on he married this second woman and for all practical purposes became the father of her children.

[31] For a good analysis of the millions of stepparents in our society, see Anne W. Simon, *Stepchild in the Family* (New York: Odyssey Press, 1964).

[32] For a review of these data see Robert R. Bell, *Marriage and Family Interaction* (rev. ed.; Homewood, Ill.: The Dorsey Press, 1967), chap. 16.

children in over 90 percent of the cases known to the courts.[33] As a matter of fact, marital failure may enhance the parental role of the mother: she now has the children more exclusively than before and probably extends the amount of time and effort she spends on them.[34]

The novelist Gold has a sketch in which a man is attempting to explain to a young daughter why he will not be living with her and her mother any more (they are getting a divorce). "I still love you," the father tries to explain, "but I no longer love your mother." He goes on to try to make it clear to the child that he still wants to be a *father* but not her mother's *husband*. This is too complex for the little girl and after a long silence she says: "I'm getting sick of big words like love."[35]

This dependence of the father role on the marital bond is often forgotten by critics of the American father. We think it needs to be kept in mind.[36]

6. *The idea that men and women are only superficially different.* In our society, since World War I, there has been a long-range tendency to regard men and women as equal—in itself a good thing in the opinion of this writer, but somewhere along the line equality became confused with *similarity*, which led to the idea that males and females at the human level are only superficially different. This is part of the togetherness approach to marriage in modern America.

It is the writer's belief that males and females at the human level are profoundly different—as Montagu argues[37]—and that this difference is most clearly seen in their diverse reactions to parenthood. The father may be delighted, indifferent, or annoyed at the idea of being a parent, and if he is not too enthralled there are often escape hatches through which he can keep his parental involvement to a minimum—longer hours of work, a second job to help with the increased expenses of rearing a family, or perhaps more time spent with his male peer group.

The mother may also be delighted, annoyed, or even appalled, but it is difficult for her to be indifferent. And it is also harder for her to escape. It is harder because of her inherent impulses as a female, and it is also harder because of society's attitude toward women who neglect their children.

[33] See Bell, *op. cit.*, p. 476.

[34] See E. E. LeMasters, "Holy Deadlock: A Study of Unsuccessful Marriages," *Sociological Quarterly*, 21 (1959), pp. 86–91; see also Morton M. Hunt, *The World of the Formerly Married* (New York: McGraw-Hill Book Co., 1966). When her marriage fails one of the common defense mechanisms of the American mother is her children.

[35] See Herbert Gold, *The Age of Happy Problems* (New York: Dial Press, 1962), pp. 27–33.

[36] This appears to be one of the findings of a study of 100 divorced men now in process at the School of Social Work, University of Wisconsin, Madison, Wisc.

[37] Montagu, *op. cit.*

This belief in male and female similarity results in criticism of the American father because he is not as close to his children as the mother. Parents, it is argued, as partners in the family enterprise, should share and share alike, and using this standard fathers are found wanting. Schaller makes it quite clear that no gorilla would ever get caught in such confusion: they know that mothers are different from fathers.[38] The male gorilla's job after procreation is to protect the group from attack. Anything else he does for his offspring represents a bonus that the group does not expect. We are not arguing that men are gorillas, although in many ways the behavior of gorillas is superior to that of man, but we are suggesting that the human male is not *entirely* different from the male gorilla and that their parental behavior reveals some similarities.

It seems to us that here again—as we discussed in chapter 3 on behavioral science—that the observers (and the critics) of fathers in our society have lost sight of man's organic nature: they overstress socialization and culture while minimizing evolution and man's place in the animal series.

Actually, judged by other mammalian and primate males, the human father is fantastically concerned about his young, but this does not mean that he is as close to them as their mother.

It might also be argued that compared to fathers in other human societies that the American father is really a very conscientious parent: he provides for his children in the vast majority of cases, he plays with them, he baby-sits with them when their mother needs help, and in general he seems to like children.[39]

The main point in this section is that the father in our society is often judged by standards that should only be applied to mothers.

7. *The American father is poorly prepared for his parental role.* This was commented on to some extent in chapter four but a few words need to be added at this point. American boys simply do not receive the socialization that helps prepare girls to become mothers. Girls get dolls and baby buggies for Christmas when the boys get guns and footballs. Later on, in high school and college, courses in home economics and child development are elected primarily by girls. And even later, the women's magazines feature child rearing material while the men's magazines feature sports and girls in scanty outfits.

As a result of all this the average American male is quite unprepared to be a father—at least socially.[40] He enjoys the process of fertilization and may even look forward to being a father but he scarcely knows what he is getting into. To some extent, of course, this is also true of many Ameri-

---

[38] Schaller, *op. cit.*

[39] The writer has over 20 newspaper clippings commenting on the interest the American armed forces men take in children all over the world.

[40] Benson, *op. cit.*, pp. 122–124, has a discussion of this.

can girls, but it seems to us that nature and our society prepare mothers for their parental role better than they do fathers.

Some problems of the American father

Many books have detailed the various problems of the woman in American society, including the reports of various government commissions established to assess the status of the female in our society.[41] We know of no similar effort to discover the status and the problems of the male in contemporary America. In fact, there are only a few books about him.[42]

In the pages following a few of the major problems of the American male will be indicated. All of these, in the opinion of the writer, have relevance for an understanding of the American father.

1. Economic problems. Although he is relatively affluent the American father is under constant economic pressure to support his wife and children on an ever and ever higher plane.[43] This pressure can be verified by reviewing the huge increase in consumer credit in recent decades or by reading the personal bankruptcy notices in the evening paper. Some families have more or less solved this problem by having the mother take a job outside of the home. This undoubtedly takes some of the pressure off of the father but may place considerable stress on the mother. There might also be some loss of maternal supervision of the children, plus the possibility of some strain on the marriage.

The strategy of the mass media in our society is to keep several years ahead of the consumer. Just when you and I have decided that a certain type of home refrigerator is all we need the advertisers begin pushing a new and bigger model that we are supposed to aim for. This can be seen in the 1960's in the tremendous drive to outdate the black and white television receivers and replace them with color sets. One father said to us: "Our black and white set works just fine but the wife and kids have been after me for six months to trade it in on a color set." He finally made

---

[41] For the latest federal government study see Margaret Mead and Frances Kaplan, *American Women* (New York: Charles Scribner's Sons, 1965). This is the report of the President's Commission on the Status of Women. In the writer's state there is an active Governor's Commission on the Status of Women—as there are in many other states. The writer is entirely in favor of such commissions but would like to suggest that the American male could stand some study also.

[42] When Kendall, *op. cit.*, began to study the American male she discovered that for every book on men in the New York City Library there were literally hundreds of books on women. For some observations on the American father and his problems, see Brenton, *op. cit.*, chap. 5, "The Paradox of the Contemporary American Father." The recent volume by Benson, *op. cit.*, is the only scholarly work in recent decades to focus on the American father.

[43] For an interesting discussion of personal bankruptcy cases, see George Sullivan, *The Boom in Going Bust* (New York: The Macmillan Co., 1968).

the trade at Christmas time and found that his old set was worth only $50 on a trade. The new color set cost approximately $500. This man works in a factory and his take-home pay does not average over $400 a month. He says that he manages to get by only because his wife works also.

For the 20 or 30 percent of fathers on the bottom of the economic system the financial problems are more stark: they are faced with not being able to provide food, clothing, or housing for their families. They are also faced with the knowledge that in a society in which most people are reasonably well off, they are not. This is the meaning of "relative deprivation"—it isn't only what you don't have, it is also what the people around you *do* have.[44] In other words, it is quite different being hungry in India where millions are on the verge of starvation than it is being hungry in the United States where most people overeat.

The writer believes that *most* American fathers suffer from economic problems of one kind or another. We even interviewed a young physician earning $25,000 a year who said that his financial pressures were almost too much for him. Only those who have sweated out economic problems know how they can affect family life: the quality of the husband-wife relationship, the feeling of the children for their parents, and the attitude of the father and mother toward being parents. A man's self-image in our society is deeply affected by this ability to provide for his family. Many times the self-image is not too positive.

2. *Marital problems.* These have already been commented on in the previous section of this chapter and only need to be noted here. For the uninitiated, however, it needs to be emphasized that the divorce rate, which is what most Americans think of when they think about marital failure, does not tell the whole story by any means. We have not only divorce, but also separation, desertion, and a fourth type: "holy deadlock"—marriages which are never terminated but are essentially pathogenic for all involved.[45] It may well be that there are more holy deadlock marriages than there are divorces. We just don't know how many American marriages are of the "shell" or "facade" type.[46]

---

[44] For an excellent analysis of poverty in our society, see the collection of essays, *Poverty: Views from the Left*, edited by Jeremy Larner and Irving Howe (New York: William Morrow & Co., 1968).

[45] In the paper "Holy Deadlock" cited earlier the writer pointed out that unsuccessful marriages that are never terminated legally are counted as successful marriages because they never show up in any other category.

[46] In their survey of upper middle-class married couples Cuber and Harroff concluded that perhaps two-thirds of these marriages had become "facade" marriages in the middle and later decades of life. See John Cuber and Peggy Harroff, *The Significant Americans* (New York: Appleton-Century, 1965). This study is marred by the fact that the authors do not bother to cite any of the previous studies of marriage in our society.

But no matter how one looks at it the failure of his marriage is a major problem for the American father.

3. *Sex life.* Kinsey and his research group found that the American male finds it difficult to confine his sexual interests to his wife.[47] Other studies have reported that the male does not think his wife is a good sexual partner.[48]

Part of the problem here is that the male adolescent peer group does not socialize for sexual monogamy: it stresses the fact that all women are legitimate sexual objects (except mothers and sisters) and that a man is a fool if he does not take advantage of any sexual opportunity. After living in this world for several years the man finds it difficult to think of his wife as the only legitimate sexual object. Girls at the office, wives of other men, divorced women—he finds many of these women sexually attractive and he often finds that they view him in the same light. In an urban society there are many opportunities for straying; the controls have to be internal because the external controls of the rural or village society are not present. A substantial number of married men find this situation somewhat more than they can manage.

In the Victorian world a married man would solve this problem by having an affair with a younger woman or a woman of a lower social class. If he was discreet, as Warren G. Harding was,[49] his wife would overlook the matter. And the man would be protected because marriage to this other woman was usually not possible.

Things are not so simple today. Men and women who become involved sexually in modern America are often from the same social class and marriage is always a possibility. Thus what starts out as an affair ends up in divorce and remarriage, with the father becoming separated from his children.

One can debate the morality of all of this endlessly. We are only interested in the father's sex life as it affects his marriage and hence his relationship with his children. It seems clear that (1) if his sex life with his wife is not satisfying that his tolerance of his marriage will be lowered, and (2) his tendency to look around for another sexual partner will be enhanced. In either event his role as father will suffer more or less.

4. *Drinking problem.* Our impression is that a substantial proportion of "bad" fathers in our society have a drinking problem. Trice reports that

---

[47] Kinsey, *op. cit.*, p. 585, estimates that perhaps one half of U.S. husbands have committed adultery at least once.

[48] For a review of some of this data see Hunt, *op. cit.*

[49] President Harding apparently was married to a sexless woman who knew that he had had at least two affairs with other women. See Francis Russell, *The Shadow of Blooming Grove: Warren G. Harding in His Times* (New York: McGraw-Hill Book Co., 1968).

various estimates conclude that fathers are three to six times more likely to drink alcohol excessively in our society than are mothers.[50]

If a man drinks too much, there are at least four ways in which this affects his performance as a parent: (a) the drinking becomes a real strain on the family budget, and this is true at almost all economic levels except for the very wealthy; (b) the quality of the marriage suffers; (c) when the father is home he is not able to function normally—he is either too good to the children or he is abusive; (d) the attitude of the children toward him changes from positive to negative.[51]

For persons who have never known alcoholism at close range the events that take place between alcoholics and their families are unbelievable. Only recently we interviewed a young mother with two children who said that during a drinking bout her husband threatened to kill her and both children. When sober this sort of behavior was never apparent in this husband-father. The wife is now afraid of her husband and has obtained a separation.

This woman has reason to be afraid of her husband. The writer, using news reports, tallied 27 children and 7 wives who were murdered in Wisconsin during 1967 by husband-fathers who were reported by the authorities to have "been drinking."

It is true, of course, that excessive drinking by American mothers is becoming more and more frequent in our society, but in this analysis we are focusing on only the father.

This excessive drinking by the father is by no means confined to any one social class. It may be found at all socioeconomic levels in substantial numbers.

5. *The male peer group.* In his study of blue-collar workers in Boston, Gans found that the men liked to spend much of their spare time with other men, away from their wives and children.[52] This sort of behavior was accepted in the particular ethnic group (Italian) and posed no great problems. But a great many American women these days view marriage and parenthood as a partnership and do not readily accept male only activities. It is the writer's belief that a vast number of American men prefer to spend their spare time with other males and that this is one of the most difficult adjustments they have to make in modern marriage. A certain proportion of them refuse to make this concession to their wives and children and continue to spend most of their spare time with the boys.

---

[50] See Harrison M. Trice, *Alcoholism in America* (New York: McGraw-Hill Book Co., 1966), pp. 19–20.

[51] *Ibid.*, chap. 5.

[52] Herbert J. Gans, *The Urban Villagers* (New York: The Free Press, 1962).

At blue-collar levels there may be a certain amount of tolerance of "segregated sex roles" (as this behavior is called) but America is becoming increasingly a white-collar world and women seem to be less and less tolerant of staying home with the children.

To resolve this sort of strain the American male has to be domesticated more than he ever has in the past. To what extent this has been accomplished, or can be accomplished, we don't know. But some men are difficult to harness, as their wives have discovered. When this is the case it seems likely that the father's role is diminished or affected negatively in some way.

6. *Resentment of women.* In the last several decades, beginning with World War I, American women have been involved in a vast social revolution, the aim of which has been to give them equality with men.[53] This drastic upheaval has thrown the two sexes into more direct competition and has taken from men some of the special privileges they once had—the exclusive right to vote, control of most work opportunities, the double standard of sexual morality, and others. While most men may recognize that women are entitled to social equality, it is not always clear that they really like the position women have won for themselves. In talking with men informally the writer has been impressed with the underlying hostility that many American men seem to have toward the modern woman. In a recent election a prominent woman in our community was defeated for the school board—a position she was eminently qualified for. We asked a male friend of ours if he had voted for her. "No, I didn't," he said. "I think women are trying to take this town over. It's about time the men began to assert themselves."

This is the way many white persons now feel toward blacks: they are getting "too equal" and something will have to be done about it. It seems to us that the analogy here between the new position of women and the new position of blacks is very real: intelligent persons recognize the need for sexual equality and also for racial equality, but their emotions need more time to get used to the change.

One husband, in criticizing his wife, said to us: "She wanted to wear the pants, now let her take the consequences." In other words, if women want equality they should shoulder half of the load, whatever it is.

To the extent that modern American men do have hostility toward their wives, the role of father will be complicated by this feeling. In some men this is very evident, but we do not know how typical or atypical these men are.

---

[53] One of the best accounts of this era is in Frederick Lewis Allen, *Only Yesterday* (Harper & Row, 1957). This is an analysis of social change in our society since 1900. For an interesting analysis of the rise of women in our society, see Brenton, *op. cit.*, chap. 3, "Notes on the Femininization of Society." See also Benson, *op. cit.*, chap. 4, "The Passing of the Patriarch."

Some general observations on the American father

1. Today's father has more leisure. It is fashionable in our society to romanticize the family system of an earlier historical period and to condemn the family of today. It is our belief that in some ways the contemporary American father is an improvement over his predecessors. A good example would be the amount of leisure time the modern father spends with his children. This will be illustrated with a case study.

We recently had a chance to interview at length a man almost 90 years old concerning his boyhood in rural Pennsylvania in the 1880's. This man's mind was quite alert and clear, even though his body was somewhat the worse for wear.

Growing up on a prosperous farm in eastern Pennsylvania in the latter part of the 19th century, Mr. D. could scarcely recall any "leisure" or "play" with his father. One reason was that leisure or recreation was considered to be bad in those days—character and salvation came from hard work.

This elderly man was quite sure that his father had never played baseball with his sons (there were five boys in this family), never went sledding or ice-skating with them in winter, never swam with them in the summer. He could remember doing all of these things, but never with either of his parents. Hunting was an exception: the father did hunt with his sons in the fall.

Mr. D. could recall his father and mother taking all of the children to the county fair in the fall; this was an annual event for the whole family and stood out in this elderly man's memory as the fun day of the year.

Vivid memories of *working* with his father on the farm were retained by this man—plowing and sowing seed in the fall and spring; harvesting the various crops; butchering in the fall; doing the endless daily chores.

Sunday was a day of rest, with only the essential work (feeding and watering the livestock) being done. Two church services were usually attended by the entire family.

In essence, this man from the 1880's has no memory of his father as a pal or companion.[54]

In contrast, fathers today go on camping trips with their children, play golf and other games with them, take annual family vacations as a group, go to drive-in movies in the family car, watch television together, and in general spend a lot of spare time with their wives and children.

In another case drawn from a later period (1900), there was a six-day week for the father—the five-day, 40-hour week had not yet become

---

[54] Another case study of a farm father and his relationship with his children will be found in chap. 11.

common in America.[55] Except for an occasional family picnic or a summer baseball game, the writer does not recall any recreation time spent with his father. And since this family lived in a small city instead of on a farm, there are also few memories of any experiences working beside the father.

In contrast to these two fathers from earlier periods in American history, we have spent literally thousands of hours in pure companionship with our two sons and in the process have seen other fathers doing the same thing.

It is not being proposed that today's father-child companionship pattern is necessarily superior to the father-child work relationship of the earlier rural America—our point is that the contemporary father *does* spend a lot of time with his children. One reason, of course, is that the time is available; he does not (as a rule) have the long work week that his father and grandfather had.

2. *Today's father is more domesticated.* There is some reason to believe that American men have changed drastically since World War II.[56] They are infinitely more domesticated than their male ancestors: they cook more meals, clean more homes, change more diapers, do more babysitting, remodel more rooms, and in general are more geared into family activities. Not everybody is entirely happy about this new American male—not even all of the men themselves—but like him or pity him, the current American male is a new breed.

In the last analysis only a "new man" can understand and live successfully with the contemporary American woman. It is simply not possible to produce a modern 20th century woman and expect her to settle for a 19th century man.

3. *The new male model is popular.* If today's American woman is unhappy with the American male she doesn't show it by refusing to marry; the marriage rate in our society is at an all-time high.[57] Even divorced men seem to be readily acceptable as marriage partners.[58] It may be that one of the factors producing the high marriage rate is the acceptability of the new male model.

It seems logical to assume that if women find the new American male acceptable as a husband that they also find him acceptable as a father. The high birthrate following World War II would certainly seem to support this line of reasoning, but the birthrate as of 1968 has dropped, indicating that a number of variables are involved in our fluctuating birthrate.[59]

---

[55] This case represents the writer's father.

[56] See Brenton, *op. cit.*

[57] These statistics are reviewed in Bell, *op. cit.*, pp. 138–139.

[58] *Ibid.*, pp. 496–501.

[59] For an analysis of these variables see Robert Winch, *The Modern Family* (New York: Holt, Rinehart and Winston, 1963 ed.), chap. 7.

4. *Social class variations in father performance.* If data were available it might emerge that American fathers are least adequate at the top and bottom of the social class structure. Although no systematic studies of the upper class father in our society have ever been made, it seems clear that their outside commitments force them to delegate much of their parental role to other persons, boarding school teachers, summer camp counselors, and the like.

At the bottom of the social class system there is considerable evidence that the lower class father (the 20 or 30 percent at the poverty level) finds his parental responsibilities overwhelming.[60] Not only does he lack the money required to support his family, he also suffers from inadequate education, poor health (physical as well as mental), slum housing, high rates of marital instability, and a host of other problems.

It might be that the best American fathers are found at the stable blue-collar level and in the vast white-collar middle class.

5. *The effects of military service.* Some 15 to 20 million American men have served in the armed forces since World War II. Almost all of these men became fathers after returning to civilian life—if they were not already fathers at the time of induction.

We do not profess to know how military service affects a man's capacity to be a good father.[61] It might be that the experience helps men to mature, and maturity is certainly an asset in being a parent.

The great variety of humans encountered in the armed forces might also help future fathers understand some of the differences they will discover in their own children.

It is also possible that the destruction one sees in military service may be functional for fathers in helping them appreciate the preciousness of human life and motivate them not only to start families when they return home but also to nourish and protect them. This may actually have been a factor in the high birthrate that followed World War II in the United States.

It is difficult to identify the negative impact of military service on future fathers. There is an obvious "crudity factor" that all men in the armed forces are subjected to—crude and obscene language, crude bedroom stories, sexual promiscuity, excessive drinking, gambling—and it is difficult to see how this sort of life prepares a man to be a good husband or a good father.

The writer confesses that he does not know the net effect of military service on future fathers. It is only suggested that this experience be remembered when critics look at the current generation of American fathers.

---

[60] See chap. 5 for an extensive discussion of social class and parenthood.

[61] The following observations are based on three years service during World War II. We doubt that it has changed much since then.

6. Differential impact of American culture. If one looks at the social deviation rates, such as crime, alcoholism, drug addiction, and desertion,[62] it is possible to conclude that the destructive impact of American society is greater on males than females. One either has to believe this or accept Montagu's claim that women are the stronger sex.[63] It seems plausible that different cultures have a differential impact on the two sexes and that ours hits men harder than women. If this is true it would help to explain some of the paternal deficiencies noted in this chapter.

Summary and conclusion

In this chapter we have noted the neglect of the American father in family research and have attempted to sketch in some of the basic facts that need to be kept in mind in thinking about fathers in our society.

In the previous chapter on the American mother it was hypothesized that the mother has become the Executive Director of the American family and that the father has been kicked upstairs to become Chairman of the Board.[64] If this is the case—and we recognize that this is only a hypothesis—then it makes a lot of difference whether the father supports the mother in her various efforts or undermines her administration. This in turn is likely to reflect the quality of the husband-wife relationship.

It is our personal belief that the American father does a better job than he is usually given credit for. But this judgment may be biased in that the writer is a father himself.

---

[62] For a review of this data see Marshall B. Clinard, *Sociology of Deviant Behavior* (New York: Rinehart & Co., 1968 ed.).

[63] Montagu, *op. cit.*

[64] Benson, *op. cit.*, pp. 99–100, writes: "a man wields power in the contemporary household only if he has the personal characteristics to pull it off or because of a unique pattern of domestic relationships, not because society backs him up with strong support."

chapter nine

Parents without
partners

I N thinking about parents it is easy to assume a model of what might be termed "the biological parent team" of mother and father. In this model two parents act as partners in carrying out the parental functions. Furthermore, both of the parents are biological as well as social parents. It is this parent team model that is analyzed in most of the chapters in this book.

What is not realized by many observers, especially by parent critics, is the fact that a considerable proportion of contemporary American parents do not operate under these ideal conditions. These parents include "parents without partners" (mostly divorced or separated women, but including a few men also); widows and widowers with children; unmarried mothers; adoptive parents; stepparents; and, finally, foster parents.

Some of the groups in the list above are amazingly large—Simon, for example, reports that in the 1960's in the United States there were about *seven million* children living with a stepparent.[1] This means that approximately one out of every nine children in modern America is a stepchild.

In this chapter we wish to do two things: (1) summarize the statistics on these parental subgroups, and (2) analyze the role complications these parents are confronted with. Some of these parents may actually have certain advantages over so-called normal parents, and where this seems to be the case we will analyze this also.

---

[1] See Anne W. Simon, *Stepchild in the Family* (New York: Odyssey Press, 1964), p. 69.

Mothers without fathers

One of the by now familiar parental types in our society is the mother rearing her children alone. As of 1960 about one household out of ten in the United States was headed by a woman.[2] In an earlier, more innocent America, this mother without father was seen as a heroic figure—a brave woman whose husband had died who was struggling to rear her brood by scrubbing floors, taking in family laundry, and so on. This was the brave little widow of an earlier day.

After the end of World War I, as the divorce rate began to climb, this picture—and this woman—underwent a radical change. With the rapid improvement of American medicine, marriages in the early and middle decades of life were no longer broken primarily by death; now the great destroyers of marriages came to be social and psychological, not biological.

With this shift the public's attitude toward the mother with no father by her side changed drastically—it became ambivalent. In some cases she might be viewed with sympathy and understanding, if she happened to be your sister or a close friend, but more often she was perceived as a woman of questionable character—either the gay divorcee of the upper social class levels or the ADC mother living off of the taxpayers at the lower social class levels.[3] In either case the image was a far cry from that of the heroic little widow of the Victorian era.

Statistically, and otherwise, these mothers without fathers fall into five different categories: divorced, separated, deserted, widowed, and never married. All of these categories overlap, so that some mothers might at some point in their lives occupy all five positions in the list.

Our procedure in discussing these mothers in their parental role will be to identify the generic patterns and problems shared by all of these mothers, and then to look at the relatively unique patterns that cluster about any specific position.

Generic features of mothers without partners

1. Poverty. It has been estimated that while households headed by a woman comprise only about 10 percent of all U.S. households, they

[2] Alvin Schorr has an analysis of this data in *Poor Kids* (New York: Basic Books, 1966). See especially pp. 16–22.

One estimate concludes that over six million children in the United States are growing up in fatherless homes. See Elizabeth Herzog and Cecelia Sudia, "Fatherless Homes," *Children*, 15 (1968), 177–182.

[3] For an excellent discussion of the changing attitudes toward divorced persons see William L. O'Neill, *Divorce in the Progressive Era* (New Haven: Yale University Press, 1967).

constitute about 25 percent of the families in the so-called poverty group in American society.[4]

In the best study yet published on divorced women, Goode found financial stress to be a major complaint.[5] At any given time approximately 40 percent of the divorced husbands in this study were delinquent in their support payments, a pattern that seems to be nationwide.[6]

Poverty is extremely relative, as is deprivation. A divorced woman receiving even $1,000 a month in support payments may have to reduce her standard of living from what it was before her divorce.

The reasons for the financial difficulties of these mothers are not mysterious or difficult to identify. Most American men cannot afford to support two living establishments on a high level. This is one reason why some support payments are delinquent. The man usually gets involved with a least one other woman, and this costs money.[7] Often his new woman is not well off financially and the man may find himself contributing to her support also.

Since a considerable proportion of divorced women are apparently employed at the time of their divorce,[8] they had what is commonly called a two-income family. The mother may continue to work after the father has left the home, but with two living establishments to maintain, two cars, and so on, the financial situation tends to be tight.

In a study of ADC mothers in Boston it was discovered that these women faced financial crises almost monthly.[9] They coped with these difficult situations by accepting aid from members of their family; by pooling their resources with neighbors and women friends in the same plight; and by occasional aid from a boy friend.

In several counseling cases with divorced women the writer was impressed with the annoying feature of the relative poverty experienced by these women—one woman didn't have the money to get her television set repaired and this created tension between herself and her children.

---

[4] Schorr, op. cit., chap. 2, "And Children of the Nation Come First."

[5] On the financial problems of divorced women see William J. Goode, After Divorce (New York: The Free Press, 1956), chap. 16, "Postdivorce Economic Activities."

[6] Ibid. See chap. 16 for a discussion of the problem of support payments after divorce.

[7] The financial problems of the divorced man were analyzed in a 1968 study conducted by the writer and several graduate students from the School of Social Work, University of Wisconsin. Eighty divorced men were interviewed at length. Financial problems were one of the constant complaints of these men. This study is not yet published.

[8] On the employment of wives at the point of divorce, see Goode, op. cit., pp. 71–74.

[9] A discussion of the financial crises of ADC mothers may be found in Sydney E. Bernard, Fatherless Families: Their Economic and Social Adjustment (Waltham, Mass.: Brandeis University, 1964).

Another woman, who lived in an area with inadequate bus service, could not afford an automobile. Any person in our society can understand how frustrating problems of this nature can be.

2. *Role conflicts.* Since these women have added the father role to their parental responsibilities they tend to be either overloaded or in conflict over their various role commitments. The presence of a husband-father provides more role flexibility than these women now have—if the mother is ill, or has to work late, the husband may be able to be home with the children.

When these mothers are employed outside of the home, as a sizeable proportion are,[10] the work hours usually conflict with those of the school system. Children leave for school too late, get home too early, and have far too many vacations for the employed mother. There are also childhood illnesses that must be coped with.

It is true that the termination of the marriage has reduced or eliminated the mother's role as wife, but she is still a woman in the early decades of life and men will be in the picture sooner or later. Thus she may not be a wife at the moment but she will soon be a girl friend, and the courtship role may be even more demanding than that of wife.

It is the writer's belief, based on numerous interviews with divorced women, that being the head of a household is, for most women, an 18-hour day, seven days a week, and 365 days a year job. It would seem that only the most capable, and the most fortunate, can perform all of the roles involved effectively.

3. *Role shifts.* Since the vast majority of the mothers being discussed here—80 to 90 percent—will eventually remarry, they face the difficult process of taking over the father role and then relinquishing it.[11] This is not easy for most of us; once we have appropriated a role in a family system it is often difficult to turn it over to somebody else.

Furthermore, these mothers operate in an unusual family system in that, for an indefinite period, they do not have to worry about what the other parent thinks. They are both mother and father for the time being.

This is not entirely true, of course, in the case of the divorced woman, but it seems to be largely true, even for this group.[12] The departed father starts out with the best intentions of "not forgetting my kids," but a variety of factors tend to reduce his parental influence as time goes on.[13]

---

[10] For an analysis of the employment of mothers with minor children see F. Ivan Nye and Lois Wladis Hoffman, *The Employed Mother in America* (Chicago: Rand McNally & Co., 1963), pp. 7–15.

[11] See Reuben Hill, *Families under Stress* (New York: Harper & Brothers, 1949).

[12] Goode, *op. cit.*, chap. 21, discusses some of the post-divorce problems of the father and his children.

[13] In the 1968 unpublished study of 80 divorced men cited earlier the lack of contact with their children was one of the problems most often referred to by these fathers.

One divorced woman talked to the writer about the problem of "shifting gears" in her parental roles: "I found it very difficult," she said. "When my husband and I were first divorced he continued to see the children and participated in some of the decisions about them. Then he moved to another state and we seldom saw him after that—but he did continue to send the support checks.

"At this point," she continued, "I assumed almost all of the parental responsibilities, except for the money sent by my former husband and some advice (of questionable value) that my mother chipped in from time to time.

"And then I met the man I am now married to. At first he stayed out of the children's lives, not being sure how long he and I would be going together. But as we moved toward marriage the children became attached to him and gradually he became a foster father to them. Now he has taken over a considerable amount of parental responsibility and I am back almost to where I was before my divorce—I am just a mother again."[14]

In the study by Hill he analyzed role shifts in a group of families in which the father had been temporarily pulled out of the home for military service. Hill discovered (a) that some of the wife-mothers could not pick up the added responsibility when the father left the home, and (b) that some of the mothers could not relinquish the father role when the husband returned from the service. One has the impression that some of the mothers being discussed here have these same problems.

Once these women have remarried there is a sort of built-in strain in that one of the parents (the mother) is a natural parent while the other (the father) is only a stepparent. This syndrome will be analyzed later in this chapter but it needs to be mentioned here.

4. *Public attitudes.*   These mothers are operating in deviant family situations, and for the most part the community tends to regard them and their children as deviants.[15] Except for the widow, all of these mothers are viewed with some ambivalence in our society. They receive some sympathy, some respect, and some help, but they are also viewed as women who are not "quite right"—they did not sustain their marriage "until death do us part."[16]

The unmarried mother, of course, never had a marriage to sustain and the public has no ambivalence about her; they simply condemn her and that's that.[17]

---

[14] This woman was a professional social worker—hence some of her language is a bit technical.

[15] For a discussion of the concept of "social deviation" see Marshall B. Clinard, *Sociology of Deviant Behavior* (New York: Rinehart & Co., 1968 ed.), pp. 3–27.

[16] On the attitudes of people toward the divorced person in our society, see Morton M. Hunt, *The World of the Formerly Married* (New York: McGraw-Hill Book Co., 1966), *passim.* See also Goode, *op. cit.,* chap. 17, "Social Adjustment."

[17] It is possible, of course, for a woman who was once married to become an unmarried mother at a later date—as a widow or as a divorced woman.

If these mothers require support from public welfare they will find the community's mixed feelings reflected in their monthly check—the community will not permit them and their children to starve, but it will also not allow them to live at a decent level.[18]

We have now examined some of the generic problems of the one-parent family system, except for the system in which the one-parent is a father, which will be looked at later. Now let us analyze the specific features of the subsystems in the one-parent family.

Specific features of the subsystems in the one-parent family

1. The divorced mother. The divorced mother has several advantages over the deserted mother: she at least has had the help of a domestic relations court in spelling out the financial responsibility of the father, also the legal arrangements for custody. In this sense divorce is a lot less messy than desertion in our society.

The divorced mother is also legally free to associate with other men and to remarry if she finds the right person—advantages the deserted woman does not have.

The divorced father, it seems to us, is not in an enviable position in his role as father. He may be happy not to be married to his children's mother any more but he often hates to be separated from his children.[19] In a sense he still has the responsibility of a father for his minor children but few of the enjoyments of parenthood. To be with his children he has to interact to some degree with his former wife—a process so painful that he was willing to have the marriage terminated.

In the unpublished study of 80 divorced men, cited earlier, one of the most frequent regrets expressed by the men was their frustration and concern about their relationship to their children.[20]

The divorced mother has one parental advantage that she shares with all other parents without partners; she does not have to share the daily parental decisions with a partner who might not agree with her strategy. In the Goode study of divorced women, the mothers seemed to think this was an advantage.[21] The parental partner can be of great help if the

---

[18] See M. Elaine Burgess and Daniel O. Price, *An American Dependency Challenge* (Chicago: American Public Welfare Assn., 1963), for data on how these mothers and their children live. See also Alvin Schorr, *Explorations in Social Policy* (New York: Basic Books, 1968) for a more recent review of the AFDC program.

[19] In the 1968 study of divorced men, conducted at the University of Wisconsin, there was frequent concern expressed by the men about the welfare of their children after the divorce.

[20] The 80 detailed interviews from this study are not yet fully analyzed since the field work was not completed until June, 1969.

[21] See Goode, *op. cit.*, chap. 21, for a discussion of how the divorced women in his sample felt about rearing children after the marriage had been terminated.

two parents can agree on how their children should be reared, but when this is not the case one parent can probably do a better job going it alone.

2. *The deserted mother.* It has already been indicated that desertions in our society are more messy than divorces.[22] There are two reasons: (1) desertion is more apt to be unilateral with the decision to pull out being made by one party alone; and (2) there is no court supervision of the desertion process—it is unplanned from society's point of view.

The deserted mother is likely to have more severe financial problems than the divorced mother because support payments have not been agreed upon.

Psychologically, desertion is probably more traumatic than divorce, partly because it is more unilateral but also because it is less planned.[23] To the extent that this is true—and we recognize that the evidence on this point is not conclusive—then the deserted mother is handicapped in her parental role by her emotional upheaval or trauma.

This woman also has other problems; she is legally not free to remarry and in a sense not even free to go out with other men since she is technically still a married woman. These feelings, of course, will tend to reflect the social class and the moral subculture of the particular woman.

3. *The separated mother.* If we assume that most marital separations in modern America have been arrived at by mutual agreement, then this mother has certain advantages over the deserted mother. One disadvantage is that her courtship status is ambiguous; another is that she is not free to remarry.[24] Psychologically, the separated mother should reflect patterns similar to those of the divorced mother: her marriage has failed but she has done something about it and now has to plan for her future life.

4. *The widowed mother.* The one big advantage of this parent is the favorable attitude of her family, her friends, and the community toward her. This tends to be reflected in her self-image, thus giving her emotional support. Once she emerges from the period of bereavement, however, she has to face about the same problems as the women discussed previously— she probably will have financial problems; she will have to be father as

---

[22] One of the better discussions of desertion is the paper by William M. Kephart, "Occupational Level and Marital Disruption," *American Sociological Review*, August, 1955. Among other things Kephart believes desertion to be more common than is generally thought. He also found that desertion was by no means limited to the lower socioeconomic levels.

[23] The writer has been unable to find any empirical research which compares the psychological trauma of divorce with that of desertion.

[24] On the courtship and remarriage problems of divorced and separated women see Jessie Bernard, *Remarriage* (New York: The Dryden Press, 1956); also Goode, *op. cit.*, chap. 19, "Steady Dating, Imminent Marriage, and Remarriage." Hunt, *op. cit.*, also analyzes these problems at length.

well as mother; she may need to get a job; and eventually she will have to consider whether or not to remarry.

It is difficult to say whether the widowed woman suffers more or less emotional trauma than the women whose husbands are still alive but whose marriages are dead. Both have experienced "death" in one form or another—either psychological or physical.

It is undoubtedly true that some of the marriages of widowed women had also failed before the husband died, but there is no way to discover how large this group is.

5. *The unmarried mother.* This is not the place to review the status and problems of the unmarried mother in our society—the literature on this woman is quite voluminous.[25] It only needs to be said here that this mother has all of the problems of the women discussed before plus a few of her own. She is more likely to be a member of a racial minority—one of the extra burdens she has to shoulder. She is also more likely to be on public welfare[26]—a major burden in itself in our society. Her chances for marriage are not as gloomy as some people once thought,[27] but her chances for a successful marriage may be more dubious.

The unmarried mother does not have to worry about what her child's father thinks, because in most of the 50 states the unmarried father has no parental privileges except that of child support.[28] As a rule his child may be placed for adoption whether or not he wishes to terminate his parental rights.[29]

The unmarried mother has one dubious advantage over the divorced, the deserted, and the separated mothers. She does not have to juggle the ambivalent feelings of the general public toward her; she knows that they disapprove of her almost unanimously.

We are talking here, of course, of the unmarried mothers who keep their children. Those who give up their children for adoption, and those

---

25 On the unmarried mother see the following: Clark Vincent, *Unmarried Mothers* (New York: The Free Press, 1961); also Robert W. Roberts (ed.), *The Unwed Mother* (New York: Harper & Row, 1966).

26 Sydney E. Bernard, *op. cit.*, states that women under 35 with no husbands in the household are responsible for more children than are the households headed by men under 35. See also Schorr, *Poor Kids*, p. 21. In chap 7, "Fatherless Child Insurance," Schorr has an excellent analysis of the economic problems faced by unmarried mothers in our society.

27 See Rose Bernstein, "Are We Still Stereotyping the Unmarried Mother?", *Social Work*, 5 (January, 1960), pp. 22–38.

28 Vincent, *op. cit.*, pp. 73–97, has a discussion of the problems faced by the unmarried father—about whom we really know very little.

29 We hear much about discrimination against women in our society because of their sex. Actually, the unmarried father is discriminated against also. The girl can choose to marry or not and still retain her parental rights, but the man loses his rights as a father unless he marries the girl. Perhaps the unmarried fathers in our society should form an organization and fight for equal rights.

who terminate their pregnancies via the abortionist, have their own problems which will not be discussed in this book.

It is interesting to note that some women in our society have occupied *all* of the positions discussed so far. They have been unmarried mothers, divorced, deserted, separated, and widowed, although not necessarily in that order. We have interviewed two such women and they both were remarkable persons.

One of these women was an unmarried mother at 16, deserted at 18, divorced at 20, widowed at 23, and remarried at 25. Along the way she had accumulated six children and had been separated any number of times.[30]

What impressed us about this woman was not only her lonely journey through the wars of matrimony but her intense concern for the welfare of her children. The general public would undoubtedly have viewed her as a "bad" mother, but our own judgment was that she did quite well with children—her problems were largely with husbands and boy friends. It is too bad that women like this don't write books, for they could tell all of us much that we need to know.

Father-only families

It has been estimated that approximately 600,000 U.S. families have only a father present in the home at any given time.[31] This figure seems large but is small compared to the 4 to 5 million American families in which only a mother is present.

There seems to be relatively little research data available on these "father-only" families. Since custody of minor children is awarded to the mother in our divorce courts in 90 to 95 percent of the cases, it seems logical to assume that the bulk of these "fathers without mothers" represent either desertion or the death of the mother.

It seems likely that these fathers do not continue indefinitely to rear their children alone, that the majority of them remarry, in which case they would experience the same problems of role shifts discussed earlier for mothers on their own.

It also seems likely that these men experience role conflicts between their jobs, their social life, and their parental responsibility.

It is doubtful that these solo fathers would suffer from poverty to the extent found among solo mothers—but the writer has no data to cite in support of this statement.

The rat race experienced by mothers rearing families without the help

---

[30] This woman was a public welfare recipient.

[31] This estimate is by Marjorie Ilgenfritz, "Mothers on Their Own," *Marriage and Family Living*, February, 1961.

of a father would likely be found among these men also; it simply reflects what might be termed "role overload."

Psychologically, judging from case studies to be presented shortly, these men probably suffer from the same syndrome found among mothers who have lost their husbands—loneliness, sorrow, perhaps bitterness, often a sense of failure, plus a feeling of being overwhelmed by their almost complete responsibility for their children. About the only effective treatment for feelings of this nature is to find a new partner and get married—the solution most adult Americans rely on for whatever ails them. These fathers are no exception to this statement.

It would appear that these men have a few problems that would be less likely to bother mothers: the physical care of preschool children and the tasks of home management, such as shopping for food and clothes, preparing meals, doing the family laundry, and cleaning the house. Some men become quite adept at this women's work after awhile, but for others a stove or an iron remains a mystery forever.

Case studies of fathers without mothers

1. Case of desertion.   A man of 45 talked to us at length about his struggle to complete the rearing of his three children after his wife had deserted him.

"I came home one night from work and she was gone. A note said that she no longer wanted to live with me and that she thought the children would be better off with me."

"Later on I had a letter from her from California with no return address."

Fortunately, one of this father's children was of high school age and could help with the younger children.

This man says that he went "through hell" for several months—the blow of being deserted, plus the added responsibility for his children, were almost too much for him.

The final solution in this case was the willingness of a widowed sister, with no children of her own, to move in with this family and take over most of the responsibility for the children. After a one year trial this arrangement seemed to be working out.

2. Case of divorce.   A man interviewed by the writer had divorced his wife because of an affair she had with a friend of his. Since he felt quite strongly that his wife was not competent to rear their four children, he applied to the court for custody of the children and his petition was approved.

This man was quite definite that he and the children managed better without the mother than they had ever done when she had been present.

"She was always feuding with either me or one of the children. She was moody and negative about life. And she hated any kind of housework.

After she left the kids and I got along fine. I did the cooking, they did the housecleaning, and we hired a woman to do the laundry. It worked out just fine."

This man—a remarkable person—even took his four children on a year's tour of Europe after his divorce. Using a combined passenger car and bus they camped all over Europe, settling down in one country for several months so the children could attend school and study a foreign language.

This man has now remarried. He still has custody of the four children and reports that "everything is fine."

3. *Case involving the death of a mother.* This man talked freely of his life after the death of his wife. He said that since only one of his three children (a boy of 10) was still at home when his wife died he had decided to "bach it"—in other words, he did not attempt to employ a housekeeper, nor did he invite any of his grown children to move back into the family home.

He said, "I felt that the boy and I could manage by ourselves and that we would be better off that way."

This was a small town and many relatives were nearby if help was needed.

This man had been very much in love with his wife and had no desire to remarry.

Eight years after his wife's death, when the boy was ready for college or a job, the father did remarry. He feels that the plan worked out well for both him and the boy—but now that the son is about to leave home the father felt the need for companionship and so he got married.

The writer does not present these cases as being typical. They simply illustrate some of the patterns to be found in the father-only family in our society.

Is the one-parent family pathological?

Most of us probably assume that the one-parent family is inherently pathological—at least for the children involved. It seems only logical to assume that two parents are better than one—the old adage that two heads are better than one.

In his text on the American family, Bell summarizes several studies that question the assumption that two parents are better than one—judging by the adjustment of the children.[32] This, however, does not say anything about the impact of solo child rearing on the parent, which is the major concern of this book.

If one wishes to debate the number of adults required to socialize children properly the question can be raised: who decided that *two*

---

[32] Robert R. Bell, *Marriage and Family Interaction* (rev. ed.; Homewood, Ill.: The Dorsey Press, 1967), pp. 419–420.

parents was the proper number? Biologically this is natural enough, but this does not prove its social rightness.

As a matter of fact, a good family sociologist, Farber, has asked the question—"are two parents enough? . . . in almost every human society *more* than two adults are involved in the socialization of the child."[33]

Farber goes on to point out that in many societies a "third parent," outside of the nuclear family, acts as a sort of "social critic" of the child.[34]

In a recent review of the literature on the one-parent family by Kadushin, the data did not seem sufficient to support the hypothesis that the one-parent family is inherently dysfunctional or pathological.[35] It has been demonstrated by Schorr that the one-parent family is considerably overrepresented in the American poverty population and also on our public welfare rolls.[36] This does not prove, however, that these families are inherently dysfunctional; it merely proves that our economic, political, and social welfare systems are not properly organized to provide an adequate standard of living for the one-parent family. A casual drive through many rural areas in America, especially Appalachia and the rural South, will soon demonstrate to an unbiased observer that the mere presence of *two* parents does not assure a decent standard of living for a family in our society.

To prove that the one-parent family is inherently pathological one would have to demonstrate that the system generates a disproportionate amount of personal disorganization. Kadushin's search of the literature did not reveal enough firm research data to support such a conclusion.[37] This, of course, does not prove that one parent in the home is as good as two—it simply says that the research to date is not adequate to answer the question.

It is obvious to any clinician that the two-parent system has its own pathology—the two parents may be in serious conflict as to how their parental roles should be performed; one parent may be competent but have his (or her) efforts undermined by the incompetent partner; the children may be caught in a "double bind" or crossfire between the two parents;[38] both parents may be competent but simply unable to work

---

[33] Bernard Farber, *Family Organization and Interaction* (San Francisco: Chandler Publishing Co., 1964), p. 457.

[34] *Ibid.*

[35] Alfred Kadushin, "Single Parent Adoptions: An Overview and Some Relevant Research," May, 1968. Available in mimeographed form from the School of Social Work, University of Wisconsin, Madison, Wisc.

[36] See Schorr, *Poor Kids*, chap. 7.

[37] Kadushin, *op. cit.*

[38] On the "double bind" and its potential impact on children see Virginia Satir, *Conjoint Family Therapy* (Palo Alto: Science and Behavior Books, 1964); also Jay Haley, *Strategies of Psychotherapy* (New York: Grune & Stratton, 1963).

together as an effective team in rearing their children; one parent may be more competent than the other but be inhibited in using this competence by the team pattern inherent in the two-parent system.

The writer happens to believe that one *good* parent is enough to rear children adequately or better in our society. It seems to us that enough prominent Americans have been reared by widows or other solo parents to prove the point.[39]

It is interesting to note that adoption agencies are taking another look at the one-parent family and that some agencies are now willing to consider single persons as potential adoptive parents.[40]

Foster parents

A relatively new type of parent in the United States is the "foster parent" utilized by social work agencies to care for children whose biological parents are unable or unwilling to assume parental responsibility. As of 1962 about 176,000 children were living with foster parents in our society. This represented about 70 percent of all American children being cared for by private and public welfare agencies.[41]

Kadushin points out that foster parents have largely replaced the "children's home" in our society: as of 1923 about 65 percent of the homeless children in the United States were living in institutions built for such children, whereas today over two-thirds are living in foster homes.[42]

This is not the place to review the whole foster home movement, but in view of the increase in foster parenthood in our society in recent decades a few observations are in order.[43]

1. *Foster parents have no parental rights.* Although about 75 percent of all foster home placements turn out to be permanent—the child never returns to his own parents—the foster parents usually have no right to

---

[39] This list includes Dr. Nathan Pusey, President of Harvard University, Dr. John Dollard, famous behavioral scientist at Yale University, and John Gardner, formerly Secretary for Health, Education, and Welfare (HEW) in the Johnson Administration.

[40] Alfred Kadushin, School of Social Work, University of Wisconsin, a well-known authority on child welfare, says that as of 1967 some adoption agencies began to accept applications from well-qualified single adults. Personal communication.

[41] Alfred Kadushin, *Child Welfare Services* (New York: The Macmillan Co., 1967), p. 363. We have relied on this source for child welfare material because when it was published in 1967 it was widely reviewed as being the best analysis of child welfare in the United States yet published.

[42] *Ibid.*

[43] See Kadushin, *Child Welfare Services*, chap. 9, "Foster Family Care," for an excellent evaluation of foster parent programs in our society; see also David Fanshel, *Foster Parenthood: A Role Analysis* (Minneapolis: University of Minnesota Press, 1966).

permanent custody of the child.[44] As a rule they cannot adopt the child, nor can they prevent the agency from taking the child away at any time for any reason. The agency is not required to "show cause" when it decides to remove a child from a foster home; there is no appeal to the courts.

About the only clear-cut right the foster parent has is the right to be paid—about 95 percent of them receive compensation for taking care of the child.[45]

2. *The foster parent role is ambiguous.* Foster parents are supposed to express instant love or affection for the foster child, but at the same time they are not supposed to become so attached to a child that they cannot give the child up at any time.

Kadushin points out that the foster parent role is quite complex: "Because foster parenthood is an ambiguously defined role," he writes, "its enactment is likely to occasion difficulty."[46]

The role is ambiguous in that it combines a commercial arrangement with an expectation of affection or a willingness to perform beyond the call of duty. When a child is sick the workday is 24 hours, with no overtime from the agency.

The foster parent role is ambiguous in that while the job pays, it does not pay very well—and yet the care of the child is supposed to be first class.

Every natural parent and every adoptive parent knows that nobody could pay enough to properly rear a child—even a million dollars would not cover the heartaches and the anguish experienced by most parents at one time or another.

The foster parent role is also ambiguous in that what is planned as a temporary placement may turn out to be permanent, while a placement that was intended to be permanent may be terminated in a few days if things don't go well.

It is the writer's belief that the foster parent role is one of the most complex roles attempted by any parent in our society, and the research seems to support this belief.[47]

Adoptive parents

As of 1963 about 120,000 children were being adopted annually in the United States.[48] Of this number almost half (47 percent) were adopted by

---

[44] Kadushin, *op. cit.*

[45] *Ibid.*, p. 425.

[46] *Ibid.*, p. 396.

[47] Both Fanshel and Kadushin agree on the difficulty of the foster parent role.

[48] Kadushin, *Child Welfare Services*, p. 437.

relatives. About two out of every 100 children in our society are reared by adoptive parents.[49]

Unlike the foster parents discussed in the preceding section, adoptive parents have all of the rights that biological parents have once the final adoption papers are signed by the court having jurisdiction. Adoptive parents not only have the same rights as natural parents, but also the same responsibilities.

In a well-known study of adoptive parents Kirk concluded that they have "very special" problems—intense worry as to how the adoption will "turn out," deep feelings of insecurity and/or inadequacy, apprehension, and so on.[50] Reading this book it seemed to us that the feelings Kirk found in adoptive parents are *universal* reactions to parenthood, not just those experienced by adoptive parents.[51]

Biological parents never really know how their children will turn out; most of them feel inadequate and insecure; and almost all of them are literally frightened when they take their first child home from the hospital and realize the awesome responsibility they have assumed—18 to 21 years of daily responsibility for another human being.

Actually, as we see it, adoptive parents have several advantages over biological parents.

1. They get to choose their child. This may not always be the case, but at least they can reject a child that they consider grossly unsuited for them. Biological parents have to accept and keep what "the Lord sends" —bright, dull, retarded, deformed, beautiful, or otherwise.

2. Adoptive parents are voluntary parents. These fathers and mothers do not become parents by accident. The adoption process is such that persons who don't know what they are doing are screened out—they never receive a child. Nobody knows how many children in our society were not actually wanted by their biological parents but the number must be substantial.

3. Adoptive parents have a probation period and can return the child if necessary. In most states there is a probationary period of six months to a year in which the adoptive parents can decide whether they wish to assume permanent responsibility for the child. With biological parents the point of no return comes at the moment of conception—except for those willing to seek an illegal abortion.

---

[49] *Ibid.*, chap. 10, "Adoption," presents a thorough review of the literature on adoption.

[50] See H. David Kirk, *Shared Fate* (New York: The Free Press, 1964). While this book is useful, we feel that Kirk would have had more perspective on parental problems if he had compared a group of natural parents with a group of adoptive parents.

[51] See E. E. LeMasters, "Parenthood as Crisis," *Marriage and Family Living*, 19 (1957), pp. 352–355. In this study of natural parents having their first child we found about the same apprehension that Kirk found in his adoptive parents. This paper received the Ernest Burgess Award from the National Council on Family Relations.

For the above reasons it seems to the writer that the role of adoptive parents is less complex and less fraught with disaster than some people think. The evidence seems to indicate that the great majority of adoptions in our society turn out reasonably well for both the child and the adoptive parents.[52] Whether this can be said for biological parenthood in our society may be debatable.

The role of stepparent

There were about seven million stepchildren in the United States as of the 1960's—this is roughly one child out of nine.[53] This is approximately double the number of stepchildren in this country in 1900. The 1960 decade was the first time in America in which more stepchildren were created by divorce and remarriage than by death. One can visualize the large number of stepchildren when it is realized that some 15 million Americans have now been divorced at one time or another.[54]

Some of the children in these families do not know how to refer to their stepparents—especially so when the father or mother has been married more than twice. One college student, a young man of 20, said to us: "My mother has been married four times. I don't even try to remember the name of her latest husband any more—I just call them by number." Actually, after the second divorce, this boy moved in with his maternal grandparents and he now calls them Dad and Mom.

A college girl said to us: "Do you have to love your stepfather? Mine wants to be real 'buddy buddy' but I can't stand him."

A divorced woman of 35, now remarried, is rearing two sets of children —two from her first marriage and two from her husband's first marriage. She finds the role of stepmother difficult and frustrating. "The other day," she told us, "one of my stepsons didn't do what I had asked him to do. When I corrected him about this he said—'You're not my *real* mother.' I got mad and belted him one." She went on to say that she also found it difficult when one of the stepchildren accused her of being partial to her own children. This woman finds her second marriage satisfying but she regards the role of stepmother as being perhaps the most difficult

---

[52] See Kadushin, *Child Welfare Services*, chap. 10, for an evaluation of adoptions in our society. In a well-designed field study in which he followed up adoptions in which the prognosis had not been favorable, Kadushin found that even these adoptions had turned out better than the experts had predicted. See *Follow-Up Study of Older Children Placed for Adoption*, School of Social Work, University of Wisconsin, Madison, Wisc. This study was completed in 1966 and is to be published by the Columbia University Press in 1969 or 1970.

[53] Simon, *op. cit.*, chap. 5, "The Child's World Changes," has a detailed review of the statistics on stepparents in our society.

[54] Simon, *op. cit.*, p. 59.

job she has ever undertaken—and especially so when there are two sets of children.

Actually, the kinds of situations in which stepparents find themselves are almost endless. In the previous case, for example, if this woman has any children by her second husband there will be *three* sets of children. At this point she is not enthused about this prospect.

A stepmother may find herself rearing a group of children from her husband's first marriage; a stepfather may find himself in the same spot; both may have children with them from a previous marriage; one or both may have had children in more than one previous marriage; they may have children in their new marriage and thus start another set of children; and so forth.

Historically, the role of stepmother has been considered the most difficult parental assignment in Western society. It was no accident that the terrible woman in Cinderella was a stepmother.

Probably the stepmother role is so difficult because children in our society are closer to their mother than their father, and this means that it is very unlikely that anybody can follow the mother without experiencing some problems.

The following factors can be identified as complicating the stepparent role in our society.

1. The stepparent is following a preceding parent. Stepfathers and stepmothers do not start with the child at birth; they follow a preceding father or mother. If the child's relationship with the first parent was positive, this creates difficulty for the stepparent—he or she has to work his or her way into the charmed circle; but if the preceding relationship was negative this also sets up problems—hostility generated in the earlier relationship may be displaced onto the stepparent.

In many different ways the child will be continuously measuring the new parent against the former parent.

2. Stepparents have a tendency to try too hard. Many college students have referred to this in term papers written for the author in which stepparents were discussed.

It seems that the stepparent is so insecure, so afraid of failure with the child, that the stepfather or stepmother pushes the relationship too fast or too hard.[55] Time is required to heal the wounds left over from the previous parent-child relationship and many stepparents don't give the child enough time.

3. Some stepparents try to replace the former parent. Simon and other writers on the stepparent role emphasize that the new parent should usually not attempt to replace the previous father or mother but should

---

[55] Simon, *op. cit.*, discusses the problems of stepparents in various chapters. See also Helen Thomson, *The Successful Stepparent* (New York: Harper & Row, 1966).

see themselves as a supplement, meeting needs of the child not met by the previous parent.[56] This is especially the case in which the child continues to see his biological father or mother.

4. *The complex sets of children to be reared by some stepparents.* This was discussed earlier in this chapter, but one can see how easy it would be for a stepfather or a stepmother to favor his or her biological offspring over the stepchildren, and even if no favoritism is involved the child may feel there is. Blood ties are very deep in human society and not all of us can rise above this in complex stepparent situations.

For all of the stated reasons, and more, the stepparent in our society has a difficult role. Simon, who probably has the best book on this subject, takes a positive attitude toward stepparents.[57] She points out that millions of children in modern America would literally have no father or mother to rear them if it were not for stepparents.

Summary and conclusion

It would seem that a sizeable proportion of American parents operate in situations that are far from ideal—they do not coincide with the dream that most of us have when we start a family.

If one fourth of all marriages in the United States end in divorce, this alone would produce a significant proportion of parents who are either rearing their children alone (those who don't remarry) or are involved in the stepparent role (those who do remarry). If we add to this the families in which a father or mother has died, we get an additional group.

And then, to all of these must be added the unmarried mothers, the separated, and the deserted who are not yet (or even) divorced.

It is not correct to just add all of these categories because almost all of them overlap at some point in time.

The writer believes that a conservative estimate would be that 25 to 35 percent of all American parents perform this role at one time or another under abnormal circumstances. In the famous (or infamous) "Moynihan Report" on the American Negro family, it was estimated that 25 to 50 percent of all black children in the United States live at least some part of their childhood with one or both of their biological parents absent.[58]

---

[56] Simon, *op. cit.*, and Thomson, *op. cit., passim.*

[57] Simon, *op. cit., passim.*

[58] See *The Negro Family*, U.S. Department of Labor, 1965. Although his name does not appear on the report, this document was written by Daniel Patrick Moynihan, hence the label "The Moynihan Report" which has become attached to this study. The report was criticized by various Negro groups when it appeared because of the feeling that Moynihan placed too much emphasis on the problems of the Negro family rather than on the broader social structure of our society. For an interesting

Actually, there are many additional deviant parent situations that we have not even mentioned: mothers whose husbands are away from home because of military service; fathers whose occupations keep them away from their children most of the time; parents who are temporarily in a mental hospital or other medical treatment facility—a tuberculosis sanitarium, for example.

It would seem, from the above, that the total number of American parents who face difficult situations in carrying out their parental responsibilities is larger than most of us realize.

An attempt was made in this chapter to analyze the problems of parents who function under deviant or abnormal conditions. The two largest groups seem to be mothers rearing children with no father present and stepparents of both sexes.

The assumed pathology of the one-parent family was questioned, and an attempt was made to estimate the total number of American parents operating under abnormal circumstances.

---

analysis of this controversy, see Lee Rainwater and William Yancey (eds.), *The Moynihan Report and the Politics of Controversy* (Cambridge, Mass: M.I.T. Press 1967).

chapter
ten

Parents, mass media, and the youth peer group

A survey of seven days of network television shows reported 81 killings in 85 hours of prime evening hours and on Saturday morning. There were 372 acts of violence or threats of violence—162 of these on Saturday morning programs viewed mostly by children.[1]

This same survey found that violent incidents occurred most frequently (every 16 minutes) between 7:30 and 9:00 in the evening when 26.7 million children ages 2 to 17 are reported to be watching television. In these early evening hours there was a murder or killing every 31 minutes—whereas later in the evening such incidents occurred about every two hours.

In another study is was estimated that the average American child has watched television some 22,000 hours by the age of 18.[2]

It is not only television and its impact on parents that we wish to consider in this chapter. We want to assess the influence of mass media in general, such as radio, magazines, and movies, and their relationship to the adolescent peer group that modern parents must cope with.

It is a mistake to dismiss these characteristics of contemporary America with the cliché that "kids have always palled around together." In his book, *The Lonely Crowd*, Riesman says: "there has been an enormous

---

[1] Survey conducted by the *Christian Science Monitor* and reported in the *Wisconsin State Journal*, Madison, Wisc., August 27, 1968.

[2] Paper given by the semanticist, S. I. Hayakawa, at the 1968 annual meeting of the American Psychological Association in San Francisco, reported in the *Milwaukee Journal* for September 3, 1968.

ideological shift favoring submission to the group . . . the peer group becomes the measure of all things; the individual has few defenses the group cannot batter down."[3]

It is also a mistake to underestimate the impact of such relatively new mass media as television on children and their parents. In a recent analysis of television the statement was made: "There is a new force in America, a force that rivals the family, the school, and the church in its influence on our values, our attitudes, and our judgements."[4]

It is the thesis of this chapter that most parents in our society have found no effective means of coping with the "mass media-adolescent peer group force" affecting their children. It is also our belief that the values of these nonfamily influences are basically in conflict with those of most American parents.

The rest of this chapter will analyze in some detail the above propositions.

Mass media and parents

One of the major themes of this book is that parents in contemporary society constitute only one set of forces operating on their children. It is true, of course, that for the preschool years parents constitute the major influence shaping the child, although some biologists and geneticists might dispute this point. But from a *social* point of view the parents have five or six years in which to implant or internalize their values before the child moves out into the larger world.

It is true, obviously, that parental influence does not cease at five or six—the point is that it ceases to be *exclusive* at that age. From then on parental values and parental attitudes are filtered or mediated by a host of nonfamily forces: the school, with its longer school year and its vastly increased number of years attended;[5] television and its "children's hour" of violence interspersed with commercials (it has been estimated that the average American is exposed to roughly 1,800 advertising messages a day);[6] and lastly the child's peer group. The power of this last force has

---

[3] See David Riesman et al., *The Lonely Crowd* (New Haven: Yale University Press, 1961 ed.), p. 82.

For a careful review of the effects of mass media on children, see Eleanor E. Macoby, "Effects of the Mass Media," in *Child Development Research* edited by Martin L. Hoffman and Lois Wladis Hoffman (New York: Russell Sage Foundation, 1964), pp. 323–348.

[4] Yale Roe, *The Television Dilemma* (New York: Hastings House Publishers, 1962), Preface, p. vii. Roe is an executive in the television industry.

[5] In 1900 only about 11 percent of the American youth of high school age were actually in school. As of 1959 the percentage was 96.6 in the ninth grade and 78.5 by the twelfth grade. See *Statistical Abstract of the United States* (Washington, D.C.: U.S. Bureau of the Census, 1967), Table 162, p. 118.

[6] Dexter Masters, *The Intelligent Buyer and the Telltale Seller* (New York: Alfred A. Knopf, 1966), chap. 9.

been greatly underestimated by many observers of the American family, in the opinion of this writer. We have already cited Riesman's belief that the power of the peer group has been increasing in modern America, and to this a few other citations of the same nature might be added. After studying the social climate of 10 American high schools, Coleman reached this conclusion: "The adolescent lives more and more in a society of his own; he finds the family a less and less satisfying psychological home. As a consequence, the home has less and less ability to mold him."[7]

Minuchin and associates, in an intensive study of low-income families, concluded that older siblings may influence their younger brothers and sisters more than the parents do.[8]

In the laboratory studies of the family life of the rhesus monkey by Harlow and his research team at the University of Wisconsin it has been discovered that interference with the normal peer group interaction may affect young monkeys as severely as a breakdown in the mother-child relationship.[9]

If the mass media and the adolescent peer group supported the efforts of parents no particular problem would exist. If a child is properly socialized (prepared for his adult roles in the society) it does not matter much who or what helped the child to mature. As Bell and many others have pointed out, the nuclear family is not the only social arrangement utilized in human society to prepare children for their place in the adult society.[10]

The problem in relationship to these nonfamily influences in our society, as the writer sees it, is that often parents are in conflict with these other forces in their efforts to produce responsible adult citizens out of their children.

It may be difficult to demonstrate that school systems are in conflict with parents, although this is not impossible,[11] but it seems to us that a good case can be made for the proposition that the mass media and the adolescent peer group subculture are in conflict with most parents in modern America.[12] The reader can judge the evidence for himself when it is presented later in this chapter.

---

[7] James S. Coleman, The Adolescent Society (New York: The Free Press, 1961), p. 312. This is a study of the social life in 10 high schools. In the opinion of this writer it is the best study to date of its kind.

[8] See Salvador Minuchin et al., Families of the Slums (New York: Basic Books, 1967), p. 219.

[9] Personal communication.

[10] Robert R. Bell, Marriage and Family Interaction (Homewood, Ill.: The Dorsey Press, 1967 ed.), chap. 14.

[11] Coleman, op. cit., p. 32, suggests that many of the facets of high school subculture are antagonistic to the values held by most parents.

[12] By mass media we refer to motion pictures, television, radio, mass magazines, commercial advertising, and popular records aimed at young people. By adolescent peer group reference is made largely to junior high and senior high school age groups, although some of the data would apply to college students as well.

In stressing the power of parental influence during the preschool years, as most psychiatrists do,[13] it is often forgotten that much of what makes the world go round is not really relevant during these early years— money, materialism, marriage, occupational choice, the use (or abuse) of liquor, crime, politics, and even sex, in spite of what the Freudians say.

One problem during these early years of socialization is that the child is unable to grasp the subtle nuances and the complexities of adult life. The parent has to simplify the world and present everything as black or white, yes or no. Honesty, for example, is presented as an absolute, never to be questioned, yet few (if any) adult Americans find it possible to be honest at all times, in all situations, to all people. Persons who question this statement should interview staff members of the Internal Revenue Service, as the writer has done.[14]

How would you explain today's complex sex code to a young child? Sexual relations before marriage are acceptable under certain circumstances with the right person, but the same behavior in other situations is bad and unacceptable.[15] This is the actual sex code that modern adult Americans live by, but from whom do young people learn the code? Not from parents or schoolteachers or college professors or ministers. They learn the code from their peer group, from the movies, magazines, television, and popular songs. We are *not* attempting to judge the code here: we are simply arguing that young Americans do not learn this complex code of sexual conduct at their father or mother's knee.

What actually happens is that much of what youngsters learn from their parents in our society has to be unlearned or relearned at a later date, as Ruth Benedict pointed out long ago.[16]

Very little, if any, of the complexities of true love between a man and a woman are learned during the early years of life. We are referring to the type of male-female relationship that makes marriage not only tolerable but enjoyable for some Americans. On television, in the movies, and in popular songs, this type of love is usually confused with sex. A man meets a woman, they go to bed together, and then the idea is implied that they have found love—actually, they have found sex, which is not a bad find in itself but is hardly to be equated with love as this term is applied to marriage in our society.

Almost all of the courtships (or love affairs) are telescoped on television and in the movies. Love is not presented as a learning process that takes time; it is not developed as something that some people *achieve*.

---

[13] Chap. 3 of this volume analyzes psychiatric theory as it affects parents.

[14] In an interview in 1967 an examiner of federal income tax returns told the writer that an "error" of 10 percent in the taxpayer's favor was considered "normal."

[15] The complexities in the current American sex code are fully analyzed in Ira L. Reiss, *Premarital Sexual Standards in America* (New York: The Free Press, 1960).

[16] See the classic paper by Ruth Benedict, "Continuities and Discontinuities in Cultural Conditioning," *Psychiatry*, I (1938), pp. 161–167.

It is presented as an accident or a twist of fate.[17] On television and in the movies people *fall* in love; it is not something that can be explained or understood—and certainly not by parents.

All this is by way of introduction to the discussion of mass media and parents. Now let us analyze the basic values presented to young people via advertising, magazines, television, movies, radio, and popular songs. We will then present what we believe to be the basic values that parents in our society would like to see their children adopt. Later we will make a few observations about similarities and differences between these two sets of values.

Values of the mass media

In looking at the mass media and the values[18] they portray to young Americans, it must be remembered that almost all of these media in our society are operated for profit.[19] And this profit is directly related to the size of the audience attracted. This means, essentially, that in order to attract readers or viewers or listeners, the program content (or the reader content) must have almost universal appeal to the audience aimed at. This explains why classical music is never heard on most commercial AM radio stations—most of their audience would tune them out if they played such music.

It is also important to keep in mind that as of the 1960's there were approximately 20 million teen-agers in the United States with a total buying power estimated at $10 *billion* a year.[20] It should also be noted that by 1970 there will be about 25 percent more youngsters under 15 and 40 percent more teen-agers altogether.

Thus the mass media are not playing for peanuts when they seek to attract and hold this audience.

How does a radio station or a television station or a movie producer reach young Americans?

The following themes seem to work rather well.

---

17 This is nicely illustrated by the lyrics of the song, "Strangers in the Night," made popular by Frank Sinatra in the 1960's.

18 On the concept of "value" see Robin M. Williams, Jr., *American Society* (rev. ed.; New York: Alfred A. Knopf, 1960), chap. 11. Williams says that "values are not the concrete goals of action, but rather the *criteria* by which goals are chosen." (p. 374.)

19 Persons interested in the precise ways in which the profit motive affects one mass medium (television) should read Fred Friendly, *Due to Circumstances Beyond Our Control* (New York: Random House, 1967). A former president of CBS news, Friendly writes: "Because television can make so much money doing its worst, it often cannot afford to do its best." (p. xii of the Introduction.)

20 For these statistics see Grace and Fred M. Hechinger, *Teen-Age Tyranny* (New York: William Morrow & Co., 1963), pp. 151–152.

Sex

These 20 million teen-agers are in the process of discovering the world of sex—their bodies and their glands are propelling them toward sexual maturity, even though psychologically and socially most of them are far from being mature.[21]

Now there is nothing wrong with sex—as most Americans will testify—and given the lack of an adequate sex education program in the United States somebody has to help these youngsters get some idea of what sex is all about. American novelists have been mining this field for a long time but in recent decades television and the drive-in movie have muscled their way into this market with great enthusiasm.

Unfortunately, as the writer sees it, sex in the movies and on television is usually on a rather physical level visually and verbally, yet is presented to the audience as love—in other words, the signals or cues are confusing. In one sense we are watching physical and genital attraction between a man and a woman but in another sense we are expected to believe that these two people are in love.

Here is an illustration: we have two sons, 16 and 18, who like the *I Spy* television series. The writer has some positive feeling for this program also, partly because the producer was courageous enough to feature a black performer (Bill Cosby) who was not a caricature of the Afro-American.

This program features very good-looking, well-built young women who are usually interested in the attractive co-star of the series (Robert Culp). These women, at least to the writer, do not seem to be nice girls—they are portrayed as aggressive in their sexual advances toward the men on the program[22] and there is often a suggestion that a sexual affair has transpired after a relatively brief acquaintance.

Once or twice, while watching such an episode with our two sons, the writer has suggested to them that the girl in this particular episode did

---

[21] In a recent newspaper series a professional observer of the Hollywood motion picture industry made the following statement: "Pictures that depict—indeed glorify—infidelity, nudity, sexual license and vulgarity are being turned out in profusion. They have achieved box office success for several film companies that had previously been near bankruptcy. . . . actors and actresses who break the established moral codes in their personal behavior find the screen moguls automatically disposed to boost the price of their services." Martin Abrahamson, United Press correspondent, *Milwaukee Journal*, September 10, 1968, Entertainment Section, p. 1.

Almost at random we select a motion picture advertisement of the following nature: "Slaves to their own strange desires. Playthings of each other's unholy passions!" *Milwaukee Journal*, September 15, 1968.

[22] Because of racial taboos on mass media white girls on the *I Spy* program are not permitted to show romantic and/or sexual interest in Bill Cosby, the black co-star of the series.

not seem to be a very nice girl. Their reaction has usually been one of surprise—*why* wasn't she a nice girl?

It seems to us that the physical attractiveness of the show—the exotic hotels and the beautiful people—makes it difficult to realize that some of the behavior is not so beautiful. Can young people (or even the rest of us) see such distinctions? It seems to us that our sons are being presented feminine models that are at best dubious.

It may well be, of course, that the end result will be quite different from what the writer fears. The research on the long-range impact of television is hardly good enough to answer such questions as yet.[23]

It needs to be said in defense of the *I Spy* television series that one very positive value is consistently portrayed—that people of different races can live and work together with mutual respect and affection.

One needs only to read the daily newspaper advertisements for movies to see that Hollywood and the foreign film makers do not overlook sex in their productions.

Violence

Survey after survey has shown the massive dose of violence presented to young and old alike on television and in motion pictures.[24] America is, of course, a violent society, and the mass media owners are always eager (a bit too eager) to point out that "We only give the customers what they want." On the same kind of logic call girls and the distributors of illegal narcotics could plead the same defense. Human beings have many self-destructive tendencies and all human societies do what they can to hold these to a minimum level. It is difficult to see how modern films and television programs are helping to achieve this end.[25]

The idealization of immaturity

In the Hechinger study of teen-age subculture cited earlier one of the major points developed is that today's teen-ager no longer worships adult heroes—his idols are just as juvenile and immature as he is. In comment-

---

23 For a thorough review of this research see Wilbur Schramm et al., *Television in the Lives of Our Children* (Palo Alto, Calif.: Stanford University Press, 1961). Schramm reports, among other things, that the average American child, 3 to 16 years of age, spends one sixth of his waking hours watching television, about as much time as he spends in school over a 12-month period; that a survey of the so-called children's programs on television revealed that one half of the 100 hours monitored from 4 to 9 P.M. featured violence. These findings are reported on the dust jacket of the volume.

24 For a merciless analysis of violence and sadism in so-called children's programs in the mass media, see Gilbert Seldes, *The Public Arts* (New York: Simon and Schuster, 1956). See also Otto N. Larsen (ed.), *Violence and the Mass Media* (New York: Harper & Row, 1968).

25 The promotion of racial and religious understanding probably represents an exception to this statement.

ing on this in the *Saturday Review*, the Education Editor, Paul Woodring, put this point in the following words:

the adolescent of an earlier age was eager to grow up, and the heroes he chose to emulate, while not always admirable, were usually adult. Today's teen-ager often chooses a model no older and no more mature than himself—a juvenile who has achieved wealth and fame at an early age with the help of just a little talent or beauty plus a hard-driving publicity agent. It is not difficult to understand why such models are chosen—they provide the basis for elaborate daydreams of what is seemingly possible for any adolescent who "gets a break," without much long waiting or hard work, without going to college or even completing high school. By comparison the prospect of a career emulating that of Abraham Lincoln or Florence Nightingale seems decidedly dull.[26]

In the face of such daydreams, parents often find it difficult to sell their children on the facts of life—that for most Americans hard work and years of training are required to compete in the society.

Materialism

In a paper cited earlier in this chapter the well-known semanticist, Hayakawa, is quoted as saying that the antimaterialism of today's youth may be a reaction to television's message that "material possessions are everything, that this headache remedy, this luxurious carpeting, this new model car" will bring happiness.[27]

American parents are themselves inclined to be materialistic—as is the whole society—but one often has the feeling that parental materialism cannot compare with that portrayed in the mass media.

The writer still has vivid memories of two mass magazine advertisements of a few years ago that seemed to have hit a new low: in one a mother, surrounded by her husband and children, is looking at a new car and says: "Our new Plymouth is the greatest thing that ever happened to this family."[28]

In the other advertisement, aimed at the Christmas trade, a father is shown heading for home (at least we hope so) pulling a child's sled on which reposes a case of a famous brand of whisky. The writer likes a drink as well as most Americans but somehow this picture was revolting.

One of the interesting features of mass media materialism is the effort made to make it seem free. You just get out the credit cards and off you go to Hawaii, with no cash needed. This is similar to what Woodring was writing about in the quotation earlier—no real effort is required to enjoy the fruits of the affluent society.

---

[26] Paul Woodring, *Saturday Review*, March 23, 1963, p. 72. Copyright 1963 Saturday Review, Inc.

[27] *Milwaukee Journal*, September 3, 1968, p. 10.

[28] We no longer have these two advertisements in our files but they both appeared in mass magazines during the period 1960 to 1965.

Hedonism

One modern dictionary defines *hedonism* as "the doctrine that pleasure is the principal good and should be the aim of action."[29]

Without debating the merits of this philosophical system, it does seem that the mass media message in our society is essentially hedonistic. This reflects the fact that the ultimate aim of most mass media is that of entertainment and escape. It is usually assumed by advertisers that Americans see enough reality in their everyday life; when they watch television they want to escape reality and be amused.

To the extent that this is true, teen-agers (as well as most other Americans) are exposed to an unreal world when they turn to the mass media.

It may well be, of course, as Riesman suggests, that the drift of our entire society is in the direction of hedonism.[30] With mechanization and automation the major problem in the affluent society may well be what people do with their leisure rather than what they do at their place of work.

The writer has the impression, not well documented, that the younger generation is considerably more hedonistic than most of their parents. If this is true it could simply reflect a deep change in basic values in our society with the youth subculture reflecting the trend more fully than the adult subculture does. Another possible explanation of the difference —if there is a difference—is that young people don't have to face adult reality as yet precisely because they are still not adults. American parents are notorious for their desire to protect young people from the harsh facts of life, and the mass media simply share this purpose.

With this background in mass media values let us turn to a discussion of parental values, after which we will try to put the two sets of values together.

Parental values

It is recognized that the list of values being discussed in this chapter are not necessarily the ones that another observer would choose to discuss.[31] This is a difficult field and subjectivity is hard to avoid. Perhaps the best approach is simply to admit the personal bias of the writer so

---

[29] *Webster's New World Dictionary of the American Language* (College ed.; Cleveland: World Publishing Co., 1956), p. 672.

[30] See Riesman et al., *op. cit.*, chap. 2, "From Morality to Morale: Changes in the Agents of Character Formation."

[31] The basic values of the American family system are discussed in Williams, *op. cit.*, chap. 4, "Kinship and the Family in the United States"; see also Max Lerner, *America as a Civilization* (New York: Simon and Schuster, 1957), Pt. 8, "Life Cycle of the American." A good analysis may also be found in John Sirjamaki, *The American Family in the Twentieth Century* (Cambridge, Mass.: Harvard University Press, 1953).

that the reader is warned. To recapitulate: the values under analysis in this chapter do not purport to be based on empirical research—they were simply chosen to illustrate certain points of conflict between parents and the mass media.

Here, then, are some parental values which we believe are not supported by the mass media.

No violence

Most American parents, regardless of what they may have done in their own lives, hope (and pray) that their children will not attack or kill other human beings. As Mead observed long ago, Americans are "counter punchers"—children are taught not to start a fight but also not to run away from one.[32] They are to fight back if they are attacked by someone else.

This is not the world of television and the movies. It is true, of course, that the bad guys always lose on *Gunsmoke* and *Bonanza*, and Hollywood has a code that crime does not pay—but nevertheless the violent, ruthless person, like the Devil in old-fashioned sermons, often emerges as a sort of "inverted hero." He may lose the girl, and even his life, but meanwhile he has captured the audience. The old gangster films made by Jimmy Cagney and Humphrey Bogart illustrate what we are talking about.

We grant that researchers are divided as to the long-range effects of such films on children,[33] but our point is that most American parents would prefer that their children not be subjected to such a heavy dose of aggression and violence.

Suppose somebody did a series of television films showing children how to shoplift from supermarkets and other stores more effectively. Even if *most* children who saw the series never actively engaged in shoplifting as a result of the series, would it be in the public interest to show such films? Actually the series might even *lower* the crime rate for juvenile shoplifters by helping them avoid detection, but one can be sure that merchants would create such an uproar that the series would be banned. Parents often feel the same way about various aspects of the mass media but they seldom are able to obtain any redress.

Mass media owners have a pat answer to parents who protest: "don't permit your child to watch our programs—or read our comics—if you don't approve of the content." Any parent who has tried this solution knows how difficult it is.

---

[32] Margaret Mead, *And Keep Your Powder Dry* (New York: William Morrow & Co., 1965 ed.).

[33] Schramm et al., *op. cit.*, has perhaps the best review of the research efforts which attempt to determine the effects of television on children. Nobody seems to know how television affects parents.

We grant that some of the mass media content is antiwar and anti-racial violence, but the net impression is one of aggression and violence in human affairs.

Sexual restraint

In our opinion most American parents in the 1960's are aware that their children, daughters as well as sons, may have sexual relations before marriage.[34] These parents did not grow up in a prudish society and have little hope that their children will be more chaste than they were. But most parents, regardless of their own sexual histories, do hope that their children will use sex constructively in their lives, and that they will subscribe to some sort of decent sex code. One element of such a code is that sex should be combined with affection and/or love.[35]

It seems to us that television, the movies, and many mass magazines do not portray sex in this way. It is presented as an overwhelming physical attraction between a man and a woman, with the individuals having little or no choice as to what they do about the attraction. And the relationships are entered into after such a brief courtship that it seems hardly appropriate to describe the interaction as love.

The girls in these programs are presented as being sexually aggressive —something that frightens the average parent.

It may well be that young Americans can still recognize love when they find it, but one has to question how much help they received from the mass media in this matter.

Lifetime monogamy

It is an interesting fact that in the 1960's the most glamorous men on American television were either bachelors or widowers—*I Spy, Bonanza, The Man from UNCLE* (while it lasted), *My Three Sons*, and so on. The married men on television, for the most part, are harried and harassed and sometimes stupid. One wonders what an image of marriage is created by such programs.

Most American parents, for better or worse, are committed to lifetime monogamy—three fourths of them are married for life and presumably hope that their children will do the same.

But the mass media take a much more tentative approach to lifetime

---

[34] For a careful study of sex attitudes among young people as well as parents, see Ira L. Reiss, *The Social Context of Premarital Sexual Permissiveness* (New York: Holt, Rinehart and Winston, 1967).

[35] On sex as love or affection, see the 1960 study by Reiss cited earlier, also Winston Ehrmann, *Premarital Dating Behavior* (New York: Henry Holt and Co., 1959). Many of these ideas are discussed in Edwin M. Schur (ed.), *The Family and the Sexual Revolution* (Bloomington, Ind.: Indiana University Press, 1964).

monogamy—many of the great stars, such as Elizabeth Taylor, have been married several times—and one reads almost daily of some young idol whose marriage has failed.

American law, of course, recognizes serial monogamy as being perfectly moral and legal, and it may well be that the drift of the society is toward serial monogamy, but divorced persons are still a minority in America and many parents must wish that the mass media might recognize this fact.

Planning for the future

Most parents in our society have come to accept the old banker's cliché that "the future belongs to those who prepare for it." Even though the parents may be in debt, they realize that some thought has to be given to the day of reckoning—not only in regard to financial matters, but also in regard to sex, alcohol, education, and so forth.

The mass media present a vague picture of the future consequence of present action. We see beautiful men and women drinking beer every few minutes on television but nobody ever gets fat. We see all the handsome males and females smoking their cigarettes on television but nobody ever gets lung cancer. We see entire families taking off for Hawaii with nothing in their pockets but a credit card, yet nobody ever goes bankrupt.

We were reminded of this never-never land of consumer economics when one of our sons asked casually whether or not we had an elaborate insurance plan that had just been described in a television commercial. This plan covered every conceivable emergency that could happen to an American family, but no mention was made of the cost. Out of curiosity we checked with an insurance agency and learned that for the writer's age group the annual premium on this particular policy would be about $2400. When we mentioned this figure to our son he was amazed; he had no idea what such things cost. And he will never learn it from television either.

Many parents today hope that their children will not smoke cigarettes—not on moral grounds but on health grounds. Such parents get little support from the mass media.

Discussion of these two sets of values

It seems to us that the major conflict between the values of parents and those of the mass media stems from the fact that parents have learned to live cautiously, with at least one eye (if not both) on the future, whereas the mass media present a world in which the more interesting people live dangerously and largely for the present.

In a sense our entire society seems to be moving toward a philosophy of living one day at a time. Since the development of the hydrogen bomb there has never been a guarantee that there will be a future for any of us to enjoy. The days of "peace and normalcy" are gone forever, and in this sense we live under a permanent psychological state of war—"let us live today for tomorrow we may die."

Another reason why the mass media tend to drive a wedge between the generations is that the mass media are actually pushing products (and ideas) that are projected 10 to 20 years into the future. A good illustration might be the miniskirt of the 1960's. This began to appear on television around 1960, yet only today (1968) has it become widely accepted in the midwestern metropolitan area where the writer lives—and even then it is worn by few mothers. Meanwhile, the mass media have moved on to new fashions—the maxiskirt, plus shorter versions of the miniskirt. This means that even parents who are relatively contemporary are made to feel out-of-date by the mass media and their youthful public.

It seems clear that most mass media content is aimed at a relatively youthful audience for the simple reason that these are the consumers of tomorrow. Thus parents, who grew up yesterday, do not often see their world reflected in the mass media.

To the writer's knowledge relatively few parents have been able to cope successfully with "the mass media problem." Efforts to legislate and/or censor have not been successful, and strong-arm methods at home have posed their own problems. One mother said to the writer: "I used to fight with my kids all the time about their television programs. Finally I gave up and decided to hell with it. Life is too short to argue about things like that all the time."

A vistor from Israel told the writer that he was appalled at the violence in American television programs viewed by children. Our reply was that many American parents were equally appalled but didn't know what to do about it.

We are not arguing that all of the values presented to young people by the mass media are nonfunctional or dysfunctional—either for the society or the youngsters themselves. For example: easy credit seems to be necessary to keep the American economy operating at a high level. If this is so, and if most Americans want prosperity, then young people need to be conditioned positively toward consumer credit—and nobody can deny that the mass media are doing a good job at that.

Even the aggression shown on television and in Hollywood films may be functional for the young viewers if you assume that a certain amount of aggressiveness is essential for success in our competitive society.

Part of the trouble arises from the fact that parents are ambivalent about many of the trends that television and the other mass media present to young people so enthusiastically. Consumer credit illustrates this ambivalence very well. Most contemporary parents use consumer credit and appreciate its convenience. But they also know that such credit can be expensive, and a lot of them also know that "easy credit" can ruin marriages and families if you use it too carelessly.

But this other side of the picture is seldom shown in the mass media— at least young people don't seem to know about it.

It is this aspect of the mass media that tends to pose problems for parents: the dreamworld that parents know can easily turn into a nightmare world if youngsters don't see the pitfalls.

Parents and the adolescent peer group

The major impression the writer has from the literature, supplemented by personal observation, is the affluence and power of the adolescent peer group in modern America. In a provocative paper Bernard points out that only a very wealthy society could support the new leisure class that these youngsters represent.[36] In the old rural America children had to work on the farm, which separated them from their peer group for most of the time and left only a few hours a week for peer group social life.

The writer's father, who grew up on a farm, used to maintain that even during the summer school recess he was lucky if he had more than three or four hours a week to visit with his friends.

Somewhat later, as America became urban and industrial, the children of immigrant parents either went into the labor force early to help their families or they worked when not in school.

Today the situation is quite different. Laws prohibit urban teen-agers from holding most jobs until they are at least 16, and with no farm chores to keep them busy they roam the streets, haunt the shopping centers, and jam into any hangout that caters to them.

Subcultures are developed by people who associate together frequently—and American teen-agers have evolved an elaborate way of life that they have created and maintained.[37] From cars to music to clothes

---

[36] See the excellent paper by Jessie Bernard, "Teen-Age Culture: An Overview," in *The Annals of the American Academy of Political and Social Science*, 338 (November, 1961), pp. 1–12. This entire issue was devoted to teen-age culture and was edited by Bernard.

A useful analysis of youth subculture will be found in Marvin Wolfgang, *The Culture of Youth* (Washington, D.C.: U.S. Dept. of Health, Education, and Welfare, 1967).

On the concept of subculture see Milton Yinger, "Contraculture and Subculture," *American Sociological Review*, 25 (1960), pp. 625–635.

[37] Actually, much of the youth subculture is created by middle-aged movie producers, record company executives, television writers, and other adults who work in the mass media.

to language, teen-agers can live in their own world almost completely isolated from the world of their parents.

In their book on teen-agers the Hechingers make the following statement:

For several decades now, the most insecure and most immature members of adult society have permitted, often in the name of self-expression and pseudo-psychology, the most insecure and most immature adolescents to establish their own independent and sovereign culture . . . the task now is to make it clearly understood that adolescence is a state of human development, not an empire . . . ."[38]

Coleman, after studying social life in 10 high schools, was impressed by the extent and power of teen-age society. He writes: "our adolescents today are cut off, probably more than ever before, from the adult society . . . our society has within its midst a set of small teen-age societies, which focus teen-age interests and attitudes on things far removed from adult responsibilities, and which may develop standards that lead away from those goals established by the larger society."[39] Coleman did not find that these high school students ignore or even reject the values of their parents—his main point is that parents are in constant competition with teen-age society and are never sure when their wishes will prevail with their adolescent children.

One can shrug off this competition with the old bromide: good parents have no trouble with teen-agers—only poor parents do. Within limits this may be correct, but the stiff competition from the teen-age society still poses severe problems for parents who have only tenuous relations with their adolescent children.

We have pointed out elsewhere in this book that some parents try to beat the teen-agers at their own game by joining them.[40] In his text on the American family Bell has a caustic observation on such parents: "it is a devastating picture of parents," he writes, "because it implies that they are still teen-agers."[41]

The Hechingers also comment on parents who try to become middle-age teen-agers. They write: "What worries us is not the greater freedom of today's youth but rather the abdication of the rights and privileges of adults for the convenience of the immature. We believe teen-age should be regarded as a phase of human development, with both pleasant and unpleasant side effects, rather than as an achievement or a disease."[42]

---

[38] Hechinger, op. cit., p. 243.

[39] Coleman, op. cit., p. 9. See chap. 1, "The Emergence of An Adolescent Sub-culture in Industrial Society," for an excellent analysis of this development.

[40] See chap. 12.

[41] Bell, op. cit., p. 431.

[42] Hechinger, op. cit., Introduction.

The writer goes along with Coleman, Riesman, Bernard, and the Hechingers, in the references previously cited in this chapter, that the power and extent of teen-age society and its resultant subculture is a relatively new force for American parents to cope with. It is also our belief that most parents are still puzzled by the rise of this new sub-society and have yet to develop means of competing with it successfully.[43]

Summary and conclusion

In this chapter we have explored some facets of mass media in our society and their impact on American teen-agers and their parents. It has been admitted in the chapter that the research on the effects of such mass media as motion pictures and television is far from conclusive. Thus Schramm and his associates, after surveying the television habits of 6,000 children, reported both positive and negative impact on children.[44]

The fact remains, however, that American parents are having a difficult time with their teen-agers and many of them feel that the mass media are contributing to their parental problems.

The chapter supported the thesis that the power and extent of teen-age society and its related subculture are relatively new forces that most parents have not learned how to cope with.

---

[43] As this book was nearly completed a provocative volume appeared: Lewis S. Feuer, *The Conflict of Generations* (New York: Basic Books, 1969). See especially chap. 7, "Generational Equilibrium in the United States."

[44] Schramm et al., *op. cit., passim.*

chapter
eleven

Parents and
social change

I T is interesting to note that in the paper by Davis on parent-youth conflict, cited so often in this book, that he discusses social change first.[1] He writes:

The first important variable is the rate of social change. Extremely rapid change in modern civilization, in contrast to most civilizations, tends to increase parent-youth conflict, for within a fast-changing order the time interval between generations, ordinarily but a mere moment in the life of the social system, becomes historically significant, thereby creating a gap between one generation and the next.[2]

In this chapter we assume that Davis was correct in this observation but we wish to push the analysis further than he does in an attempt to see *how* rapid social change affects parents in our society. Before proceeding to the analysis, however, it may be helpful to make a few observations about the concept of social change.[3]

The concept of social change

1. Social change is not synonymous with social progress. It is important to remember that in social science analysis, social change is not

---

[1] Kingsley Davis, "The Sociology of Parent-Youth Conflict," *American Sociological Review,* **5** (August, 1940), pp. 523–535. For extensive analysis of the process of social change see *Social Change,* edited by Amitai and Eva Etzioni (New York: Basic Books, 1964).

[2] Davis, *op. cit.,* p. 523.

[3] A useful book on the family and social change is *The Family and Change* edited by John N. Edwards (New York: Alfred A. Knopf, 1969).

equated with social progress or social deterioration. It can easily be proven, for example, that the divorce rate in America has increased since 1900, but the evaluation of this change is quite a different proposition. Almost all of the changes discussed in this chapter are of this same nature: they have had both positive and negative impact on American parents.

2. *The rate of social change is not constant.* Societies and their way of life (their cultures) do not change at a fixed or steady pace. The United States, for example, has probably changed more from 1900 to 1960 than it did in the previous two or three centuries. In many ways the rate of change seems to be cumulative—it follows a curve of acceleration.

3. *Social change in a society is not even or symmetrical.* Many years ago Ogburn pointed this out in his concept of "cultural lag."[4] His thesis was, essentially, that some parts or aspects of a culture change more rapidly than others, and that this creates imbalance and stress in the system.

In this chapter we will see that the parental role in modern America has been complicated by uneven social change—an example would be the urban school year. This developed originally for the benefit of farm parents who wished to have their children help with the farm work during the summer months—but the long summer school recess is not functional for either urban parents or their children. And for the employed mother it is almost disastrous.

Another good example of uneven social change in our society might be the deep social revolution that American women have been going through since World War I in contrast with the slower and less pervasive changes American men seem to have experienced in the same period. To the extent that this has actually been the case—and we recognize that it is merely a hypothesis, not a proven fact—then fathers and mothers would have more difficulty in agreeing how they should rear their children.

The term *differential social change* is useful in referring to uneven change in our society.

4. *Social change is not usually planned.* In most societies major social changes are not actually planned; they simply evolve in response to some need or they occur as the result of some crisis in the system. An example would be the American public welfare system, which is currently being subjected to severe criticism. Until the economic disaster of the 1930's the United States had no modern public welfare system. Voluntary or private social work agencies met family emergencies and did most of

---

[4] The concept of "cultural lag" or unequal rates of social change within a society was originally developed by W. F. Ogburn in a book called *Social Change* (New York: B. W. Huebsch, 1922).

the family counseling, with local public welfare agencies meeting the minimal economic needs of the chronically indigent. When this system broke down because of mass unemployment in the 1930's a new system of local-state-federal public welfare services was hastily improvised. Today it is becoming increasingly clear that this system, designed to help the temporarily unemployed of the 1930's, is not adequate for the 1970's. The clients of today are different and their needs are different.[5] The failure of the welfare system to be properly planned and organized has posed great problems for low-income and minority group parents, as we have seen in earlier chapters.

5. *The total results of social change are not often anticipated.* In social systems, also families, a change in one part of the system forces change in other parts, for the simple reason that the various aspects of the system are interrelated. Prohibition is often cited by American social scientists as a prime example of the unanticipated results of social change: it was not realized in advance that prohibiting the legal sale of alcoholic beverages would channel hundreds of millions of dollars of revenue into the underworld, thus creating a vast empire of syndicate gangs that still pose problems in urban America.[6]

A good example of unanticipated change in the American family would be the impact of the automobile on parents and children. Not only was the budget of the family drastically altered, but supervision of dating couples became literally impossible. Chaperones at dances, for example, became mere symbols once couples could come and go in automobiles.

6. *Social change is often not desired—it is forced on people.* It is doubtful that most American men really wanted to grant equal social status to women at the end of World War I. In a very real sense the change was forced on the men. This means that social changes of this nature always create conflict, and even after the battle is over, pockets of resistance will be found. Some husbands and fathers in the United States today are still convinced that American political life began to deteriorate the day women began to vote.

Only recently the writer heard a so-called educated person make this remark at a public meeting. "Don't you agree with me," he said to a mixed group of men and women, "that the American family began to decline when the women began to wear the pants?" The women present greeted this remark with cold silence but a few male heads nodded in agreement.

Parents are often caught by this ambivalence about social change.

---

[5] See Alvin Schorr, *Explorations in Social Policy* (New York: Basic Books, 1968).

[6] For a good analysis of the impact of prohibition on American society, see Andrew Sinclair, *Prohibition: The Era of Excess* (Boston: Little, Brown & Co., 1962).

Some parents may go along with the change, while others try to resist it. One parent may accept the change while the other is still fighting it. Another possibility is that the children will welcome the change while the parents deplore it. The "going steady" dating system that swept through American high schools after World War II has been popular with young people but not with parents.[7]

7. *Social change is usually not reversible.* It is rare indeed when a social system, or a family, reverts to a previous state of organization. The American divorce rate, for example, never returned to the prewar level after World Wars I or II. Some sort of permanent change had taken place in the American marriage system during these national crises.[8]

This same principle does not seem to hold for parent models, however: there is, at least in the United States, a certain cyclical pattern to child rearing. Lerner, for example, comments that the extreme permissiveness of American parents that developed during the 1920's and the 1930's seems to have tapered off in the 1950's and 1960's.[9]

These fads or fashions in parent models pose certain problems for fathers and mothers—should they go along with the current fashion or stick to older patterns? What if one parent is contemporary while the other is traditional? American parents have been plagued with dilemmas of this sort in recent decades.

With this background let us now turn to an analysis of a massive social change that American parents are still struggling to cope with—urbanization.

The impact of urbanization on American parents

We do not intend to commit the error so common in sociology textbooks—to present the modern city as the den of iniquity. It is true that all of our crime syndicates are to be found in our large cities, but it is also true that all of our great art museums are found in these same cities. Later in this chapter we will present some of the positive aspects of the city as it affects parents, but at this point we wish to analyze some of the problems American parents found themselves facing once they had left the farm and had settled in the city.

It needs to be kept in mind that these new urban parents composed several distinct groups: (*a*) newly arrived immigrant groups, such as the

---

[7] On changes in the dating system after World War II see Robert D. Herman, "The Going Steady Complex," *Marriage and Family Living*, 17 (1955), pp. 36–40.

[8] The best analysis of the increase in divorce in the United States is probably Paul H. Jacobson, *American Marriage and Divorce* (New York: Rinehart & Co., 1959). See especially chap. 7.

[9] Max Lerner, *America as a Civilization* (New York: Simon and Schuster, 1957), p. 569.

Italians, most of whom settled in the large cities even though they came from rural areas in Europe.[10] There was a simple reason why they settled in the city: there was no free land left for them in rural America, and few jobs were open in agriculture. The jobs were in the big cities; (b) black families moving into the cities as the need for farm laborers declined because the farms were being mechanized; (c) white families moving into the cities because Henry Ford was paying $5 a day and economic conditions were not good on American farms after World War I had ended.

In this chapter we do not wish to analyze the problems of minority group or immigrant parents—that has been done in a separate chapter. Here we wish to focus on the generic problems of all parents operating in an urban environment. And by urban we do not have in mind a small community of 2,500 which meets the definition of urban as used by the U.S. Census Bureau. We are concentrating on metropolitan areas, which are defined as consisting of a central city of at least 50,000 population surrounded by a number of smaller, satellite communities. As of the 1960 Census the great majority of all American parents functioned in such a setting.

As we see it, the following characteristics of the metropolitan community system posed certain problems for parents.

1. *Pluralistic nature of the city.* The city has been the great melting pot in our society. This means that urban fathers and mothers have had to function in close proximity with parents of diverse ethnic, religious, and racial backgrounds. While this is a source of richness and variety in urban life, it is also a potential source of conflict. Sons and daughters form friendships across cultural and racial lines and parents are not always sure how to react to this. Young people also fall in love across these lines to the consternation of parents.

In such a pluralistic community children are exposed to all sorts of "competing models"—such as Catholics, Jews, Italians, Negroes, middle class, or lower class. Children exposed to such a variety of people may question why their own parents think and behave as they do, and this may threaten the parents.

It is true, of course, that the urban communities tend to be segregated by social class and by race, but to some extent the pluralistic nature of the metropolitan community has to be faced by all who live there, parents as well as their children.

2. *The increased leisure of urban youth.* One great advantage of the farm parent has always been that the children could be kept busy. The opposite situation faces urban parents: school adjourns at 3:30 and

---

[10] For an excellent discussion of American immigrant parents and their child rearing problems, see Oscar Handlin, *The Uprooted* (Boston: Little, Brown & Co., 1952). See especially chap. 9, "Generations."

children roam the streets; during vacations or the long summer period urban children find themselves with time to spare. In the more affluent neighborhoods or suburbs this problem is easier to cope with, but in the low-income areas solutions are difficult to find. The present school year was never designed for urban parents and conflicts with the work schedules of both fathers and employed mothers. The urban school should offer at least a half-day program during the summer months, plus some evening and weekend programs.[11]

3. *A more powerful youth peer group.* One of the results of more leisure time and close physical proximity in the city has been the rise to power of the youth peer group.[12] Urban children may spend 30 to 50 hours a week talking and playing with members of their peer group, and out of this youth society emerge norms of behavior and loyalties that challenge the power and influence of parents. This is a relatively new development of urban America that rural parents did not have to cope with.

4. *The impersonality and anonymity of the city.* Parents in the urban community often do not really know with whom their children are associating. Not only do they not know their childrens' friends, they also do not know the parents of these other children. Very often all they know about the peer group of their children consists of what the children choose to tell them. This means that in planning their strategy or making decisions concerning the peer group they are forced to operate with inadequate or biased data. Any business executive today will tell you that the most modern computer is no better than the information fed into it. The same principle applies to parents.

In an interesting passage in his textbook on the family, Farber points out that parents are forced to take a risk in almost every decision they make—they never have complete knowledge or understanding of any particular child, nor do they ever have all of the facts affecting the particular problem facing them.[13] While this observation applies to all parents, it seems especially to be a condition faced by fathers and mothers in the modern urban community. One mother said to the writer: "All I know about the boys my daughter dates is what she tells me. How am I supposed to help her choose her boyfriends when I don't know anything about them?" It's a good question.

5. *The pervasive nature of urban mass media.* It is true that no American today, except a few hermits and some religious minority groups,

---

[11] An excellent analysis of the deficiencies of the urban school may be found in Peter Schrag, *Village School Downtown* (Boston: Beacon Press, 1967).

[12] This data was analyzed in the preceding chapter and the references will be found there.

[13] Bernard Farber, *Family: Organization and Interaction* (San Francisco: Chandler Publishing Co., 1964), pp. 493–495.

can escape the massive attack of the mass media—radio, television, newspapers, magazines, and billboards. To some extent rural parents have to contend with such forces also, but not to the same extent as urban parents. There is something about the physical crowding of people that heightens the communication process.

Urban parents are often in conflict with the values of the commercial groups who seek to influence and exploit their children: Hollywood movies that flaunt traditional sex norms; television programs that pound away daily and nightly promoting a way of life that parents may or may not believe in; radio announcers who become folk heroes of the young and use their popularity in behalf of some sponsor.

In a very real sense urban parents today operate in an atmosphere of the circus or the carnival. Their children are surrounded by hundreds of pitchmen selling some product or some idea. It is only the very skilled father or mother who can prevail against the highly paid men and women from Hollywood and Madison Avenue.

6. *The urban ghetto.* The problems of minority group parents were analyzed in a separate chapter, but a few words about urban slums and the problems they pose for parents are appropriate here.

As the affluent white families migrate to the suburbs, the central city of the metropolitan community comes to be composed primarily of low-income whites, blacks, Puerto Ricans, Mexican-Americans, and American Indians. This central city is badly financed because the well-to-do taxpayers live out in the suburbs. This means that schools and other public services are not maintained at desirable levels. Housing is almost universally substandard—the *U.S. Riot Commission Report* says that at least 70 percent of the housing occupied by black families does not meet minimum standards.[14]

It is clear that only superior parents could rear children successfully in such an environment. It is not odd that school dropout and juvenile delinquency rates are high in such areas—the amazing thing is that such behavior is not universal.

The positive aspects of urbanization

The city is often portrayed as the center of evil in our society but in a very real sense it has been the center of hope—for the millions of immigrants from Europe who got here too late for the free land; and more recently for the American black family.

With all of its problems for parents, the urban community actually offers many advantages: better school systems, with special classes for

---

[14] For a discussion of housing in the ghetto, see the *U.S. Riot Commission Report* (New York: Bantam Books, 1968), pp. 467–482.

the handicapped child; better social welfare services, both private and public; better medical and public health facilities; more tolerance for racial and religious minorities; and a greater chance for vertical social mobility.[15]

It can be argued, with considerable logic, that the impoverished rural parent in modern America is in an even more difficult position than the urban ghetto parent. There is no place in the rural agricultural economy for most of the low-income farm children; their parents lack the knowledge and experience to help these children make a successful move to the city; and, finally, the rural community lacks the network of health, welfare, and educational services available to low-income urban parents.[16]

It can be demonstrated that the urban black family has made social progress since 1940, but it is difficult to prove this for the poverty stricken rural families of America.[17]

It is an interesting fact that the minority group that has achieved the highest socioeconomic position in the United States—the Jews—is almost entirely metropolitan in residence. And contrary to what millions of Americans think, the majority of these Jewish families entered the socioeconomic system at the bottom.[18] It was their utilization of urban services, such as the urban university, that enabled them to attain a comfortable position in our society.

We have been analyzing the impact of urbanization on parents. Because of the massive move to the city since World War I, farm parents now constitute less than 10 percent of all parents in the United States. In a sense they have become a minority group—not only in a statistical sense but also sociologically. We now turn to an examination of the special problems of farm parents.

The special problems of rural parents in modern America

It could well be true that rural parents in our society are in a more difficult position than urban parents. In some ways the rural revolution in the United States in recent decades has been deeper and more widespread than changes taking place in the city. The mechanization of the farm has greatly reduced the demand for farm laborers, and the increased productivity per farm worker has meant that in each of the recent

[15] Some of these positive features of urban life are discussed in Herbert J. Gans, *The Urban Villagers* (New York: The Free Press, 1962).

[16] Some of the superior features of the urban welfare system are discussed by Schorr, *op. cit.*

[17] On the progress of the American Negro see Thomas F. Pittigrew, *A Profile of the American Negro* (Princeton, N.J.: D. Van Nostrand Co., 1964), pp. 178–201.

[18] A good analysis of some of the problems faced by Jewish parents in America may be found in Nathan Glazer and Daniel Patrick Moynihan, *Beyond the Melting Pot* (Cambridge, Mass.: M.I.T. Press, 1963), chap. 3, "The Jews."

decades the percentage of the American population engaged in agriculture has declined.[19] As of the 1960's this figure has been somewhere between 6 and 10 percent.

All of this means that a majority of our farm youth today will be forced to resettle in the urban world.

Historically, the farm family in the United States has been romanticized. The image most of us have is that of the prosperous middle-class farm owner—the one usually portrayed on the cover of mass magazines at Thanksgiving. Americans don't like to think about the lower class farm families—the farm tenants, the sharecroppers, the farm laborers, or the migratory farm workers. These families, on the average, are probably worse off than most low-income urban families.[20]

In the next few pages we wish to focus on some of the special problems faced by farm parents.

1. The urbanization impact. Because of mass media, the automobile, the consolidated school, and general population mobility, farm children are increasingly being subjected to urban values and the urban way of life. This means that a considerable amount of social distance is being created between farm parents and their children. To the extent that the parents are attempting to internalize rural values and a rural way of life in their children, the parents are struggling against the stream—the whole drift of the society is in the other direction.

2. Farm parents are preparing their children for an urban-industrial world. Farm parents today face many of the problems American immigrant parents used to face; they have to prepare their children for a world they do not understand themselves. On the farm, historically, a man who was willing to do hard physical labor could get by. Formal education was not very essential. The ability to handle animals was more crucial than the ability to handle people.

These conditions do not prevail in urban America, and to a considerable extent they no longer prevail in rural America either. Trade unions, sex equality, racial integration—ideas that have never been too popular in rural America are dominant today in urban America. Farm children will have to understand and adjust to this world of the city, but their parents may not be too much help in the process.

---

[19] One of the best accounts of the farm revolution is Lauren Soth's *An Embarrassment of Plenty* (New York: Thomas Y. Crowell, 1965).

See also the paper by Lee G. Burchinal, "The Rural Family of the Future," in *Our Changing Rural Society* edited by James H. Copp (Ames, Ia.: Iowa State University Press, 1964), pp. 159–197.

[20] We find that most college students are unaware of the fact that the poverty rate is higher in rural America than in our cities. They also do not realize that about three fourths of the rural poor are white. See *White Americans in Rural Poverty*, Agricultural Economics Report No. 124, U.S. Government Printing Office, 1967.

3. *The rural economy.* There is simply no place for most of the farm children in the farm economy of tomorrow. Only the well-educated, well-financed farm youth can hope to survive in the agricultural world of tomorrow. Farms of today are larger, more expensive, more mechanized, and more scientifically managed than ever before. The poor farmer has no place in such a world unless he plans to earn his living in a nearby city and run a small farm as a sort of hobby or moonlight operation.

4. *The rural social class barrier.* Because of the farm revolution, the farm boy or farm girl from a low-income family has little chance for vertical social mobility. Migration to the city offers the best hope for most of these children. The more intelligent farm parents know this. The children of the others will have to find it out the hard way—by experience.

Interview with a farm parent

The following interview was with a dairy farmer who had recently sold his farm, his dairy herd, all his farm equipment, and had quit farming. It should be noted that this man did not give up farming because he was unsuccessful—his farm had always provided a living for himself and his family, and at his retirement his net worth was in excess of $100,000.

"I quit because it no longer seemed to be a good way of life. For over 30 years I worked from sunup to sundown—and later—7 days a week, 365 days a year. Dairy cows don't take Sundays or holidays off—not even Christmas—and small dairy farmers don't either.

"In all of those years we took only one family vacation—and that was made possible by a brother of mine who had just been discharged from the service and took care of the cows while we took a trip to New York."

We asked him: "What made you finally decide to quit farming? You're too young to retire."

"I quit because my son just laughed at me when I suggested that he could take over the farm in a few years. He said he wouldn't want it even as a gift.

"My son said: 'All of your life you worked like a dog with those cows and now you want me to do the same thing. No thanks. I want a job with an 8-hour day and a 40-hour week—and time and a half for overtime. I want Christmas off and all the other holidays.'"

His son apparently said even stronger things: that as long as he could remember his father had not had time to play with his children because the farm kept him too busy. The boy also complained that he had always had to rush home from school to help with the farm chores while the city children attending the same school had been free to play.

This son went into an apprentice program to become a machinist after graduation from high school.

After selling his farm, the father joined a real estate firm specializing in farm property and has been quite successful. He built a lovely new home and recently took a month's trip to California. "I'm beginning to live like the rest of you guys," he said, smiling.

This man is in his middle fifties. It seems to us that he and his family are good illustrations of the "rurbanization" process: their farm was gradually being enveloped by the nearby city. Their children no longer attended a rural school—they went to a brand-new school located near the family farm but with a student body composed largely of suburban children. Only one of the teachers in this school lived on a farm.

These factors, plus television and other mass media, meant that the rural world was disappearing for this family. When this farm father saw that his son had been converted to the urban way of life he decided to make the switch also. He could see, of course, that the physical labor demanded by the farm operation would become more of a strain as he got older. He could also see that the operation would be less profitable if he had to hire the labor to do the work his son had done for several years.

This man does not actually regret his many years on the farm. As he says, "I started with practically nothing and came out of it with over $100,000 clear. It was hard work but I was my own boss and was never unemployed."

A great many farm parents find themselves in the same position as this man. But not all of them can make the move to an urban way of life as easily as this family did.

Parent defense mechanisms against social change

How do successful parents—at least those who *seem* to be successful with their children—cope with rapid social change? How do they communicate across the chasm that separates the generations in our society?[21] As we see it, there are many ways that parents attempt to do this, five of which are listed here.

1. Early marriage. Americans have been marrying earlier in recent decades. There are various reasons for this, but one of them seems to be the desire to start their families in their twenties.

---

[21] One of the best analyses of this is that of Lewis S. Feuer, *The Conflict of Generations* (New York: Basic Books, 1969). Even though Feuer focuses primarily on student movements, the book is relevant for all parents and all family sociologists. One of the interesting concepts employed by Feuer is that of "deauthoritization." By this he means that the so-called wisdom and prestige of parents is undermined under conditions of rapid social change. Discussions of this process will be found in almost every chapter of his book.

See also J. Mogey, "A Century of Declining Paternal Authority," *Marriage and Family Living,* 19 (1957), pp. 234–239.

2. Early parenthood. Women today are having most of their children by the time they are 30 years old. Many of them can be heard to say: "I want to have them while I am still young enough to enjoy them."

There are, of course, many potential disadvantages in assuming the parental role at an early age, but one of the advantages is that it does reduce the social distance between parent and child.

3. The buddy system of parenthood. In a sense these parents adopt the attitude that "if you can't lick 'em, join 'em." They virtually become teen-agers themselves and seek to bridge the generation gap in this way.

To some extent such parents resemble the social workers assigned to work with street gangs in our larger cities—they mingle with the young people and try to influence the group from within. One college girl described a mother of this type in this way: "My mother is a real pal. You can do almost anything with her—she fits right into the group."

Some parents seem to achieve a certain amount of success with this buddy approach, but others simply make themselves look ridiculous.[22]

4. Don't try to understand the younger generation—it's hopeless. One mother told the writer: "I don't even try to understand my children's generation anymore. My only concern is that they understand *me*."

These parents take the position that basic values do not change in our society and they hammer away at these in rearing their children. "Honesty and decency and cleanliness don't change," one father said to the writer. "As long as you stick to things like that you can't go wrong. And you'll never be out-of-date."

Essentially, these parents hold themselves aloof from the current fashions in child rearing and stick to the "eternal verities." They remind one of a woman who refuses to raise or drop her hemline just because Paris says to wear the skirts short or long. One woman said to us: "What do I care about what Paris says? My knees are big and bumpy and I don't intend to show them if I can help it." Some parents adopt this approach in their roles as fathers and mothers.

5. The radar system of child rearing. Riesman argues that most American parents hedge against social change by using the "radar system" of child rearing.[23] Not being sure of what is right or wrong, these parents train their children to "fit in," to "be adjusted." They equip their children with a built-in radar antenna that provides them with a constant flow of signals as to what is happening in their significant reference groups, and all these children need to do to be adjusted is to alter their values and their behavior to fit the current fashion. Almost all of us do this in choos-

---

[22] For a criticism of parents as pals see Robert R. Bell, *Marriage and Family Interaction* (rev. ed.; Homewood, Ill.: The Dorsey Press, 1967), p. 431.

[23] David Riesman et al., *The Lonely Crowd* (rev. ed.; New Haven: Yale University Press, 1961), pp. 45–55.

ing our clothes, but Riesman says that "fashions" now include values and norms as well as hemlines or shoe styles.

Whyte develops a similar argument in analyzing the "social ethic" of the middle-class suburbanites reported on in his best seller, *The Organization Man.*[24]

Riesman believes that parents in an earlier America really didn't care what other parents were teaching their children.[25] These pioneer fathers and mothers, says Riesman, knew what was right and they internalized these values and norms in their sons and daughters. In any new or difficult situation, then, all these children had to do was to look *inward* to find the solution to their dilemma.

This system of child rearing may work well in a deeply religious society in which parents can operate with "revealed truths" that are assumed to be "eternal." But in a society in which the revealed truths come from the secular priests, who seem to change their truths almost every decade, how can parents find any absolutely certain values or norms to internalize? The answer seems to be that they can't.

Faced with this neat little problem the smart parent falls back on an even more eternal principle—the law of the jungle, which is to *survive.* "Don't be a sucker, or a martyr," the child is told. "Go along with the group and you can't get too far out of line." In a sense this represents the wisdom of the old sergeant (or the old chief petty officer) when he tells the raw recruit: "Keep your nose clean and you won't get into any trouble."

Riesman has an interesting comment on the inner-directed method of child rearing. "Homing pigeons," he writes, "can be taught to fly home, but the inner-directed child must be taught to fly a straight course *away* from home, with destination unknown; naturally many meet the fate of Icarus.[26]

In an earlier discussion in this chapter we said that some parents try to solve the problem of social change by falling back on the values and norms that are not temporal—they are supposed to apply at all times everywhere. When pressed by the writer in parent discussion groups such parents usually cite words such as "honesty," "decency," "cleanliness," and so forth. But none of these words, it seems to the writer, mean today what they did in the America of 1910 or 1920. Our grandparents, for example, felt themselves to be clean when they bathed once a week— or even once a month in winter. No body deodorants were used by these

---

24 William H. Whyte, Jr., *The Organization Man* (Garden City, N.Y.: Doubleday & Co., 1957). See especially chap. 29, "Conclusion."

25 Riesman et al., *op. cit.,* pp. 40–45.

26 Riesman et al., *op. cit.,* p. 42. For the non-Greek scholars it might be pointed out that Icarus crashed into the sea and never made it back home.

men—or the women either. The aroma of honest sweat was not considered offensive. On the contrary, its presence proved that a man or a woman was not afraid to work.

Today, children begin in junior high, if not earlier, to use deodorants, and on television it sometimes seems that the worst sin a father can commit is to take the family's deodorant with him on a business trip.

Would a small-town merchant of the 1920's recognize the word *honesty* if he came back and saw how consumer goods are advertised and sold today?

Would a nice girl of 1910 accept the definition of a *nice girl* that seems to be current today?

It is difficult to see where fathers and mothers in contemporary America would find any eternal truths to teach their children. In a Protestant church known to the writer a careful survey of the membership conducted on an anonymous basis by an outside research organization found that about 60 percent of the members were "not sure they believed in God."[27] This seems strange since to join this church new members have to stand up in front of the congregation and take an oath that they *do* believe in God.

What should a modern parent teach his children about lifetime monogamy when some of the best people in our society no longer practice it?[28]

What should a Roman Catholic mother teach her daughter about birth control? Recent surveys show that the average American Roman Catholic no longer supports his church's position on contraceptives.[29] What position should parents take?

In view of the "relativity" of modern values and norms it is understandable that modern parents turn to a radar system of rearing their children. "After all," one mother said to us, "if radar is good enough for the airlines it should be good enough for parents."

Parents who can't cope with social change

Although the point is difficult to document, it seems likely that parents who cannot cope with social change must face insuperable barriers in rearing children in modern America.

Riesman makes the point that some parents may be preparing their children for a world that no longer exists. He writes: "parents who try

[27] This survey was done in a metropolitan "liberal" Protestant church in the Midwest in 1967.

[28] In recent years divorces have been reported in the public press for the following elite families: Ford, Rockefeller, Kennedy, and Roosevelt.

[29] See *New Catholic Thinking about Family Planning* published by the Planned Parenthood Federation of America, New York City, 1967.

in inner-directed fashion, to compel the internalization of disciplined pursuit of clear goals run the risk of having their children styled clear out of the personality market. Inhibited from presenting their children with sharply silhouetted images of self and society, parents in our era can only equip the child to do his best, whatever that may turn out to be."[30]

This point might be illustrated in relationship to the sex conditioning of daughters in contemporary America. If a father and mother were able, somehow, to rear their daughter to believe that she should not neck until she was engaged to be married, it seems likely that such a girl would be priced out of the high school or college dating system—unless by some odd chance she found a boy who had internalized the same norms. The writer has actually interviewed one college woman who reported—and we have reason to believe that she was being honest—that she never necked until she was engaged to be married in her senior year of college.

It needs to be noted, however, that this girl reported very few dates in high school or college until she met her future husband at the beginning of her last year of college, and that this is the *only* college woman ever interviewed by the writer who said she adhered to such a stringent sexual code.

It is true, of course, that parents may teach their children almost any set of values they wish to, but if they deviate too much from the current model they run two types of risk: they may damage their relationship with their child; or their child may be isolated from his (or her) peer group and be considered odd or peculiar. This is not always undesirable but it does pose special problems for adolescents with their great fear of nonconformity.

Some parents seem to have difficulty coping with social change because one parent is more contemporary than the other. Not all married couples change at the same rate, so that a traditional father may find himself paired with a modern mother—and this can pose problems in a role such as parenthood that demands teamwork. Actually one of the complexities of the parent role is that we usually have to work at it *in pairs*. This is not easy when we have differential social change between parents.

Some studies indicate that mothers in our society may be more contemporary than fathers.[31] If this is true, then a built-in strain between American parents would be expected. The writer does not believe that

---

[30] Riesman et al., *op. cit.*, p. 47.

[31] For an interesting discussion of modernity among fathers and mothers in their parental roles, see John R. Seeley et al., *Crestwood Heights* (New York: Basic Books, 1956), chap. 9, "Parent Education."

the current research is adequate to conclude whether this is the case or not.[32]

Of course, if the American father is as "shadowy" in our family system as some observers seem to think, then whether he is modern or traditional wouldn't make much difference. As we stated in an earlier chapter, however, we doubt very much that fathers in our society have ceased to affect the rearing of their children.

Parents as salesmen and negotiators

If we assume that parental authority has declined in America in the last several decades, the question needs to be posed: how do successful parents manage to perform their role without traditional power and authority? It seems to us that the answer must include the following hypotheses:

1. Successful parents (those who have relatively little difficulty rearing their children) do such a good job in the early years that the children never seriously question the values of the parents—in other words, the socialization process has been so complete that the values of the parents have been internalized and seem to the child to be his own.

2. Or, the successful parents are skilled salesmen and negotiators. We live in a society that in a very real sense survives by a process of "selling"—the economy in particular has reached the point at which production is no longer a problem. The major problem in the economy is to sell the product and keep the consumer convinced of his brand.[33]

It seems to us that parents, lacking real power, have been forced to develop their skills as sellers: they have to convince their children, at least at the high school and college levels, that the way of life of the parents is the best way.

When persuasion (selling) fails, then the skilled parent resorts to negotiation. One can see an analogy here in the current college and university scene: the old-fashioned, tough dean or college president is being replaced by the skilled negotiator who can keep in mind the desires of his student, his faculty, his alumni, and his trustees.[34] Such men seem

---

[32] In one of the more elaborate modern studies of parents almost half of the mothers reported disagreements with their husbands over discipline problems with children, with the father reported to be "tougher." See Daniel R. Miller and Guy E. Swanson, *The Changing American Parent* (New York: John Wiley & Sons, 1958), p. 225.

[33] For an interesting analysis of influence versus power, see William A. Gamson, *Power and Discontent* (Homewood, Ill.: The Dorsey Press, 1968).

[34] Shortly after he had settled a campus revolt at the Madison campus of the University of Wisconsin, Robben W. Fleming, a labor dispute arbitrator, was offered the presidency of two of the largest state universities in the country. He is now president of the University of Michigan.

to resemble the labor negotiators employed by trade unions and corporations. Having great patience, they strive to get the best deal for their client. We feel that the more successful parents in modern America employ a somewhat similar approach.

Parents who cannot (or will not) operate in this fashion would seem to be in a difficult spot in contemporary America. If they attempt to fall back on traditional authority they run the risk of having their children revolt. Their parental model is being displaced by a new model and their children may tend to compare them unfavorably with parents who have adopted the new approach.

It would appear that white-collar parents would have an advantage over blue-collar parents in using the new model in that white-collar jobs place considerable stress on the manipulation of people. In the Miller and Swanson research there is some evidence that blue-collar parents employ somewhat different child rearing models than white-collar parents —the so-called working class parents try to rear their children to fit into the industrial system, whereas the white-collar parents attempt to teach their children how to operate within the system.[35]

Parents and resocialization

In a society dedicated to rapid social change and progress, as the United States is, the dilemma of parents is clear: they themselves grew up in the world of yesterday, a world that is now largely dead, even if not buried, and this is the world they internalized; they rear their children in the world of today, a world they only partially understand and only partially accept; but they are rearing their children for the world of tomorrow, a world that nobody understands as yet. These conditions are some of the reasons why even intelligent and capable parents often feel confused and bewildered in modern America.

In his paper on parent-youth conflict, Davis refers to the phenomenon of "decelerating socialization."[36] By this he means that parents have already passed the peak of their learning curve by the time they become parents. Thus their efforts to keep up with the world of their children are handicapped by their relatively slow rate of learning in their twenties and thirties. At the same time their children are at the peak of their learning curve.

The situation is even more complex than Davis described it, because the learning of adults (parents) actually involves *resocialization*—that is,

---

[35] Miller and Swanson, *op. cit.*, various chapters.

[36] Davis, *op. cit.*, p. 524.

they have to unlearn what they absorbed earlier in order to take in the new knowledge.[37]

In a famous paper the anthropologist, Benedict, analyzed this process of resocialization.[38] She used the term *discontinuity* to describe what happens: a girl learns that sex is bad and something to avoid, yet later as a wife she is supposed to think that sex is good and something to be enjoyed. How does she ever make the transition from Stage I to Stage II?

Parents face this type of situation almost daily:[39] something they were taught as children that would "never change" is suddenly out of style— for example, that college students don't get married until they have completed their undergraduate degree. Another good illustration would be the old saying that "violence never solves anything." Some black parents are finding this old truism harder and harder to sell to their children.

Summary and conclusion

In this chapter we have tried to analyze the nature of social change and to see its impact on modern parents. The problem of differential social change was explored, also some of the positive aspects of social change related to urbanization. The conclusion was reached that deep and pervasive social change is one of the most difficult factors that American parents have to cope with.

In the next chapter, the concluding one, our attention will be focused on the process of parent counseling.

---

[37] For an analysis of the process of resocialization, see Orville G. Brim, Jr. and Stanton Wheeler, *Socialization after Childhood* (New York: John Wiley & Sons, 1966).

[38] Ruth Benedict, "Continuities and Discontinuities in Cultural Conditioning," *Psychiatry*, 1 (May, 1938), pp. 161–167.

[39] An interesting paper is that by Kenneth Keniston, "Social Change and Youth in America," in *The Challenge of Youth* edited by Erik Erikson (New York: Doubleday & Co., 1968), pp. 191–222.

chapter
twelve

Counseling
with parents

I N his book, *Games People Play*, Berne makes the following statement: "Raising children," he writes, "is primarily a matter of teaching them what games to play."[1]

In this chapter on counseling with parents we are adopting a stance somewhat similar to that of Berne: counseling with parents is primarily a matter of helping them see explicitly what parental model they have been using; examining that model with the parents to see how well it fits them and their children; suggesting alternate models that might work better for them; and, finally, teaching the parent (or parents) how to implement the model decided on. The rest of this chapter will attempt to explain how this counseling system works.

The attitude of the counselor

Before proceeding to parental models and their implementation, a few words need to be said about attitudes that social workers, teachers, ministers, judges, psychologists, and psychiatrists tend to have toward parents.

Parents are often assumed to be guilty before they even get a hearing with the counselor.[2] The child has been doing something wrong, therefore the parents have been doing something wrong. The professional counselors forget that parents are *amateurs*—very few of them

---

[1] Eric Berne, *Games People Play* (New York: Grove Press, Inc., 1964), p. 171.

[2] Orville G. Brim, Jr., *Education for Child Rearing* (New York: Russell Sage Foundation, 1959). See especially chap. 9, "Aims of Parent Education."

ever had any training for the parental role. This means that the professional counselor[3] is usually using professional norms to assess the performance of nonprofessionals.

Counselors who have never been parents tend to underestimate the complexity and hazards of being a parent in our society—they are too willing to condemn parents if a child is having difficulty.[4]

Almost all counselors, including this writer, have feelings and attitudes from their own family experience that sometimes intrude on the counseling situation—appropriately or inappropriately. Some of these attitudes and feelings may be conscious but others are subconscious or unconscious.

Brim makes it clear that most workers in the family life education field reflect a built-in middle-class bias.[5] It seems likely that parent counselors have the same bias.

Most American parents seen by counselors are already suffering from a deep feeling of inadequacy. Regardless of how hard they may have tried, the results of their parental efforts have not been satisfactory. Therefore, it does not seem appropriate or desirable for the counselor to add to this crushing weight of failure. It may help the counselor if he remembers that even unsuccessful parents have often tried hard to rear their children properly—their efforts have simply not paid off.

Finally, parent counselors need to watch that they do not become "child worshippers"—people who seem to be willing to do almost anything to parents "if it will help the child." Parents are people too, and they have as much right to consideration as children have.

With this background let us examine various parent models and attempt to see how better knowledge of them might help parents.

Parent models

Whether they realize it or not, all parents adopt one parent model or another. In the rest of this chapter we wish to examine some of these models to see what their essential characteristics are and to discuss how parent counselors can use the models in working with parents.

The martyr model

Many parents, without realizing it, adopt the martyr model. "Nothing is too good for my children," they will say, or "I would do *anything* for my child."

---

[3] The term *counselor* is being used generically here to denote any member of the helping professions who works with parents.

[4] This observation is based on contacts with graduate students who are not yet parents in a school of social work.

[5] Brim, *op. cit., passim.*

The following characteristics are usually found in this model.

Parental guilt. For some reason these parents usually exhibit guilt and the counselor needs to explore this with them.

Overprotection. Guilt is often accompanied by overprotection. The parent is afraid that something will happen to the child and attempts to set up a "super safe" world for the child. This, of course, almost invariably produces problems for all parties concerned—parents as well as children.

It is our impression that divorced parents, or those whose marriage has failed even though it is still intact, are especially subject to the guilt-overprotection syndrome. Parents with handicapped children will often exhibit this pattern also.

It hardly needs to be said that these martyr parents spoil their children. They cannot set realistic goals for their children, or if they do, the goals are not adhered to.

Revolt or meek submission by the child. A healthy reaction by children living under this parental model is that of revolt—they almost instinctively reach out for a normal life and this inevitably brings them into conflict with the parent or parents. At this point the martyred parent assumes the posture—"look what you are doing to me—and after all I have done for you." Berne analyzes this game as it is enacted between marital partners.[6]

A child that does *not* revolt against the martyr model is a sick child —he will be crippled for life if he does not revolt. This might not be true in some societies but it is certainly true in the open-class, competitive, impersonal society American children will graduate into.

As a youngster the writer grew up with a boy who submitted to a mother who had adopted the model of the martyr.

George was an only child—not unusual in this model—and his father had died when this boy was about 10 years old. The boy did not participate in male peer group activities, and later on in high school he never dated. As soon as school was out he would hurry home so that his mother "wouldn't worry" about him.

After high school graduation George never moved into the open adult society. During the economic boom of World War II he did not enter the labor market but remained at home with his mother.

When the writer was visiting his home community several years ago this "boy" (now about 50 years old) was to be seen on the front porch of the family home, with his mother sitting nearby.

This case is not presented as being typical of what happens when parents adopt the martyr model, but it does illustrate how severe the crippling of the child can become.[7]

---

[6] Berne, *op. cit.*, pp. 104–107.

[7] In another case studied by the writer a woman of 65, in good physical health, entered a home for the aged because both of her parents were now deceased and she could not face the world alone.

Hostility and resentment by the child toward the parent. In the event of revolt this will be open and obvious. In cases of submission it will be covert and repressed. Martyr parents can never understand this reaction by their children: "Look at that attitude after all I have done for them."

It is the writer's belief that the martyr model is perhaps the most destructive one found in American parents. In some ways it is even more destructive than the model of parent neglect—the neglected child is at least free and has a chance of finding a substitute parent.

On an ethical level it is simply not right that a parent should serve as a martyr for a child: it denies the parent his right to a life of his own as an adult; furthermore, it places the child in the inevitable role of the ungrateful offspring.

Some of the most difficult counseling situations in working with martyr parents are found when one parent adheres to the martyr model while the other one rejects it. This can be described as a "split model" situation. When this is found the counselor has to be careful not to be seduced by the martyred parent, and to see the split as an asset—it means that conflict is present and out of this conflict change can be generated.

The best strategy in dealing with martyr parents is to be honest and direct: unless they can be made to see what they are doing to themselves as well as their children the prognosis is not pleasant. These parents have thick defenses and the counselor will often need to be provocative and/or aggressive to get any movement.

The buddy or pal model

A certain number of parents in modern America seem to have adopted the buddy or pal model—they apparently feel that this is a solution to the gap between the generations.

Some students of the family have been rather caustic in their comments on this model. Bell, for example, has this to say:

The middle-class belief that a parent should be a "pal" to his children reflects a social value which gives importance to a common world for parents and children. The belief in a common world has developed around notions of democracy between parents and children and implies they are equals socially, psychologically, and intellectually. If this is true, it is a devastating picture of the parents because it implies that they are still teenagers.[8]

Bell goes on to point out that the pal approach to parenthood is not the only area in which the lines between generations have been blurred in our society.[9]

---

[8] Robert R. Bell, *Marriage and Family Interaction* (rev. ed.; Homewood, Ill.: The Dorsey Press, 1967), p. 431.
[9] *Ibid.*

In a sense the parents who adopt the buddy or pal models are follow-ing the old saying, "if you can't beat 'em, join 'em." They are trying to infiltrate the youth peer group and work from within. In some ways they resemble the social workers assigned to work with juvenile gangs on the streets of our large cities.[10] These social workers have no authority: they simply attempt to influence the gang leadership. This is not only a difficult role but also a dangerous one—and the writer has a hunch it is no easier for parents.

It is possible that the pal or buddy model received its impetus from the rush of early marriages that followed the end of World War II. The writer interviewed a mother of 20 a few years ago who was taking care of her two preschool children. She just laughed when we asked her if she felt mature enough to be rearing a family.

"Nobody is grown up in this house," she said. "My husband is 20 also and he certainly isn't very grown up."

After a pause she looked at her two children and said: *"I guess we're all growing up together."*

It struck us that her generation—at least some of them—do not accept the traditional idea that you have to be grown up to get married. On the contrary, all you need is somebody who wants to grow up with you. The writer does not know how many young parents in America sub-scribe to this point of view, but for those that do the pal model may be functional: they would only be kidding themselves if they pretended to be mature adults rearing a family.

Another impetus for the pal or buddy model may have come from the rejection of middle age or old age in our society. Americans do not revere the older person, or assume that he has any great store of wisdom to offer young people. If anything, we tend to pity the older person—and by older the society means anybody over 40. Thus, by the time American parents are dealing with adolescents, they are near (or over) the dividing line between youth and old age. Many of them are tempted to conclude that they might as well pretend to be a pal or buddy because there is nothing to gain by acting your age. Millions of women in our society use this strategy (with some success) and some parents apparently use it also.

The writer happens to believe that the pal or buddy model of parent-hood is difficult and risky. Its major problems follow.

It is extremely unrealistic. Our society holds that parents are re-sponsible for the rearing and guidance of their minor children. Parents can be imprisoned for neglect or mistreatment of their children. They can also have their parental rights terminated under certain circumstances.

In view of the "generation gap" in our society it seems unlikely that

---

[10] Some of these problems are reviewed in Richard A. Cloward and Lloyd E. Ohlin, *Delinquency and Opportunity: A Theory of Delinquent Gangs* (New York: The Free Press, 1964).

any children are going to be fooled by the pal model of parenthood.[11] They know who the enemy is—and their motto seems to be: "never trust anybody over 30."

As we pointed out earlier in this chapter, the pal or buddy model may be realistic for some teen-age parents who are still children themselves, but the model hardly fits the vast majority of American parents.

The roles called for in the model are quite complex. Few of us can cross generation lines effectively and convincingly enough to make this model work. One has to penetrate or infiltrate the youth peer group, understand its subculture, and be accepted by the group. Pal parents cannot fall back on parental authority when the going gets tough—they have to sustain the pal role consistently if the model is to work. Very few parents can achieve this level of role performance.

The pal model requires superior parents to make it work. In World War II we had an opportunity to study at close range two types of officers in the U.S. Naval Air Corps.[12] The traditional officer maintained considerable social distance between himself and his enlisted men—a model that the Navy had found to be effective over the years. This traditional model was well defined and made no great demands on the imagination or creativity of the officer. All he had to do was to follow the rules and not much could happen to him. In the bomber air groups, however, with their long missions and close physical proximity, some officers abandoned the traditional model and adopted a pal or buddy model—their enlisted men did not have to salute officers, first names were used, regulation clothing was not insisted on, and so forth.

It was the writer's impression, based on three years of participant-observation, that only the *superior* officers could adopt the buddy model and get away with it. If the officer was average or below average in ability the flight crew soon deteriorated and order had to be restored by some subordinate, such as a chief petty officer, if the crew was to function properly.

It is our belief that the same conditions hold for parents: only the superior parent can play the buddy game with his or her children without losing their respect and their obedience.

The pal or buddy model involves considerable risk. This was quite clear in the Naval Air Corps in the opinion of the writer. Several tragic plane and crew losses might have been avoided in the writer's air group if crews had been held under more strict discipline.

We have the impression that the pal model is equally risky for parents: if things don't go well they have to retreat to a more formal, author-

---

[11] For an interesting analysis of the generation gap see Richard Lorber and Ernest Fladell, *The Gap* (New York: McGraw-Hill Book Co., 1968).

[12] The observations on officer models in the U.S. Naval Air Corps are based on three years service during World War II.

itarian parent model—and this retreat or shift in role is extremely difficult to manage without damaging the parent's image in the eyes of his children.

A professor known to us had been using the buddy model with a graduate seminar. Among other things he told the class that they didn't have to come to class if they didn't want to. One day this professor went to class and found only one student out of fifteen present. He was furious and immediately posted a notice that attendance would be compulsory in the future. The class reacted with resentment and the semester was completed in the atmosphere of an armed truce.

One of the advantages of the traditional authoritarian parent model is that it allows the father or mother to relax the rules occasionally without damaging the relationship with the children—in fact the relationship should be enhanced. This is not the case when the pal model has been adopted.

It should be clear to the reader by now that the writer has grave reservations about the workability of the pal or buddy parent model. The counselor should explore with the parents the complexity and hazards of the model and help them consider other models that appear to be less complex and less hazardous.

The policeman or drill sergeant model of parenthood

Some parents seem to conceptualize their role as that of the policeman or drill sergeant. They are alert to punish the child for the most minor offense, making sure that he obeys the rules at all times. These parents seem to believe that this system of parenthood will keep their children from getting into trouble.

In some ways this policeman model is a foolproof defense system for the parents: if the child does get into difficulty the parents can always say—"we told him not to do it."

In our opinion this model will not work for most parents in the United States for the following reasons.

Americans tend to be "cop haters." Almost any book on police in the United States, or even casual reading of the daily newspaper, will reveal how unenviable the position of the policeman is in our society.[13] Except on television shows the police are the bad guys. In a recent incident in the Midwest a group of citizens stood by while a patrolman was beaten up by several men who had been creating a disturbance. Not one citizen offered to help the police officer.[14]

---

[13] See, for example, Arthur Niederhoffer, *Behind the Shield: The Police in Urban Society* (New York: Doubleday & Co., 1967).

[14] In a university city in which the writer was teaching, a group of young people watched passively while a patrolman was beaten up by three men he had tried to arrest for creating a disturbance.

Vacancies in almost every urban police department testify to the reluctance of most Americans to assume this role.

In the armed forces the drill sergeants are no more popular than are policemen in the civilian community.

From the earliest colonial days Americans have been allergic to authority, and the allergy seems to be increasing, not decreasing.

The adolescent peer group is too powerful. Parents may get away with the policeman model while their children are quite young, but eventually the parents will be confronted by the adolescent peer group—and as we have seen in earlier chapters, this is a formidable opponent in modern America.

In some ways the policeman and drill sergeant have an advantage over parents: the legal structure is usually on their side. Parents are not always sure of a friendly reception in court—most judges and social workers will identify with the "helpless child." As Lerner says, there are no "bad children in our society—only bad parents."[15] In this sort of atmosphere it is difficult, if not impossible, for the extremely strict or harsh parent to win in our society.

A great deal of love is needed to make the policeman model work. If the parent can achieve the image of the "benevolent despot," strict or even harsh discipline will be tolerated by many children. But warmth and love have to be so obvious and plentiful that the child can never doubt that the parent has the child's best interests at heart.

It is our impression that many parents who adopt the policeman or drill sergeant model simply do not have enough love for the child to make the severe discipline tolerable. Or if they *do* have the love it does not get communicated to the child.

Parenthetically, it can be said that much of the open hostility of the poor and minority groups in our society toward the police stems from the fact that these people are convinced that the police do not have their best interests at heart—they view the police as their enemy, not their friend.[16] It appears that many American parents who adopt the policeman model are viewed in a similar way by their children.

The pluralistic nature of our society, discussed in earlier chapters, also poses problems for parents using the policeman model—the norms are not that clear or that specific; there are often divergent or competing norms of behavior, and the child may challenge the right of the parent to select a particular norm to be enforced. Here, again, the policeman and drill sergeant have an advantage over parents—the laws governing

---

[15] Max Lerner, *America as a Civilization* (New York: Simon and Schuster, 1957), pp. 560–570.

[16] One of the major findings of the *U.S. Riot Commission Report* (New York: Bantam Books, 1968), was the feeling of hostility (if not hatred) that the urban racial minorities have toward the police. See chap. 11, "The Police and the Community."

communities and the regulations in the armed forces are more specific than those that parents operate with.

This model is not functional in our society. If the United States is actually an open-class, competitive society, then a premium would be placed on parental models that emphasize such qualities as initiative, aggression, and competitiveness—qualities that appear to be minimized in the policeman or drill sergeant model. It needs to be remembered that the police and the armed forces are primarily concerned with maintaining order and discipline, hence the model is functional for those systems. But to the extent that America is still an open-class, competitive society the model is dysfunctional for parents; it would not meet the basic needs of either the society or the child.

It is possible, however, to view the situation in an entirely different light—that America has become primarily a socioeconomic system of large bureaucratic organizations, both public and private, and that these systems maximize obedience, discipline, reliability, and conformity, qualities that appear to be attainable with the policeman or drill sergeant model.

Miller and Swanson found that the middle and lower class parents in their sample appear to be preparing their children to "fit into" large bureaucratic organizations.[17] When one remembers that the most expansive sector of the U.S. economy in recent decades has been that of public employment, these parents may be preparing their children very realistically for the America of today and tomorrow.

In reading Riesman and Whyte one gets the same message—American parents are preparing their children to live and work harmoniously in a tightly organized mass society.[18] Whyte does not like what he sees— nor does Riesman—but the picture they report is quite clear: American society today has more room for the conformist than it has for the innovator.

It may well be that the policeman or drill sergeant parental model is functional for the lower class and most of the middle class in our society, but that it is dysfunctional for other groups. This appears to be the finding of Miller and Swanson.[19]

The writer believes that the policeman or drill sergeant model has limitations that are not necessary. This will be seen later in the chapter

---

[17] Daniel R. Miller and Guy E. Swanson, *The Changing American Parent* (New York: John Wiley & Sons, 1958), chap. 4, "Child Training in Entrepreneurial and Bureaucratic Families."

[18] On conformity in our society see David Riesman et al., *The Lonely Crowd* (New Haven, Conn.: Yale University Press, 1961), *passim;* also William H. Whyte, Jr., *The Organization Man* (New York: Doubleday & Co., 1957), especially Pt. 1, "The Ideology of Organization Man."

[19] For a discussion of the functionality of the two systems of child rearing analyzed in their study, see Miller and Swanson, *op. cit.*, pp. 109–118.

when the fifth and last parental model is analyzed. But before that let us look at the fourth model, the teacher-counselor.

The teacher-counselor parent model

This is the developmental model.[20] The child is conceptualized as an extremely plastic organism with almost unlimited potential for growth and development. The limits to this growth and development are seen as the limits of the parent (and other teachers) to tap the rich potential of the child. Parents themselves are regarded as expendable—only "the child" counts. Discipline may be firm but never harsh—and punishment should be psychological, not physical or corporal.

The model presumes that the parent (as teacher-counselor) knows all the right answers—the only problem is to motivate the child to find out what they are.

The good teacher-counselor (parent) always puts the need of the child first—within the tolerance limits of the classroom or the school system itself.

This model has deep historical roots in our society—Christ is usually presented as a teacher or counselor; Benjamin Franklin and Abraham Lincoln, both folk heroes in America, reflect some of the teacher-counselor image. The dedicated (and underpaid) schoolteacher is a warm symbol in the United States, and in these days of social work and psychiatry the image of the counselor casts its shadow across the land.

This model reflects the progressive school era inspired by John Dewey, also the psychiatric viewpoint pioneered by Sigmund Freud. The child is seen as fragile and plastic but capable of infinite growth and development if enough parental love and guidance are applied. The uniqueness of each child is stressed—not his similarity with other children.

At the middle-class level this model has probably been dominant in the United States in recent decades. While it has many fine features the writer believes it also poses the following problems.

Parents are not viewed as ends in themselves. In this system the needs of the child are always paramount. Parents are expected to sacrifice themselves gladly for the welfare of "our children." Such a value system, in the opinion of the writer, can have devastating effects on fathers, mothers, marriages, society, and even the child himself. It is a great burden in later life for a son or daughter to be told—"I sacrificed everything for you." This takes us back to the martyr model discussed earlier in this chapter.

This model is often too permissive. American parents are often ac-

---

[20] For a delineation of the child development parent model, see Evelyn Duvall, "Conceptions of Parenthood," *American Journal of Sociology*, 52 (1946), pp. 193–203.

cused of "spoiling" their children.[21] This is easy to do in the teacher-counselor model because of the great stress placed on the uniqueness of each child and his needs—relatively little is said about the needs of the parent or the needs of society. Thus the child may get the impression that he is the center of the universe.

The model tends to produce anxiety and guilt in parents. Middle-class parents in modern America appear to be afflicted with anxiety and guilt. Lerner doubts that *any* human society has ever produced parents as anxious and threatened as those in our society.[22] Some of the reasons for this have been explored in earlier chapters in this book. Brim argues that one of the chief products of the massive parent education program in the United States has been parental guilt.[23]

The writer believes that most American parents are reasonably conscientious and competent in their parental role and holds the teacher-counselor model partly responsible for these fathers and mothers being made to feel guilty and inadequate.

The model tends to view parents as experts. Parents are *not* experts. Most of them have never had any formal training or education for their parental role—and by the time they have learned enough from their experience as parents to feel like experts their children are grown up and they are on the sidelines watching other young couples struggling with the same problems they struggled with.

When parents try to become experts they are courting trouble—they can never really learn all of the mystique known to the psychiatrist, the psychologist, the home economist, or the social worker, and if anything goes wrong they will be told, "but that's not what we said. You misunderstood us." In a very real sense a little knowledge is a dangerous thing.

What also happens is that the professionals (the designated experts) begin to judge parents by professional standards—parents should know this or that or something else.

This model does not adequately present the needs of the society. Since the model focuses primarily on the needs and development of the individual, the requirements of the community and the larger society are necessarily downgraded. This has been one of the factors that has produced a generation which displays relatively little respect for parents or other representatives of the social order.

It would seem that in any society a balance must be struck between the imperatives of the society and the needs of the individual—and it is our judgment that this parent model fails to pass this test.

---

21 See Lerner, *op. cit.*, pp. 562–568 for a discussion of spoiling of children by American parents.

22 *Ibid.*, pp. 562–563.

23 On the production of guilt in parents see Brim, *op. cit.*, *passim*.

The athletic coach model

It seems to the writer that some of the most successful parents in our society employ a model derived from the role of the athletic coach. As we have analyzed this model it appears to have the following characteristics.[24]

Physical fitness. The players must be physically fit for the contest. This involves not only vigorous physical activity but also abstention or moderation in smoking, drinking, late hours, and so on.

Mental fitness. The athlete must be psychologically fit—that is, he must have confidence in his ability and a feeling that he can compete successfully.

Knowledge of the game. The player must know the rules of the game and the penalty for violating them. At times he may knowingly and deliberately violate the rules—but only after calculating the chances of getting caught and the potential gain if he is not caught.

Basic skills and techniques must be painfully learned. There are no "born" star athletes—they may be born with potential but only hard work will permit them to realize that potential. A player that refuses to practice, no matter how gifted, will not be tolerated on the squad.

The player must have stamina. He must not give up or reduce his effort—even when he is tired. As Woody Hayes, coach of the Ohio State football team, once said: "Victory in football means getting up one more time than your opponent does."[25]

Aggressiveness and competitive spirit. The athlete must desire to compete and to win. There are no "happy losers" among first-rate athletes or their coaches.

The player must accept strict discipline. Regardless of his status on the team—star or substitute—each player must submit to strict discipline. Violation of basic regulations usually results in suspension or dismissal from the squad.

Subordination of self to the success of the team. Each player is expected to put the success of the team ahead of his personal glory. Failure to do this not only brings repercussions from the coach but also from the other players.

The coach is expected to have the welfare of his players in mind at all times. In order for the tight discipline system in this model to work the coach must never order a player to do anything that might threaten his welfare—an injured player, for example, no matter how essential to the

---

[24] The athletic coach model used here was derived from several weeks the writer once spent with a group of coaches at Ohio State University. This group included two men who later became nationally famous for their winning teams—Paul Brown and Woody Hayes.

[25] Athletic banquet speech reported in the *Milwaukee Journal*, November 14, 1965.

team, must never be ordered to play if his future may be jeopardized. Most coaches would not even permit a boy to play—even though he requested permission—if further injury at this time could result in permanent damage.

The coach cannot play the game—this must be done by the player. The coach's position here is quite analogous to that of parents: once the game has begun it is up to the players to win or lose it. The coach has some advantages over parents—he can send in players and he can substitute one player for another. But he faces the same prospect as parents of sitting on the sidelines and watching players make mistakes that may prove disastrous.

Discussion of the athletic coach model

The writer submits that this model has much to recommend it to American parents. The overwhelming popularity of competitive sports in our society seems to indicate general acceptance of the model among large numbers of youth as well as by the general population.

The model seems to contain a nice balance of aggression, competitiveness, and cooperation. The developmental theme is included in the expectation that each player will realize his full potential. The model emphasizes success but the players, as well as the coach, must also learn how to live with defeat.

The model has some limitations, however, due to the fact that the role of parent is not exactly the same as that of an athletic coach. Some of these limitations are as follows: (1) the coach has had professional preparation for his role—most parents have not. (2) The coach can select his players from a pool of talent—parents have to work with the children they have, talent or not. (3) The coach can substitute one player for another. Parents cannot. (4) The athletic contest for which the coach is preparing his team is more specific than "the game of life" for which parents are preparing their children. The athletic contest is less subject to deep social change than is the society for which parents are training their children. The time span is shorter for the coach also. He does not have to wait 20 years to see whether his efforts paid off. (5) The coach can quit if the situation seems hopeless—parents are not supposed to resign their roles as father or mother. Coaches can also be discharged or fired—something that is legally possible for parents but not common. (6) Coaches are expected to like or at least respect their players—but parents are supposed to love their children.

In an interesting passage Brim says that "if a social role *requires* characteristics such as friendliness or love, it is almost self-defeating."[26]

---

[26] Brim, *op. cit.*, p. 98.

He goes on to say that "certain acts might be required in a role . . . but that love and similar expressions of feeling cannot be deliberate or contrived."[27] In this respect the athletic coach has an advantage over parents.

With all of these limitations it still seems to the writer that the athletic coach model has much to recommend it to American parents.

The use of these models in counseling parents

It would seem that these models can be used by counselors to help parents see what they are doing. The technique is similar to that used in the client-centered counseling system developed by Rogers—the counselor reflects back to the parents the model they are using.[28] At an appropriate time the counselor should point out that several parent models are available in our society and that perhaps this father and/or mother might do better using another model.

It is recognized that this approach assumes that the parents desire to improve their role performance and are willing to consider modification of their behavior. If this proves not to be the case, then the counselor would have to explore other problems that would seem to be blocking the treatment.

Other functions of the parent counselor

As we said earlier in this chapter, it is important that the counselor approach parents with the right attitude—they should not be judged guilty without a fair hearing. Even the most inept parents have often tried hard to live up to their obligations as fathers and mothers.

It is also essential that the counselor use reasonable expectations in dealing with parents. Most of them have had to function under adverse conditions; most of them had no preparation for their role as parent; they are not social workers or clinical psychologists or psychiatrists. The fact that they could conceive and produce a child did not automatically endow them with any insight into themselves, their child, or their world. There is really no social test for parenthood in our society—only a biological test.[29]

It is the writer's conviction that marital conflict is a basic factor in

---

[27] *Ibid.*

[28] See Carl Rogers, *Client-Centered Therapy* (Boston: Houghton Mifflin Co., 1951). For a good analysis of the Rogerian counseling system, see Calvin S. Hall and Gardner Lindzey, *Theories of Personality* (New York: John Wiley & Sons, 1957), pp. 467–502.

[29] There is a "social competence" test for adoptive and foster parents. This is why the writer believes that in some ways these parents have an advantage over biological parents.

preventing good parent performance in the two-parent family. If this is true the counselor will often need to focus on the husband-wife relationship rather than the parent-child relationship.[30]

Inadequate and/or distorted communication networks are typical of families in which parents are not functioning well. Indeed, recent trends in marriage and family counseling, as represented by Satir and Haley,[31] indicate that improvement of communication is one of the most important functions of the marriage and/or family counselor.

It needs to be understood that improved communication does not necessarily resolve husband-wife or parent-child conflicts—but it does sharpen and clarify these conflicts so that they can be dealt with more effectively.

Some fathers and mothers will need some type of psychotherapy. It needs to be remembered, however, that there are "sick families" in which the various individuals themselves are not sick—the pathology is not intrapsychic but interpersonal.[32] This is often obvious in counseling with married couples, but it is not so obvious in parent-child counseling.

The writer has found that it often helps to explore the parent's childhood and how his parents handled him or her. We are all apt to forget or repress our own childhood—or to romanticize it. The writer has always been impressed, for example, with the inability of parents who grew up in the 1920's or the 1930's to remember any serious necking or petting—yet the sexual revolution in our society was well along by then. Parents need to be reminded of some of the things they did as young people. This should make them somewhat more tolerant of the current generation.

In view of the great burden of guilt and anxiety carried by most American parents it is hoped that the counselor will not add unnecessarily to this load. It may be that some parents could benefit from being made to feel guilty, but the writer believes these to be a small minority.

Finally, there is much to be said for counseling parents in groups.[33] They often have quite similar problems; some parents feel more comfortable in a group counseling situation; they get perspective on their problems by listening to other parents; and they can learn from each other.

---

[30] For a statement of the functions of the marriage counselor see Gerald Leslie, "The Field of Marriage Counseling," in Harold T. Christensen (ed.), *Handbook of Marriage and the Family* (Chicago: Rand McNally & Co., 1964).

[31] See Virginia Satir, *Conjoint Family Therapy* (Palo Alto, Calif.: Science and Behavior Books, 1964), and Jay Haley, *Strategies of Psychotherapy* (New York: Grune & Stratton, 1963).

[32] Nathan Ackerman, *The Psychodynamics of Family Life* (New York: Basic Books, 1958), chap. 8, "Behavioral Disturbances."

[33] See Satir, *op. cit., passim.*

Summary and conclusion

In this chapter five parent models were presented and analyzed with the hope that these might be useful to counselors working with parents. Ideas from Berne and Rogers were utilized in the analysis. Our hypothesis has been that parents follow a certain system of performing their parental role whether they realize this or not. One of the basic functions of the counselor, as we see it, is to help parents understand what model or system they are using.

The chapter concluded with a brief statement of several other functions of the parent counselor.

Index

227

Birth rates
 among minority groups, 114–15
 and parenthood, 73
Black parents; see Afro-American parents
Blood, Robert O., Jr., 20, 29, 67, 122, 141
Blue-collar parents, 81–83
 special problems of, 82, 83
Borgatta, Edgar F., 128
Bossard, James H., 2, 97
Brenton, Myron, 56, 123, 138, 148, 152, 154
Brim, Orville G., Jr., 2, 10, 25, 27, 35–38, 42, 43 51–53, 64, 127, 143, 209–11, 220, 222
Broom, Leonard, 34
Brophy, William A., 102, 105, 108, 109, 111, 114, 116
Burchinal, Lee G., 200
Burgess, Ernest W., 22
Burgess, M. Elaine, 104, 162

C

Caplow, Theodore, 66
Carmichael, Stokely, 71
Carter, Richard, 130
Caudill, Harry, 75
Cavan, Ruth S., 28, 70, 73, 94, 125
Cayton, Horace R., 75, 102
Childless couples, 19, 27, 28
Children and marital adjustment, 27–29, 70
Chinese-American parents, 113–17
Christensen, Harold T., 14, 25, 224
Churchill, Randolph, 21, 96, 134
Churchill, Mrs. Winston, 21
Churchill, Winston, 21, 96, 134
Clark, Kenneth B., ix, 115, 117
Clarke, Helen, 62
Clinard, Marshall B., 37, 72, 133, 156, 161
Cloward, Richard A., 3–5, 214
Cobbs, Price M., 101
Coleman, James S., 9, 115, 178, 190
Collier, John, 110
Conant, James, 65, 72
Cottrell, Leonard S., Jr., 28, 33
Cottrell, W. Fred, ix
Counseling with parents, 210–25
 counselor's attitude, 210, 211
 functions of the counselor, 223, 224
Cowley, Malcolm, 106
Cuber, John F., 88, 149
Cult of the child, 6, 25

D

Darrow, Clarence, 41
Daughters vs. sons, the rearing of, 21, 22
Davis, John D., 94
Davis, Kingsley, 2, 4, 5, 15, 16, 30, 107, 108, 114, 144, 192, 208

Day care facilities, lack of, 75
Dependency of children, length of, 62–64
Diaper determinism, 43
Drake, St. Clair, 75, 102
Drucker, Peter F., 122
Duvall, Evelyn Millis, 63, 219

E

Educational level, effect on parenthood of, 75, 76
Edwards, John N., 192
Ehrmann, Winston, 186
Ellis, Albert, 17
Employment, impact of on parents, 74, 75
Environmentalism, use by social scientists of, 33–35, 37
Erdman, Joyce M., 108, 111
Erikson, Erik H., 111, 209
Ethology, 47
Etzioni, Amitai, 192
Etzioni, Eva, 192
Evaluation of parents
 by other parents, 6, 7
 by professionals, 6, 7, 58, 59
Experts on child rearing, 9, 10

F

Fanshel, David, 169, 170
Farber, Bernard, 168, 197
Farnham, Marynia A., 120, 126
Fate and parenthood, 25, 26, 37
Father-only families, 165–67
Femininization of American society, 56
Ferguson, Charles W., 123, 138
Feuer, Lewis S., 15, 191, 202
Fine, Benjamin, 65
Fishman, Jack, 21
Fladell, Ernest, 215
Folklore about parenthood, 17–31
Foote, Nelson N., 33
Fosdick, Raymond B., 95
Foster parents, 169, 170
Fragmentation of parental functions, 14
Frazier, E. Franklin, 101, 124
Freedman, Ronald, 12, 64
Freidin, Seymour, 38
Freud, Sigmund, 24, 38–47
Freudian theory and parents, 10, 36, 38–47
Friedan, Betty, 23, 38, 119, 123
Friendly, Fred, 180
Frost, Robert, 57

G

Galbraith, John Kenneth, 17
Gamson, William A., 207
Gans, Herbert, 70, 76, 79, 81, 85, 88, 129, 151, 199
Gelb, Arthur, 18, 123

Gelb, Barbara, 18, 123
Gillin, John, 34
Glazer, Nathan, 74, 100, 102, 103, 105, 112, 113, 199
Gold, Herbert, 93, 146
Golden, Harry, 100
Goldscheider, Calvin, 112–14
Goldstein, Sidney, 112–14
Gomberg, William, 81
Goode, William J., 22, 23, 37, 65, 72, 77, 84, 103, 132, 140, 159–63
Gordon, Milton M., 116
Gorer, Geoffrey, 37, 119
Goslin, David A., 139
Green, Arnold W., 19, 34, 53, 67
Grier, William H., 101
Gunther, John, 95, 134

H

Hagan, William T., 109
Haley, Jay, 48, 168, 224
Hall, Calvin S., 34, 40, 42, 47, 103, 223
Hamilton, Charles V., 71
Handlin, Oscar, 13, 76, 102, 105, 114, 133, 137, 196
Harding, Warren G., 150
Haroff, Peggy, 88, 149
Harrington, Michael, 60, 71, 73, 82, 110
Hayakawa, S. I., 176
Hechinger, Fred, 9, 180, 190
Hechinger, Grace, 9, 180, 190
Heer, David, 141
Hemingway, Ernest, 138
Herberg, Will, 112
Herman, Robert D., 195
Herzog, Elizabeth, 158
Higher standards for parents, 5, 52, 54, 59, 64, 65
Hill, Reuben, 125, 130, 144, 160
Historical romance about parenthood, 22
History of parenthood in America, 42, 59
Hobbs, Daniel F., Jr., 20
Hoffman, Lois Wladis, 7, 48, 53, 82, 121, 130, 160, 177
Hoffman, Martin L., 48, 177
Hollingshead, August B., 72, 78, 85, 92, 126
Horney, Karen, 47, 127
Housing and parenthood, 74
Howe, Irving, 75, 82, 149
Human genetics, 48
Hunt, Morton M., 132, 146, 150, 161, 163

I

Ilgenfritz, Marjorie, 165
Illness and parenthood, 77
Immigrant parents, 13, 65

Inkeles, Alex, 35
Instinct concept
  new concept of, 47
  as used by Freud, 42

J

Jackson, Don D., 17, 48
Jacobson, Paul H., 132, 195
Japanese-American parents, 113–17
Jeffers, Camille, 75
Jones, Wyatt C., 127

K

Kadushin, Alfred, 26, 28, 62, 74, 80, 104, 105, 141, 168–72
Kaplan, Frances B., 122, 148
Kazin, Alfred, 100, 117
Kendall, Elaine, 123, 138, 148
Keniston, Kenneth, 209
Kennedy, John F., 96
Kephart, William, 163
Kinsey, Alfred C., 22, 24, 72, 139, 150
Kirk, David, 171
Kirstein, George C., 95
Kluckhohn, Clyde, 47
Komarovsky, Mirra, 21, 81, 125, 129
Kramer, Judith R., 100, 113
Kriegbaum, Hillier, 49

L

LaBarre, Weston, 35
LaPiere, Richard, 39
Larner, Jeremy, 75, 82, 149
Larsen, Otto N., 182
Lederer, William J., 17
LeMasters, E. E., 10, 17, 19, 40, 51, 84, 85, 88, 105, 132, 142, 146, 149, 171
Lerner, Max, 2, 5, 6, 23, 25, 64, 72, 84, 121, 127, 184, 195, 217, 220
Leslie, Gerald, 224
Leventman, Seymour, 100, 113
Levi, Carlo, 99
Levine, Irving R., 24, 134
Lewis, Oscar, 71, 99, 105–7, 145
Liebow, Elliott, 35, 75, 104, 129
Lindzey, Gardner, 34, 40–42, 47, 103, 223
Litwak, Eugene, 84
Lorber, Richard, 215
Lorenz, Konrad, 35, 47, 133
Love and parents, 27
Lower class parents, 71–81
Lower middle-class parents, 83–85
Lower upper-class parents, 92–94
Lundberg, Ferdinand, 120, 126
Lunt, Paul S., 85, 92
Lynd, Helen, 84
Lynd, Robert S., 84, 127

232   Parents in modern America

This book has been set in 10 and 9 point Caledonia, leaded 2 points. Chapter numbers are in 14 point Craw Modern. Chapter titles are in 18 point Craw Modern. The size of the type page is 27 x 45½ picas.